Church and Parish

Batsford Local History Series

Church and Parish

AN INTRODUCTION FOR LOCAL HISTORIANS

J. H. Bettey

B. T. Batsford Ltd · *London*

© J. H. Bettey, 1987.

First published 1987.

Typeset by Progress Photosetting Ltd.,
and printed in Great Britain by
Biddles Ltd
Guildford and Kings Lynn.

Published by B. T. Batsford Ltd.,
4 Fitzhardinge Street, London W1H 0AH.

British Library Cataloguing in Publication Data.

Bettey, J.H.
  Church and parish: a guide for local historians—(Batsford local history series).
  1. Church of England 2. Parishes—England
  I. Title
  254'.0342'002497   BX5153.5.P3

  ISBN 0-7134-5101-7
  ISBN 0-7134-5102-5 Pbk

CONTENTS

ACKNOWLEDGEMENTS

Any study of the possibilities and sources for the history of parish churches and church life must rely heavily on the work of others, and especially on the labour of local historians and of those who have produced editions of parochial and diocesan records. The major sources which have been used, together with the main studies and articles which have been consulted, will be found in the references to each chapter and in the bibliography.

I am also grateful to numerous friends and colleagues with whom I have discussed particular topics or sections of this book, and especially to Michael Aston and Dr Robert Dunning, who together with Anthony Seward of Batsford, have read earlier drafts of each chapter, and have made valuable comments and suggestions for improvements. Gordon Kelsey provided help and advice with the illustrations, and Jim Hancock and Michael Lansdown both allowed me to use photographs from their collections.

J. H. Bettey
University of Bristol

INTRODUCTION

The cathedrals, abbeys and parish churches of England remain the largest
and most impressive buildings in most towns and villages, and are a constant
reminder of the part which the church has played in the religious, social,
educational, cultural and charitable life of parish communities over more
than twelve centuries. Even in the twentieth century the church buildings
dominate their surroundings, and in earlier centuries their size was even
more impressive. Everywhere towers can be seen rising above fields and
streets, while not even the remotest moorland or the most secluded valley is
out of ear-shot of the church bells. From a purely economic standpoint it
seems perverse that societies lacking in technology and living close to
subsistence should have spent so much time, effort and wealth on the
construction of enormous church buildings, or that so many men should
have withdrawn from productive employment and devoted their lives to
the conduct of religious worship; but it was common theological belief and
united community endeavour which provided the framework of life
throughout the Middle Ages, and which only very slowly distintegrated
thereafter. Religion is not only concerned with people's beliefs or with what
they thought and did inside churches or on Sundays; religious belief
affected human relationships, work, leisure, superstitions and all the
manifold activities in which common attitudes find an echo. For successive
generations, the church with its festivals, saints' days, processions, rituals,
dramas and imagery, provided a pattern for the progress of each year and
brought colour, music, light, hope and holiday to lives which would
otherwise have been uniformly hard, monotonous and uncertain. Common
concern for the parish church building, its enlargement, decoration and
adornment, provided a focus for community life and an object for
fund-raising, merry-making and recreations of all kinds. The church thus
provided the focal point for almost all communal activities.

For the local historian, interested in the development of a particular
parish, district or region, the church building and the records of church
organisation and legal system provide what is often the single most fruitful
source of information. Yet the right questions are often not asked, and the
evidence which can be obtained from the diocesan records is not explored;
and many parish histories continue to be written without making adequate
use of these rich sources. The parish church, its site, structure, architectural
features and furnishings, the churchyard and associated buildings, the
situation of the church within the parish and its relationship to prehistoric
features, boundaries, roads, footpaths, settlements and manor house, can

provide numerous insights into the growth, expansion, decline or even disappearance of local communities; the written records associated with the work of the church in the parish, with control by the bishop and diocese, or with the multifarious activities of church officials and church courts, can give a unique insight into the life of the parish community and into the most intimate concerns, beliefs and attitudes of individual parishioners.

This book is written with two objects in mind. The first is to describe the historic role of the church in all aspects of community life, and the ways in which this has changed over the centuries; to discuss the changing framework of belief, and the impact of the church and clergy on communal activities, religious worship, official ceremonies, civic functions, cultural, charitable and educational provision, games, plays, processions and recreations, most of which were for many centuries inextricably linked to the parish churches. The second aim is to explore the wealth of sources and evidence of all kinds, archaeological, architectural and documentary, which local historians can use to elucidate the religious ideas, controversies, social concerns, superstitions and community life of parishioners; and also to suggest some of the questions which should be asked and to give examples of the sort of answers which may be obtained concerning the people who built, enlarged and decorated the parish chuches, who worshipped and were baptised and married within them, who were buried beside or beneath them, and for whom the church, its doctrines, sanctions, feasts and fasts, ceremonies, rituals and obligations, provided the central focus of their lives.

The sources for the history of the nonconformist churches are not dealt with here, since both the records themselves and the important influence of these various churches on the religious, social and economic life of many towns and villages is a separate study in its own right. For most of the twelve centuries or more during which England has been a Christian country, religious life has centred upon the parish churches, and this book is concerned with what their records, architecture and furnishings, and the records of the dioceses of which they formed part, can reveal about the successive generations of the parish community and the ways in which the parish churches' role has changed and developed over this long period.

It must be made clear at the outset that not all parishes or dioceses will possess all the records which are discussed in the following pages, that many ecclesiastical records, especially diocesan archives and the proceedings of the church courts, are not easy to use, and that although examination of the architecture and furnishing of a parish church will often reveal a good deal about its history, only detailed and expert investigation will disclose the full story of their development. The survival of records has been uncertain and haphazard, and although many parishes and dioceses possess a wealth of material, there are inevitably numerous gaps. Diocesan administration was complex, many of the earlier records are in Latin, and the proceedings of the church courts, although extremely informative, are often lengthy and difficult. Moreover, the apparently neat system of parishes, deaneries, archdeaconries and dioceses, is complicated by the existence of many anomalies and especially by 'peculiars', which were parishes exempt from the jurisdiction of the diocesan bishop and under the control of monasteries, cathedral chapters or some other authority and whose records will not be among the diocesan archives but must be sought elsewhere.

There is much to be said for exploring the history of several adjacent parishes, for example along a river valley, in a particular district, or those which were formerly linked to a minster church, rather than concentrating, as many local historians do, exclusively upon one parish. In this way deficiencies in the records or architecture of one parish may be supplied from those of a neighbour, and the religious history of the whole neighbourhood may be investigated. Above all, however, it is only through posing the right questions that the full potential of church sites and buildings as a source of local history will be revealed; and only by careful examination of parish, diocesan and national records can the rich possibilities and unique information of these sources be uncovered.

Location of records

The documentary sources which are discussed in the following pages will be found in several different record offices. The records of the parish officers such as churchwardens and overseers of the poor, as well as the parish registers, are most likely to have been deposited in the county record office. Some county record offices also house the diocesan records, and these will include material such as the bishops' registers, the records of diocesan administration, visitations, faculties, the records of the ecclesiastical courts together with wills, inventories and other material relating to probate. Other evidence, particularly for those parishes which formerly were part of the possessions of a monastic house, a cathedral chapter or of some great estate may have to be sought in one or more of the great national repositories such as the Public Record Office, the British Library, the House of Lords' Library or the Bodleian Library. Essential guides to possible locations and to the use of such national collections include Philip Riden, *Local History: A Handbook for Beginners,* Batsford, 1983; W. B. Stephens, *Sources for English Local History,* C.U.P., 1981; and Philip Riden, *Record Sources for Local History,* Batsford, 1987.

Chapter One

SAXON CHRISTIANITY

Christianity was established in Roman Britain by the fourth century, with an organised structure of bishops and local churches. Although Christians remained a small proportion of the population, they were not insignificant, especially in the towns, and the existence of the British Church is evident from the attendance of its bishops at several ecclesiastical councils in Europe.

The late-Roman Christians in Britain had few distinctive buildings for public worship, and have left little archaeological evidence, but recent work on this period has left no doubt of the widespread acceptance of Christianity or of its importance. The number of villas which contained Christian symbols, like those at Lullingstone (Kent), Frampton (Dorset), Littlecote (Wilts), Chedworth and Cirencester (Glos), Icklingham (Suffolk), and above all the discovery in 1963 at Hinton St Mary (Dorset) of a mosaic showing a male figure with the Chi-Rho monogram which must surely be a depiction of Christ, show how far the influence of Christianity had penetrated into the lives of the wealthy, educated villa-owners of fourth-century Britain! But the hold of Christianity appears to have been largely confined to the educated classes and to urban dwellers, and for the most part it was rapidly submerged under the tide of Germanic heathenism during the successive invasions of the fifth century; the Christian religion disappeared from many places, and most of England saw the return of a vigorous paganism, whose ideas and symbolism were to remain a potent force underlying later Christian belief. The British Church survived in the west, in Ireland, Wales and in Cornwall, but it developed in isolation from the main stream of Christianity, with its own customs, liturgy and characteristics, giving birth to saints and missionaries, of whom the most notable was St Patrick, the founder of the remarkably influential Irish Church; other outstanding figures included Illtud who founded the important religious site at Llantwit Major on the coast of south Wales in c.500, and whose pupils included St Samson and St David; the Cornish saints Piran, Petroc, Fingar, Ia, and that host of vigorous preachers of the faith who have given their names to so many of the churches of Wales and the West Country. From Ireland, where numerous monastic houses, a central feature of Celtic Christianity, had preserved the great traditions of classical learning and education, St Columba and his companions came in 563 to settle at Iona to begin the conversion of the North. Columba died at Iona in 597, the year in which Augustine came to Canterbury with his forty monks to bring the faith to the heathen Saxon kingdoms of England?

Most local historians are unlikely to find much evidence for the earliest beginnings of Christianity. For a few, indications may survive in the lives or legends of the saints, the references in Bede's *Ecclesiastical History of the English People,* which was written during the early eighth century, in the *Anglo-Saxon Chronicle,* or in the difficult and specialised evidence of charters, in place-names such as the numerous *eccles* names, or in church dedications. Elsewhere the survival of carved or inscribed stones, either memorials or fragments of crosses such as the numerous examples in Wales and Cornwall, or those at Wareham (Dorset), Bewcastle (Cumberland), Hexham (Durham), Eyam (Derbys) and many others, may give some indication of early Christian devotion. Above all, the most fruitful evidence is likely to come from archaeology, and as will be shown later, this ranges from Christian burials, symbols and ornaments, to complete church sites and foundations, often lying beneath much later church buildings.[3]

It is not necessary to tell again here the well-known story of the Conversion of England, nor to detail the differences between the Celtic and the Roman forms of Christianity and the eventual triumph of Rome at the Synod of Whitby in 664; but of great significance for the future, and of particular interest for local and regional historians, was the way in which the manner of the Conversion left an abiding mark upon the character and organisation of the English church, and continued to be reflected in its administration, in the arrangements, furnishing and decoration of its churches, and in the attitudes and beliefs of congregations throughout the Middle Ages. In this, as in so many other ways, the history of the English people was for many centuries profoundly affected by what happened during the Anglo-Saxon period.

A remarkable feature of the Conversion of England was the rapidity with which the missionaries were able to spread their message and make converts. Partly this is to be explained by the vigour and enthusiasm of the preachers; partly by the efficiency of their organisation, which will be described shortly; but not least by their success in converting the royal households. For example, Augustine and his followers depended heavily upon the support of King Ethelbert of Kent and his Christian queen, Bertha; King Edwin of Northumbria supported the Christian missionaries there; and King Sigbert of East Anglia greatly encouraged the preaching of Christianity in Suffolk. In these places, as elsewhere, the Conversion proceeded from the leading figures downwards through society. Likewise in Cornwall a life of St Samson records that the saint's preaching converted a pagan chief who thereupon 'made all his people undergo first baptism, then confirmation, by St Samson'.[3] In view of the speed of the Conversion, however, it is difficult to escape the thought that perhaps the heathen religions were no longer strong or that their hold upon the people had relaxed. But against this must be set the fact that many pagan ideas and symbols remained as part of the beliefs of the newly-converted English Christians and continued throughout the Middle Ages to be used in the decoration of churches; the names of the heathen gods survive in the days of the week and in numerous place-names; the Christian calendar was greatly influenced by pagan ceremonial occasions and observances, while the pagan goddess Eostre gave her name to Easter, the greatest of all the Christian festivals. Holy wells were taken over from pagan religions and dedicated to local saints, and pagan fertility cults survived not only in the decoration of churches with figures such as the Green Man or the *Sheila-na-Gig,* but also in the symbolism of mummers' plays, May Day ceremonies and dances such as the Bromley Horn Dance or the Helston Floral Dance?[5] Law makers continued to find it necessary during the seventh century to forbid the worship of heathen gods, even in Kent where Christianity was strong; In Essex the old temples were repaired and pagan worship was resumed during the stress of a great plague in the 660s; Raedwald, king of East Anglia, erected pagan and Christian altars in the same temple during the early seventh century, while Bishop Wilfred, landing in Sussex after a visit to Gaul in 666, was set upon by heathens led by their priest, who attempted unsuccessfully to bind the bishop's hands by his magical arts. In view of all the evidence there seems no reason to doubt that 'heathenism was both widespread and deeply rooted among the English when Augustine reached Canterbury in 597'[6]

Minster churches

The fight against pagan beliefs, and the Conversion of the English, was accomplished through the organisation of the church into monastic houses, many of which became influential centres of religious life and learning; and the faith was spread through 'minster' or district churches, the missionary centres where priests lived a communal life, and from where they journeyed out to preach and teach, to celebrate mass and to baptise converts in the surrounding pagan countryside. The system of parishes, which was to become such a permanent and essential feature of church life and organisation, was a later development and was still not complete by the time of the Norman Conquest. The picture which emerges from the greatest of all the early narratives of the Conversion, Bede's *Ecclesiastical History of the English Nation,* written early in the eighth century, is of small companies of secular priests living in communities or *monasteria* and preaching in the surrounding countryside. For example, describing the situation in Northumbria after the Synod of Whitby in 664, Bede wrote of the people flocking to hear the clergy.

> ... and if any priest happened to come into a village, the villagers immediately gathered together and sought from him the word of life. For those priests and clerics went into the villages for no other reason than to preach, baptise, visit the sick, and in short, take care of souls[7]

Likewise Bede wrote of St Cuthbert undertaking preaching tours, and commented that

> in those days the English people were accustomed to gather together whenever a clerk or priest came into their village, at his call, to hear the Word.

Writing of the situation in Sussex in 680, where pagan beliefs and practice remained strong, Bede described the successful preaching of St Wilfred who administered to the people 'the word of the faith and the baptism of salvation'. He also described the failure of the priests in a minster or *monasterium* at Bosham, in a pagan land,

> surrounded by woods and sea, and in it five or six brothers, serving the Lord in a humble and poor way of living. But none of the people of the province cared to imitate their life or to listen to their preaching[8]

The areas served by some minsters were very large, and required several priests. A charter granted to Christ Church, Canterbury in 805 shows that the minster there had two senior clergy, eight priests and four clerks. Slightly earlier, a grant to the minster at Worcester reveals that it consisted of nine priests, four deacons and five clerks[9] The reasons for establishing minsters are set out in a charter of *c.*680 whereby a Mercian landowner, Friduric, granted land to the abbey of Medeshamstede, later known as Peterborough, so that the abbey might provide a minster at Breedon-on-the-Hill, in Leicestershire. His purpose was that

> in view of the growing and multiplying of the number of Christians in the island of Britain ... a minster *(monasterium)* and oratory of monks serving God should be founded, ... and also a priest of honest life and good reputation instituted, who should bring the grace of baptism and the teaching of the Gospel doctrine to the people committed to his care.

Breedon remained an important minster throughout the pre-Conquest period, and some notable eighth-century sculpture survives in the building[10]

This system of itinerant preachers operating from minsters, which could be extended further and further across the land as paganism retreated, and as ever more converts embraced the faith and were baptised, was ideally suited to a missionary church and well adapted to the task of spreading the gospel among a heathen population. It was the army of unknown missionary priests working from the minster churches over several generations which broke the power of the belief in pagan gods and finally effected the total conversion of the English people.

> We allow our attention to be riveted too much on the great names, on Augustine, Paulinus, Aidan and Birinus. But these were the leaders, the generals, of a large army, of which most have left no name behind them![11]

From the minsters, daughter churches were established, some of which continued for many centuries to pay allegiance to the mother church, while from the eighth century onwards, local landowners began building churches on their estates, so that in this way the whole countryside was provided with churches. It is likely that there were many hundreds of small churches and chapelries in late-Saxon England, many of them built by local lords, often beside their own halls, and serving the spiritual needs of a small community. Not all survived to become parish churches; some remained as chapels or subsidiary churches in outlying parts of large parishes, others ceased to perform a useful function as settlements moved or farmsteads were abandoned, and were allowed to fall into ruin and disappear. In late-Saxon England the possession of a church was an important attribute of rank, and the majority of local churches, many of which were later to become parish churches, came into existence through the initiative of the local lord. This explains why numerous churches are still to be found in such close proximity to one another, especially in towns, and why so many are beside a manor house, moated site, or former fortification, often at some distance from the village.

King Edgar's Laws, promulgated at Andover in 970 but no doubt reflecting a situation which had existed for many years, distinguished three different kinds of church: minsters, churches with a burial ground, and churches without rights of burial. A code of laws issued by King Ethelred in 1014 listed four kinds of church, the chief minster or cathedral, minsters, a daughter church with rights of burial, and a 'field church' established by a landowner on his estate but without burial rights![12]

The pattern of early churches

For most places in England, any attempt to reconstruct the early history of Christianity is beset with difficulty and frustration, for unless a fortunate accident has provided some reference in a charter, letter or other documentary source, or unless recognisable Saxon remains survive in the structure of the church building, only archaeological excavation, probably beneath the existing church, can reveal firm evidence, and such excavation is seldom possible![13] A more practicable project for local historians is to attempt a reconstruction of the early pattern of minster and subsidiary churches in the district. Clues may be sought in the structure and surroundings of the churches themselves, in place-names, in documentary sources such as charters and land-grants and in the later ecclesiastical organisation of the area. In many places, the ancient minsters for long retained to themselves the rights of baptism and burial, or continued to demand various dues and forms of allegiance from their daughter churches, even long after these had attained parochial status.

At the time of the Domesday Survey in 1086, the minster at Thatcham in Berkshire was listed as part of the royal estates in the county, with a well-endowed church and two priests, serving the whole of the large hundred of Thatcham. Gradually, numerous daughter churches and dependent chapelries were established which in time became separate parishes, including the town of Newbury, but the process was not completed until the nineteenth century when Midgham and Greenham achieved parochial status![14] At Crewkerne in south Somerset the parishioners of the former daughter churches Misterton, Wayford and Seaborough continued until the nineteenth century to pay dues to their mother church and to bury their dead there, while the parishioners of Wayford brought the key of their church to Crewkerne each year on the patronal festival (St Bartholomew, 24 August) and solemnly laid it upon the high altar of the mother church as an acknowledgement of their dependent status.[15] When the antiquary John Leland visited Chew Magna near Bristol in c.1540 he noted:

> There be dyvers paroche chirches there aboute that once a year do homage unto Chute (Chew Magna) their mother chyrche.

As late as the eighteenth century the responsibility of repairing specific sections of the churchyard wall of the ancient minster at Chew Magna still remained with the four daughter churches, who continued to bury their dead at the former minster although in other respects they had long since become separate parishes.[15] In a dispute during the late-sixteenth century over the collegiate church at Bromyard in Herefordshire it was stated that

> the stalls yet in the choir were not only for the prebends (Portionists) there, but also for the 15 other priests of the 15 inferior churches thereabouts which came continuously once a year upon Whitsun monday to help to say service in the Collegiate (Portionist) church confessing the same to be the Mother Church.[16]

Similar evidence for former minsters and their daughter churches, and for the gradual development of the parochial system, has been found in many other places including the huge *parochia* or minster areas of Leominster (Herefordshire), King's Somborne (Hants), the Vale of Berkeley (Gloucestershire), north Yorkshire, Kent, Lincolnshire, Leicestershire, Shropshire and elsewhere, while many others await detailed investigation by local historians.[17] The sources of such investigation include charters, monastic and cathedral records, bishops' registers, court proceedings, later ecclesiastical divisions and practice, place-names and the study of church structures and parish boundaries. Following a detailed study of the evidence for the minsters and their dependent chapelries in the Kesteven region of Lincolnshire, Dorothy Owen summarised the value of such local study:

> The English parochial system as we still know it seems to have crystallized in the late Anglo-Saxon period and it therefore retains a picture of the chronology and density of settlement, at least in some areas. Certainly it can be used to demonstrate what were the principal centres of population and which the satellite or daughter communities of the tenth or early eleventh centuries.[18]

Since the minsters were frequently established on royal or other large estates, and many subsidiary chapelries were built by lesser landowners to serve the tenants on their lands, the parochial boundaries may well follow the divisions of much earlier land units, and provide for the local historian some insight into earlier Saxon or even Roman estates, economic units and divisions of territory.[19] Evidence of former minsters also survives in place-names such as those in Dorset including Yetminster, Charminster, Wimborne Minster and Iwerne Minster. Early documentary sources, especially the evidence of charters, confirms that in Devon there were minsters at Axminster, Crediton, Braunton, Plympton and Coryton. Likewise documentary evidence reveals that in the region around

Canterbury there were minsters at Reculver, Minster-in-Sheppy and Hoo, as well as in other parts of Kent?[20]

Archaeological and architectural evidence

Evidence of early minster churches is also provided by archaeology, by the survival of pre-Conquest architecture and stone-carving, and occasionally also by the siting and dedication of churches. Again, these are subjects where the detailed knowledge and research of local historians can make an important contribution. Substantial parts of several early churches survive, especially in south-east England, and others which have since been demolished or totally rebuilt are known from archaeological excavation or from surviving descriptions. They include Bradwell-on-Sea (Essex), which was founded by Cedd in 653 within the Roman fortress of Othona, and in Kent there are the foundations of St Andrew's, Rochester, St Mary's, Lyminge, SS Peter and Paul at Canterbury, and a description of the notable church at Reculver which was built in c.670 and demolished in 1805. Similarly in Northumbria, parts of seventh-century churches survive or are known from excavation or description at Monkwearmouth, Escomb, Jarrow, Corbridge, Hexham and Ripon. All these churches were small, and none could have accommodated more than a priest and a very few worshippers. Those in south-east England, and others in the Midlands such as Brixworth (Northamptonshire), Wing (Bucks), and Breedon-on-the-Hill (Leicestershire) were distinguished by numerous internal divisions creating several *porticus* or side chapels and chambers, and this continued to be a feature of Saxon churches, even of the larger buildings erected during the century or more before the Norman Conquest?[21] St Andrew's at Hexham was one of the four churches built there by St Wilfred late in the seventh century, and although only the crypt now survives, the Life of Wilfred written by a follower, Eddius Stephanus, soon after the saint's death in 709, provides a vivid glimpse of the complex and subdivided interior of the church:

> My feeble tongue will not permit me to enlarge here upon the depth of the foundations in the earth, and its crypts of wonderfully dressed stone, and the manifold building above ground supported by various columns and many side aisles, and adorned with walls of notable length and height surrounded by spiral stairs leading up and down..[22]

The characteristics of Saxon architecture and building techniques and the arrangement of church interiors, as well as the problems involved in the dating of these structures, have been authoritatively examined and discussed by H. M. and J. Taylor, and their work is the essential starting point for any local investigation of this subject?[23] The evidence of recent work in church archaeology has been admirably summarised by Dr Warwick Rodwell, and no local historian can ignore the remarkable evidence which recent archaeological work has produced concerning early churches and the alterations to which existing churches have been subject, even though such excavation can be carried out on very few churches and church sites?[24] It is important to remember that most churches have undergone successive alterations, enlargements and restorations over the centuries, and that few retain more than a vestige of the original church which once occupied the same site. Excavations at St Paul-in-the-Bail, Lincoln, have revealed at least seventeen different phases of church building, from the seventh century to the present; the church at Rivenhall (Essex), which was once thought to be Victorian, has been shown to be of Saxon origin and to stand on a Roman building: excavation of St Martin's church at Wharram Percy in east Yorkshire has uncovered twelve stages of building from the late-eighth century to the present.

The proliferation of churches

At first the places regularly visited by the missionary priests from the minsters were marked by stone crosses which served as the focus of worship for the surrounding area, or which stood beside the early wooden or stone churches, and many of these survive, either entire like the great crosses at Bewcastle (Cumberland), Rothbury and Hexham (Northumberland) or the Reculver Cross, now in Canterbury cathedral, or as fragments within later churches. In north Yorkshire, for example, notable Saxon crosses or cross fragments survive at Masham, Brompton-in-Allerton, Sunnington, Middleton and several other places, while the finest example, the Easby Cross of c.860 is now in the Victoria and Albert museum. More than 350 early stone crosses survive in Cornwall, and many are beside the sites of later churches. An eighth-century biography of St Willibald states that in Somerset it was customary for visiting priests to preach and celebrate mass by a cross set up outside the lord's hall?[25] The next stage in the long process whereby the whole country was covered by a network of parishes, each with its own church, was the building of a church by the local lord, as a place where the priest from the minster could say mass, preach and baptise converts. Many of these early daughter churches were of wood, like those described by Bede as *more Scottorum. non de lapida* (after the manner of the Scots, not of stone), the wooden church at Doulting (Somerset), into which St Aldhelm, bishop of Sherborne, was taken when he died in 709, or St Michael's church, Thetford (Norfolk), which excavation has shown was originally built of wood but was replaced by a stone structure during the eleventh century. Excavation of the early eleventh-century church at Stafford which was dedicated to St Bertelin, a Saxon saint of the eighth century, showed that a large wooden cross which had previously stood within a timber church was buried beneath the later stone building[26] Excavations at St Mary's, Tanner Street in Winchester, at Raunds (Northants), St Paul-in-the-Bail, Lincoln and elsewhere have revealed the way in which small Saxon churches were gradually replaced by larger, more elaborate buildings, and how the process of rebuilding and extension continued without a break during the eleventh century. The Norman Conquest led to renewed efforts to build on a grand scale, and the prosperity and population growth of the twelfth and thirteenth centuries brought even grander schemes; only the catastrophic plagues and recession of the fourteenth century brought a temporary halt to the steady growth in the size of many churches?[27] For the landowner, the establishment of a church could be quite profitable, for as well as the spiritual benefits he and his family might expect to acquire, and the convenience for his tenants, he retained the proprietary rights to the church, the *advowson* or right to appoint the priest; moreover the tithes, offerings and other dues of his tenants were retained within the estate, although in some places the rights of the minster continued to be recognised.

Similarly, in the Anglo-Saxon towns, churches proliferated, especially during the century before the Conquest, although many of the urban churches were very small. Norwich, for example, had 49 churches and chapels by 1086, London must have had even more, and towns such as Winchester, York, Worcester, Bury St Edmunds, Lincoln and Chester were abundantly provided with churches?[28] In selecting the site for a church it seems probable that many landowners chose the place which had previously been used for pagan worship, and, although the answer will not often be forthcoming or definite, it is important for local historians to consider whether there is any evidence that a church stands on a prehistoric site or place of pre-Christian worship. A frequently-quoted letter of Pope Gregory written in 601 to Abbot Mellitus, who was later to become Bishop of London, instructed that the pagan temples and sacred places should not be totally destroyed, but rather that they should be sanctified with holy water and that Christian altars should be set up within them; so that in surroundings which already had powerful and familiar religious associations, the people would be more easily won to the new faith. Early Christian leaders were anxious not to impose too heavy a conflict of loyalties upon the new converts, and Pope Gregory was no exception, for he ended his letter to Mellitus with the astute observation that if a man wished to climb he should do so by steps and not by leaps.[29] An eighth-century life of St Samson records how, when on a missionary journey through Cornwall, the saint broke down the idol in a pagan temple and replaced it by a stone which he marked with a cross. It seems likely that a similar process occurred in many other places, although only rarely does documentary or archaeological evidence exist to confirm this. The early church at Knowlton near Cranborne (Dorset), now a ruin, is situated in the centre of a notable neolithic ritual earthwork; likewise the church at Oldbury-on-Severn, near Thornbury in the lower Severn valley, is on a hilltop and within a circular earthwork, while its dedication to a local Saxon saint, Arilda, is further evidence of its early origin. At Berwick (Sussex), the church is situated beside a large barrow, as it is at Maxey (Northants). Rudston in Yorkshire has a prehistoric monolith 19 feet high beside the church, and Edlesborough, Taplow and West Wycombe, all in Buckinghamshire, are situated within or beside prehistoric earthworks or burial mounds, as are also Ludlow in Shropshire, Wickham St Paul in Essex, Avebury in Wiltshire, Brentor in Devon, St Issey in Cornwall and many others. There must be even more for which the evidence is no longer so clear, where the Christian Church took over and adapted the former sites of pagan worship. Elsewhere, many churches are situated close to manor houses, ancient roads and boundaries or beside former castles, monastic establishments or even Roman villas. The tendency for a parish church to remain in its original position means that it often provides the earliest fixed point in the history of an area, and thus gives a unique insight into the post-Roman development of the landscape and settlement. The local historian should therefore look carefully for prehistoric remains or burials, signs of a surrounding bank and ditch, a circular churchyard, evidence of prehistoric occupation or use from archaeological excavations, chance finds or place-name derivations, as well as examining the relationship of the church site to the settlement pattern of the locality, even though the evidence to be found is likely to remain inconclusive[30] It is, of course, important not to push the idea of pagan origins too far, as was sometimes done by over zealous antiquarians in the past. Not all church sites were the former scenes of pagan ritual, nor should it be supposed that there is any essential resemblance between pagan cults and Christian worship, in spite of all the pagan symbolism absorbed by the Church[31]

Following the destruction caused by the Viking invasions and the long Danish wars, beginning with the attack on Lindisfarne in 793 and the plunder of Jarrow in 794 and continuing throughout the ninth century, the tenth century saw a remarkable revival in the English Church. It was a movement associated with such figures as Dunstan, first as abbot of Glastonbury and later as archbishop of Canterbury (960-980), Oswald, bishop of Worcester (961-972) and archbishop of York (972-992), Ethelwold, abbot of Abingdon (954-963) and bishop of Winchester (963-984); with the homilists and preachers, Aelric and Wulfstan; with new dioceses; with a revived monasticism based on the *Regularis Concordia,* the reformed Benedictine rule (probably the work of Ethelwold), which was approved by a Council at Winchester in 970. The reforms and revival of the tenth century were marked by the foundation of many new monastic houses, by an outburst of literary and artistic work, by a revived structure of bishoprics and cathedrals, and by a wave of church building throughout the country, so that by the beginning of the eleventh century there were few places in England not within walking distance of a church. It is from these churches that most English parish churches are descended[32]

The pre-Conquest Church

For the local historian the last phase of the Anglo-Saxon church during the century and a half before the Norman Conquest is easier to study than is the earlier history of Christianity in England. There are more documentary sources in the form of charters, land grants, letters, lives of saints, sermons, chronicles and works of art, which may provide evidence for local studies. Also despite the fact that many Saxon churches continued to be made of wood and have long since been replaced, and notwithstanding the Norman enthusiasm for demolishing and reconstructing Saxon architecture, a great deal of late-Saxon sculpture and decoration survives in English parish churches. Recent painstaking investigation has revealed that the architecture of no less than 267 churches is wholly or partly Anglo-Saxon, that many more churches contain fragments of Saxon cross-shafts, carving or decoration, and that even more later churches stand upon Saxon foundations.[33] The survival of so many Saxon churches, ranging from large, complex buildings like Brixworth (Northants), Deerhurst (Glos), Barton-on-Humber (Lincs), Breamore (Hants), Worth (Sussex), Milborne Port (Somerset), or Stow (Lincs), to small village churches or chapelries like Bradford-on-Avon (Wilts), St Martin's, Wareham (Dorset), Brigstock (Northants), Escomb (Durham) or Bradwell-on-Sea (Essex), with their characteristic high walls, narrow windows, doors and arches, and small, dark chancels evidently not designed for an elaborate ritual, provide abundant evidence of the high level of piety and also give a good indication of the surroundings and atmosphere of late Anglo-Saxon worship. The Saxon period also saw the introduction of towers and bells, both of which were to become characteristic of English parish churches. Numerous Saxon towers survive, for example at Earls Barton (Northants), Deerhurst (Glos), St Bene't (Cambridge), North Leigh (Oxon), Sompting (Sussex) or St Martin's, Wareham (Dorset), and there are references to bells and bell-ringing in the *Regularis Concordia*. The enthusiastic way in which kings, nobles, bishops and landowners founded churches in both towns and countryside during the tenth century is a remarkable tribute to the strength of the religious revival, and to the zeal and enthusiasm of the clergy. Some indication of this is apparent in late-Saxon manuscript decoration and stone-carving emphasising the dramatic struggle between the forces of good and evil, or in inscriptions such as that on the tub-shaped Saxon font at Potterne (Wilts) with the Latin verse from Psalm 42 around its rim, which in English reads:

Like as the hart desireth the water-brooks,
So longeth my soul after Thee, O God.

Likewise, the inscribed sundial at St Gregory's Minster, Kirkdale (N. Yorks) shows a remarkable enthusiasm for renewal in this area, which was particularly badly affected by Danish raids and by long continuing warfare. The inscription records that Orm rebuilt the church in the days of King Edward the Confessor (1042-1065) and Tosti, Earl of Northumberland (1055-65), thus giving a precise dating for the work.

Orm, son of Gamal, bought St Gregory's Minster when it was all broken down and fallen, and he let it be made anew from the ground to Christ and St Gregory, in the days of Edward the King and Tosti the Earl, and Haward wrought me, and Brand the Priest.

This is the day's sun-marker at every tide.

At Odda's chapel, the small building close to the large Anglo-Saxon church at Deerhurst in Gloucestershire, a dedication stone survives, marking its dedication in 1065 in honour of the Holy Trinity and St Peter. The church which provides the most striking evidence of the fervour and enthusiasm of the Saxon priests and of the tenth-century revival is the minster of Breamore in Hampshire. In this large late-Saxon church, an archway leading into the south porticus has deeply cut around it the words HER SPUTELAD SEO GECPYDRAEDNES DE, — 'In this place the Word is revealed unto thee'. Above the entrance to the church at Breamore is another notable feature of Saxon religious art, the rood or figure of the crucified Christ, with body twisted in the agony of crucifixion, still a powerful sculpture in spite of the mutilation it received at the hands of iconoclastic reformers during the sixteenth century. Similar Saxon roods survive at Headbourne Worthy and Romsey (Hants), Langford (Oxon), Wormington (Worcs), Daglingworth (Glos), Bitton (Avon) and elsewhere.

Projects and questions

It is of great importance for the local historian to remember that although rebuilding and alterations to a parish church over the centuries may have destroyed most, if not all, of the easily observable evidence, the probability is that the site of the church may well have been used for Christian worship and burial for far longer than the architecture of the present church might suggest. Since archaeological excavation is not possible for most churches, it is important to look carefully for any surviving evidence of Saxon work, such as remnants of carving or stonework or fragments of cross-shaft, or blocked-up windows and doors, both inside and outside the church. Examples of what can be found by careful investigation in apparently unpromising buildings may be cited from three churches in the Bristol region. At Chew Stoke, the church was very largely rebuilt during the nineteenth century and although some features survive from the fifteenth century there seems to be nothing earlier; but close investigation of the churchyard wall has revealed two stones with very clear Saxon inter-lace carving, giving a strong indication of a much earlier church, or at least a cross or grave-slab on the site. At Banwell, almost the whole church appears to have been rebuilt during the fifteenth century, a period of great prosperity in the west country when many churches were totally refashioned in the grandest style, but recent work on the repair of the south doorway revealed a large stone slab covered with Saxon carving. The church at Holcombe, remote in a field, has some Norman work, but is largely late-medieval in date, with notable Georgian furnishings; but careful examination of the Norman doorway shows that part of a late-Saxon inscribed stone has been re-used and turned around, so that on the outside it forms part of the carved Norman arch, but part of the back of the stone can be seen with a Saxon inscription turned upside down.

The dedication of a church may also give a clue to its early origins. Dedications to a Saxon or Celtic saint, to the Holy Cross, Holy Rood or Holy Ghost — all common early dedications — or to local saints such as the Celtic saints of Wales and Cornwall, or to saints such as St Alban, St Pancras, St Petronilla, St Helen, St Ethelreda, St Candida or St Wite,

St Guthlac, St Ethelbert, St Frideswide, St Aldhelm and many others, to missionary-saints such as Chad, Cuthbert, Martin, Felix, Wilfred or Aidan, or to one of the saintly members of the Saxon royal houses, are all strongly indicative of an early foundation.

To place the church under the protection of a specific saint, and to keep and venerate the relics of that saint, were important features of Anglo-Saxon religious life. Since there was no regular procedure for canonisation, many local saints, missionaries and founders of chantries were venerated. The relics of the saint gave a special significance to prayers and oaths made in the church, and it was Harold's oath of loyalty to William of Normandy, made on the relics of saints, which provided the religious justification for the Norman Conquest. Church dedications were frequently changed during the Middle Ages to more popular or better-known saints, but it may be possible to establish the earlier dedication of a church from place-name evidence, charters, monastic cartularies or bishop's registers. Bishop's registers sometimes record the change of dedication; medieval wills commonly name the church where burial was to take place and other local churches to which bequests were made; and the date of the village feast or annual fair often coincided with the patronal festival and may give evidence of an earlier dedication.[34] It has been suggested that during the Saxon period, and perhaps later, new churches were aligned so that east was at the point of sunrise on the day of the patronal festival. There are difficulties in the way of examining this theory. The church is likely to have been enlarged, the original alignment may be uncertain; but on the other hand the hypothesis can only be tested by local experiments, and forms an interesting subject for local study as well as a possible way of recovering the original dedication.[35]

For many local historians the earliest documentary reference to a church may be in the Domesday Survey, although it is important to remember that the Domesday commissioners were primarily concerned with financial matters, and the absence of any reference does not necessarily mean that no church existed. Moreover, the commissioners in different parts of the country interpreted very differently the need to record churches; thus in Suffolk and Huntingdonshire most churches were included, whereas very few are recorded, for example, in Essex or Staffordshire. It may be true that the prosperous areas of Huntingdonshire and Suffolk were well-supplied with churches, but it is unlikely that the contrast was so great as the record of Domesday would suggest. In Cambridgeshire, for example, apart from four monastic houses, churches and/or priests are mentioned at only eleven places; and the fine Saxon church at Great Denham (Norfolk), is not mentioned by the Domesday Survey.[36]

The main proof of the omission of many churches from Domesday, however, is the absence from the Survey of several churches with clear Anglo-Saxon architecture, and the case of Kent, where other eleventh-century sources list numerous churches which are ignored by the Domesday commissioners. To take merely one county, Wiltshire, there are at least seven churches which must have been in existence at the time of the

Domesday Survey, but which are not mentioned by the commissioners. Warminster, as its name suggests, had an ancient minster church, and is mentioned as a royal residence in the tenth century, but no church appears in the Domesday Book; the churches at Somerford Keynes, Burcombe, Limpley Stoke, Bremhill and East Knoyle all have clear remains of Saxon work in their structure, while at Bradford-on-Avon there is one of the best-preserved of all small Saxon churches, but none of these appear in the Domesday Survey.[37] For Kent, there are two twelfth-century lists of parish churches, one made for the Canterbury diocese (the *Domesday Monachorum*), the other for Rochester, (the *Textus Roffensis*). Together these give the names of 365 churches, while Domesday Book records only 147 churches.[38] But although the Domesday Survey does not record all the existing churches, it nonetheless warrants careful study by local historians who wish to understand the origins and development of parishes. It is clear from the Survey that in 1086 minster churches with several priests were still functioning in many places, notably in Devon and Cornwall, and in the Welsh borderland. But in many other parts of England, the division of the countryside into parishes, although not complete, was already far advanced, and even in the terse entries of the Domesday Book the continuing process of church building can be recognised. At Offenham in Worcestershire, oxen were kept to draw stones to the church; at Bermondsey in Surrey, there was a new and beautiful church; at Thorney in Suffolk, four brothers had built a chapel because the mother church could not contain all the people; while in Wiltshire, the normally formal entry becomes almost lyrical with the description of Wilcot in the vale of Pewsey, where the landowner, Edward of Salisbury, had built a new church, an excellent house and a good vineyard (*ecclesia nova, domus optima et vinia bona*).

Chapter Two

CHURCH AND COMMUNITY IN THE EARLY MIDDLE AGES

The period between the Norman Conquest and the Black Death of the mid-fourteenth century saw numerous developments in the Church, with reorganisation and re-location of diocesan centres, the completion of the parochial system, a flowering of monasticism and the appropriation by monastic houses of many parish churches, together with the quickening zeal in the Church which was marked by a massive wave of building and extension in cathedrals, monasteries and parish churches alike. Most parish historians will, however, find little documentary evidence about the life of individual churches during these centuries and will be compelled to rely upon archaeological evidence of the testimony of the parish church building itself. Most of the surviving documentary records give a clear picture of the Church hierarchy, organisational structure and routine administration, but, with a few important exceptions, they are silent about the parish congregations, about what went on within the walls of the churches and about church life and beliefs at a parochial level. Until the appearance of church-wardens' accounts during the later Middle Ages, all ecclesiastical records such as bishops' registers, visitations, licences, grants, and monastic cartularies or records of property rights, were compiled by clerics, and parishioners appear, if at all, only as providers of wealth, as persons with duties to perform and dues to render, or as delinquents who have by their conduct, objections or petitions, interfered with the smooth running of the ecclesiastical machinery.

> Parishes were viewed, not as spearheads for pastoral activity, but as steady sources of income... the revenues deriving from parochial churches figured largely in both registers and cartularies. Advowsons, pensions and tithes loomed large, but very little attention was paid to the pew-fodder, or more often groundlings, who provided these nonstop funds willingly, or otherwise. Such records represent administration and finance, and indeed the whole apparatus of the clerical hierarchy, as ends in themselves, rather than as a means to an end!

Early medieval sources of information

Three early medieval sources provide lists of benefices and give some indication of their income; they were compiled for purposes of ecclesiastical taxation, and all three are available in print. They are the 'Taxation (or Valuation) of Norwich' 1254, which lists the returns for eight dioceses in England and Wales (Bangor, Durham, Ely, Lincoln, Llandaff, London,

Norwich and St Asaph); the 'Taxation of Pope Nicholas IV' 1291, which includes some 8,500 churches and chapels, listing all benefices valued at more than six marks (£4.00), and has been described as 'the most comprehensive directory of medieval benefices in existence'; and the 'Inquisition of the Ninths' 1341, which also lists benefices and their income throughout most of the country?

Although the architectural evidence of parish churches throughout England bears abundant witness to the amount of church building, both in the reconstruction and enlargement of Saxon churches and in the creation of a multitude of new parish churches, most of them founded by laymen on their estates, it is not possible to find detailed documentary evidence of this process nor to date precisely the foundation of most parish churches. Bishops' registers which survive from the thirteenth century provide details of consecrations, rededications after rebuilding work, changes of patron saint, the establishment of chapels-of-ease or private oratories, and also give invaluable details of the institution of rectors or vicars; they are, therefore, an extremely important source and one which is too little used by local historians. Although they are in Latin, many of the entries are formalised and are not too difficult to translate, and many of the registers have been printed by local record societies or by others such as the Canterbury and York Society. (A list of the many surviving registers may be found in D.M. Smith, *Guide to Bishops' Registers of England and Wales 1981*.)

Architectural evidence

Before the thirteenth century, however, the most fruitful source of evidence is the church building itself. This should be examined as thoroughly as possible, both inside and out in different lighting conditions, including any crypt or vaults, the walls, roof and tower. The production of an accurate, measured plan and elevations will reveal much about the building, its alignment, discrepancies, additions, and the pattern of its development, which might otherwise remain hidden. Likewise, careful examination of the structure may reveal additions, straight-joints in walls, blocked-up windows and doors, re-used stone, older roof-lines and other evidence of addition and alterations. Most English parish churches were originally constructed as simple buildings, consisting of a nave and small chancel; many have developed by enlargements, extensions, the addition of aisles, side chapels, a tower and other features, and the local historian should look carefully for the evidence of earlier buildings now submerged beneath later developments, since for most parish churches this will be the only record of their early history and development we possess. Nor should the amount which can be learnt from such careful and systematic examination be underestimated. Recent work on churches such as Deerhurst, (Glos), St Peter's, Barton-on-Humber (Lincs), Little Somborne (Hants) or the three Essex churches of Hadstock, Rivenhall and Asheldam, have demonstrated the complex way in which the plans of apparently quite ordinary churches developed. It has been shown that what appeared at Asheldam to be an 'undistinguished, small medieval church, typical of many in the area, with no outstanding architectural features, nor overt evidence of early origin', was, in fact, a complex series of stone structures which had grown by successive alterations and enlargements over the centuries. Such studies emphasise the conclusion that

> No matter how well a church's history and architecture have been documented and studied in the past, there is invariably a great deal more to be learned from an exhaustive study of the up-standing fabric, coupled with analysis of the church and its graveyard in the parochial landscape.[3]

Norman churches

The scale and extent of church building of every sort during the century and a half after the Norman Conquest is stupendous. In their concern to sweep away what they regarded as cluttered and unsatisfactory Saxon buildings and to provide a new setting for the worship of a reformed Church, the Normans rebuilt almost every cathedral, erected hundreds of new monasteries and thousands of parish churches, in an outburst of building activity of which the like was not to be witnessed again until the nineteenth century. The establishment of new parishes with their own churches, often by local landowners, led to the final extinction of the supremacy of the old minster churches, although a few continued to receive dues from the parishes within their former sphere of influence, and others long retained rights such as those of baptism or burial. More often these rights faded with time and the minster church lost its primacy. A few former minsters continued to have several priests and remained collegiate foundations: these included St Buryan and St Endellion (Cornwall), Leominster (Herefordshire), Ripon (Yorks), Beverley (Humberside), Southwell (Notts) and Wolverhampton (Staffs); others became colleges of secular canons, generally Augustinian, such as Taunton (Somerset), St Frideswide (Oxon), Hexham (Northumberland), Hartland and Crediton (Devon) and Christchurch (Hants).[4] The minster church of St Paul at Bedford was still being served at the time of the Norman Conquest by a group of secular canons who were the successors of the priests who served the minster there in the seventh century.[5] At Leominster, the collegiate church maintained a force of four priests at the end of the twelfth century 'on account of the dispersal of the parishes'.[6] At Morville (Shropshire), the break-up of the minster *parochia* was not completed until the twelfth century, as chapelries were established in the outlying villages and hamlets, and of these six developed into churches for separate parishes.[7] There is similar evidence for rapid growth in the number of churches in towns, and by the end of the twelfth century there were already over 100 churches in London, 35 in Lincoln, 14 in York and similarly remarkable numbers in other towns.[8] It was often one or more landlords who paid for the erection of a church, endowed it with land (glebe) and a house (parsonage), and who thereafter 'owned' the profits of the obligatory tithes and offerings, and possessed also the *advowson* or right of choosing the priest. The churches which are recorded in the Domesday Book as attached to particular estates and as having their profits or income divided into half, quarter or even sixth parts, are accounted for by the fact that they were erected by a group of landowners. Likewise, the multiplicity of churches in some medieval towns such as York, Exeter, Bristol, Norwich, Stamford and others arose because a single landowner or wealthy merchant founded a church for himself and his men, or because a group of neighbours collaborated in building and endowing a church. Such men adopted a proprietorial attitude to their churches and rebuilt or enlarged them, changed the site or bequeathed the church and its profits to a monastic house, apparently regardless of the sentiments of the parishioners. For example, in c.1180 the local landowner gave the profits of the church of Sutton-in-Holland (Lincs) to Castle Acre priory and agreed that the church building should be demolished and a new one built on a different site, which he also gave:

> ...three acres of land in Sutton, in the field called Heoldefen next the road,
> to build a parish church there. And my wish is that the earlier wooden
> church of the same vill, in the place of which the new church will be built,
> shall be taken away and the bodies buried in it shall be taken to the new
> church?

This proliferation of new churches and energetic reconstruction of old ones is impressive evidence of the devotion, wealth and practical concern for the church among the laity, and of the zeal and enthusiasm of that army of parish clergy of whose work in the Saxon and post-Conquest period so little else survives, and about whose activities the documentary records are almost completely silent.

The Church in the landscape

The negative evidence is also important, for the structural development of the church and its situation within the settlement may be a reflection of the fortunes of the community which it served. Thus the fact that so many Norman churches in Sussex, Berkshire, Shropshire, Herefordshire and the whole of the Welsh borderland were not subsequently rebuilt or enlarged is an indication of the continuing poverty of those regions throughout the later Middle Ages, just as many ruined or deserted churches of Norfolk provide evidence of late-medieval conditions there![10] An isolated medieval church is almost always an indication that the settlement has moved or been deserted, for the value of the parish church in landscape studies lies in the way in which it tends to cling to its original site and thus provide a fixed point in the landscape, notwithstanding all later changes in settlement patterns, population or economic life![11] At Maxey (Northants), the medieval parish church is isolated from the village, but aerial photographs reveal that it was formerly close to the Saxon and later settlement; similarly at Kempley, on the Gloucestershire-Herefordshire border, the fine Norman church with its remarkable series of wall-paintings shows clear evidence of the wealth lavished upon it in the twelfth century, but the modern village is more than a mile away and only the earthworks in the fields surrounding the church survive from the earlier settlement. Great Walsingham, Weasenham St Peter, Longham and West Dereham as well as many other churches in Norfolk are now isolated, because of the way in which the habitation has moved, but were originally beside or surrounded by the settlements which they served![12]

The importance of the church site in elucidating the settlement history of a town can be seen at Abingdon, where the early minster church of St Helen was the focal point of the original settlement; it was founded close to the confluence of the Thames and Ock rivers, and three medieval streets converged upon the church. Later, a Saxon abbey was established on a site to the east of St Helen's, and the subsequent growth and considerable prosperity of the abbey attracted settlement and a market, and completely altered the lay-out and focus of the town![13] Likewise, there are many parish churches which show evidence of reduction in size by the demolition of the chancels, aisles, transepts, side chapels or parts of the nave, such as Ovingdean (Sussex), Upavon (Wilts), Merton (Oxon), Eastleach Turville (Glos), Chepstow (Mon), Little Malvern (Worcs) or Lastingham (Yorks) and many others. The naveless chancel at Winchelsea, with the ruins showing fine and expensive architectural features, is a stark reminder of the startling decline in the town's fortunes; likewise, the great church at Cley-next-the-Sea (Norfolk), with its ruined south transept, provides remarkable evidence of the former prosperity of this now abandoned but once-important seaport.

Church organisation

One effect of the new spirit and new personalities brought to the Church by the Norman Conquest was the reorganisation of the diocesan structure under Willian the Conqueror's archbishop of Canterbury, Lanfranc, who had been abbot of Caen. At a Council held at Windsor in 1072 it was ordered that those Saxon bishoprics situated in villages or remote rural situations should be moved to major towns. The see of Dorchester-on-Thames was moved to Lincoln, Selsey to Chichester, Lichfield to Chester; Ramsbury and Sherborne were amalgamated and the bishopric moved to Old Sarum; the see of Elmham was transferred to Thetford and afterwards to Norwich, and Wells to Bath. During the reign of Henry I two new dioceses were created—Ely and Carlisle. Thus was established the basic diocesan framework of the English Church which survived without further major alteration until the Reformation.

As early as the tenth century the payment of tithe was made compulsory, and the laws of Edmund (939-46) and Edgar (959-75) added the power of the Crown to that of the Church to enforce payment. The need to define each man's responsibility for the payment of tithes as well as of other offerings and dues such as church-scot or plough-scot, levied on burials for the benefit of the deceased person's soul, and the need to make it clear to which church or priest such dues had to be paid, made it necessary to delimit parish boundaries precisely. It was also important to make it clear which church each person was to attend to hear Mass on Sundays and the great festivals, where he should take his children for Baptism and Confirmation, where his daughter's marriage should be celebrated, or where he should be buried. During the eleventh and twelfth centuries the development of canon law laid increasing stress upon the financial obligations of the laity towards their parish church. These duties became even more formalised as more and more parish churches were appropriated by monasteries, which were often situated far from the parish, so that the parishioners were regarded by the monks as an additional source of income, and the monastic responsibility consisted only in the appointment of a vicar to care for the spiritual welfare of the parish. This widespread transfer of parishes and parochial income to monastic houses is one of the most remarkable features of early-medieval church life; it has been estimated that before 1200 a quarter of the parish churches of England had already been appropriated by religious houses, and about half of all parishes were eventually to pass into the hands of the religious orders![14]

For those appropriated churches and for other parish churches which owed dues of various sorts to monastic houses, the monastic cartularies provide an admirable source of information. Cartularies often supply the earliest reference to the existence of a church, give the names of the incumbents, note dependent chapelries or offerings due to a mother church, and the rights established for the vicar when a monastic house became the rector of the parish. Like the bishops' registers, these are a source of information on church life which are too often neglected by local historians. Many monastic cartularies have been published and a list can be found in G.R.C. Davis, *The Medieval Cartularies of Great Britain*, 1958. For example, the Great Cartulary of Glastonbury abbey, compiled in *c.*1340 and listing all the properties, charters, rights, privileges and estates of one of the richest and most ancient of all English abbeys, gives details of the appropriation of eleven parish churches with their chapelries during the twelfth and thirteenth centuries, and of another five churches to which Glastonbury had rights of patronage and appointment, and of several others which were obliged to pay various dues to the abbey. For all these churches the cartulary provides detailed information which would otherwise be quite unobtainable![15]

In the appropriation of the revenues of parish churches by monasteries or cathedrals, as in so many other aspects of ecclesiastical administration, the wishes or preferences of the parishioners were totally subordinate and they were not consulted. The church and its revenues were regarded as the property of the patron, to be bestowed on whichever person or institution he wished. The appropriation of parish churches and the establishment of vicarages depressed the standard of living of many of the parochial clergy, for normally the monastic house which became the rector took the great tithes of corn and hay, tithes which were profitable and relatively easy to collect, and left to the vicar the lesser tithes such as milk or cheese, garden produce, fish, wildfowl, eggs or industrial products which were all much more difficult to assess and collect and much less valuable. When the monks of Muchelney abbey in Somerset established a vicarage for the parishioners at Muchelney in 1308, the rights and emoluments due to the vicar were carefully recorded in the register of Walter de Haselshaw, bishop of Bath and Wells (1302-9). The vicar was to serve the parish church which the monastery had built right beside and almost touching the great monastic church, as well as the dependent chapelry of Drayton, and he was to live in the charming vicarage house which survives beside the church. He was to have the lesser tithes, and the bread, eggs and other offerings at confessions, marriages and purifications and at Mass on Sundays, except on the great festivals, the times when the largest congregations might be expected, when the offerings were reserved for the abbot. The vicar was also to be supplied with bread and two gallons of best conventual ale from the abbey, and to have a dish of flesh meat on Sundays and Tuesdays, and of eggs or fish on other days, from the monastic kitchens. As well as the vicar's house there survives among the stonework found in the abbey ruins a late-medieval carving showing one of the vicars, carrying his two-gallon barrel of ale and three loaves of bread.[16] Similarly, the priory of Cistercian nuns at Stixwold in Lincolnshire established a parish church and vicarage beside their own church at the end of the thirteenth century, and the arrangement is recorded in the register of the diocesan bishop (Oliver Sutton, bishop of Lincoln 1280-99). The nuns agreed that the vicar was entitled to

> fourteen gallons of ale and seven pricked loaves for his boy, twenty shillings per annum for a robe, fourteen shillings for his clerk's stipend, and for his larder eight hundred eels, two stones of cheese, one stone of butter, half a stone of soap, two hundred turves, and a suitable lodging near the church.[17]

The total transfer of all income, property and rights, both spiritual and temporal, in a parish church by appropriation to a monastery or cathedral, and the completely passive role of the parishioners in the transaction can be ilustrated from the case of Pucklechurch (Avon). The parish church, which was in the patronage of the Crown, was given to the Dean and Chapter of Wells cathedral; on Sunday, 12 November 1396 two canons of Wells, Richard Harewell and Richard Bruton, arrived at Pucklechurch with both royal and papal licences, and when the parishioners were assembled for Mass, entered the church and

> advancing to the high altar took possession of the church in the name of the Dean and Chapter, and in sign thereof took in their hands the books, missals, chalices and ornaments of the church, rang or caused to be rung the church bells, and remaining in the chancel while the High Mass was celebrated caused the said papal and royal letters to be published, and their effect to be declared before a great concourse of people in the vulgar tongue, and on the same day entered and took possession of the rectory manse; and after on 13 November held a court of the church tenants in the hall of the said rectory, who appeared before the said proctors and acknowledging the said Dean and Chapter for their lords, gave their oaths of fealty.[18]

The formal words of this statement do not conceal their dramatic effect, nor the fact that the parishioners, the 'great concourse of people', had no say in this matter which was to have such an impact upon their church, and which was to mean that henceforward the greater part of their tithes would go to Wells, twenty-five miles away and in a different diocese, in order to provide additional food for the canons, or, as the deed of the appropriation put it, to sustain 'the charges of the Chapter table', while the spiritual care of the parish would be entrusted to a lowly-paid substitute, a vicar or chaplain![19]

The beliefs of laity

In spite of the silence of most official records such as bishops' registers about the beliefs of the parochial clergy and the parishioners to whom they ministered, some clues can nonetheless be found. The early-medieval carving and decoration which survives in so many parish churches reveals the continuing strength of the popular belief in an incessant conflict between the forces of good and evil in the world. The omnipresent forces of evil are also shown in the many examples of exuberant Norman stone-carving, full of monsters, demons, grotesques, biting beasts and fierce dragons, such as those at Kilpeck (Herefordshire), Iffley and Barford St Michael (Oxfordshire), Adel near Leeds (Yorks), Ault Hucknall (Derbys), Barfreston (Kent), Studland (Dorset) or Elkstone (Glos). The imminence of Doom and Judgement is powerfully portrayed in twelfth-century wall paintings like the Judgement scene at Clayton (Sussex) or Christ in Majesty at Copford (Essex) and Kempley (Glos), in the battle of the virtues and vices at Claverley (Salop), or in the examples of The Three Living and The Three Dead which depicts three prosperous young men or three kings meeting with three skeletons.[20] The protection afforded by the Church and its sacraments to an otherwise helpless soul, and the incessant conflict with the powers of darkness, is emphasised in the many carvings of the battle between St Michael and the devil-dragon, as at Stoke-sub-Hamdon (Somerset), Luppitt (Devon), Ruardean and Moreton Valence (Glos) or Hoveringham (Notts). The same idea of the unceasing battle for the human soul can be seen in the carving on many fonts, as in the conflict between the seven virtues and their contrary vices depicted on the twelfth-century fonts at Stanton Fitzwarren (Wilts) and Southrop (Glos). The virtues are depicted trampling upon their contrary vices, and at Southrop, the figures of the vices each have their names carved back to front or in 'mirror-writing' as a further indication of their wickedness; around the top of the font are shown the heavenly mansions to which the soul may aspire by holding fast to the virtues through the help and sacraments of the Church, while eschewing all the vices. At Lullington near Frome (Somerset) the ornate font is surrounded by demons, monsters and a horned god, as well as by flowers and the heavenly mansions, and has a deeply-cut inscription around it: 'Hoc fontis sacro pereunt delicta lavacro' (in the sacred washing of this font are sins cleansed). The vigorously-carved font of black Tourai marble at East Meon (Hants) shows the Creation and Expulsion of Adam and Eve from Paradise amid a collection of dragons, birds and beasts; on the font at Avebury

(Wilts) the dragon is overcome by a bishop with crozier and book, while at St Mary's, Southampton, the font shows grotesque beasts confronted by the symbols of the four Evangelists. Medieval gargoyles and grotesque figures, beasts, monsters, demons, mermaids, crude satires, coarse humour in stone and frankly pagan symbols such as the Tree of Life or the almost universal Green Man or, more rarely, the hideous and sexually-explicit female figure known as a *Sheelagh na Gig*, or a male fertility carving, all these throw light on otherwise hidden beliefs. They reveal the powerful subculture which, in spite of the teachings of the Church and the denunciations of the clergy, continued to hold fast to many superstitions and pagan ideas[21]

The close contact and intimacy between priest and people is evident from the design of pre-Conquest and Norman parish churches, where the undivided nave and chancel and the small size of the building must have brought clergy and laity together in a way quite different from the remote, screened chancels and large impersonal churches of the later Middle Ages.

A good idea of the sort of church which served many English parishes during the twelfth century can be obtained from the few surviving examples which, unlike the majority of parish churches, were not enlarged or extensively remodelled during the later Middle Ages. Such churches include Winterborne Tomson (Dorset), Boarhunt (Hants), Kilpeck (Herefordshire), Manningford Bruce (Wilts), Hales and Intwood (Norfolk), Avington (Berks), Birkin (Yorks), North Marden (Sussex) and Bengeo (Herts). The dark interiors and profusion of wall-paintings can be seen at Claverley (Salop), Stoke Orchard and Kempley (Glos), Gussage St Andrew (Dorset) or Sutton Bingham (Som). Larger and lavishly-carved Norman churches survive at Iffley (Oxon), Stewkley (Bucks), Elkstone (Glos), Great Tey (Essex), Melbourne (Derbys) and at Castor (Northants) where an inscription records the consecration of the church in 1124.

Relics and saints

In an age which had few stone buildings even in towns, and when art was a rarity, the visual impact of the parish church, its architecture, stone-carving, decoration, paintings, bright colours and stained glass was inevitably great; and in a society in which religious belief, however inarticulate or superstitious, underlay all the precariousness and uncertainty of a harsh life, the power of the Church's message was immense. The cult of relics, and changes in the dedication of parish churches, often from obscure Saxon saints to more popular figures who might possibly be more powerful advocates with the Almighty, also cast light on popular beliefs and attitudes. Relics had the additional merit of attracting pilgrims and offerings, and were the prized possessions of parish churches, as well as of the greater churches, cathedrals and abbeys. The church of Stanford-in-the-Vale (Berks) still has the reliquary which once contained a bone of St Denis, the patron saint. Grantham (Lincs) possessed the relics of St Wulfram; St Edmund's, Salisbury had a piece of the skull of St Wolfride. At Whitechurch Canonicorum (Dorset) the shrine still containing the bones of St Wite is built as an altar in the north transept of the church, and was a place of pilgrimage throughout the Middle Ages. A reliquary containing the bones of St Piran was kept in the church at Perranzabuloe (Cornwall) and on festivals was carried in procession by the parishioners to various places in the vicinity in order to attract the offerings of the faithful. An inventory made of the goods of the church in 1281 includes the head of St Piran as well as the teeth of St Brendan and St Martin. Changes in the dedication of parish churches are commonly recorded in bishops' registers; the Normans had little respect for many of the Saxon saints and Archbishop Lanfranc himself wrote that he had strong 'doubts about the quality of their sanctity'. Bishops' registers, charters, monastic cartularies and wills may all provide evidence for the earlier dedication of a church, and thus also provide a clue to its early origins.[22] To take just two examples from Shropshire, the church at Atcham retains its dedication to St Eata (d.685) a companion of St Aidan, whose mission played such an important part in the conversion of the midlands and the north; this dedication links Atcham with the beginnings of Christianity in that region, even though none of the surviving architecture of the church is earlier than the twelfth century. Wistanstow, north of Ludlow, takes its name from the Mercian saint, Wistan, who was martyred in 849, and a cartulary of Lilleshall abbey refers to the church there as St Wistan's; but after the Norman Conquest, the church was completely reconstructed, leaving no trace of the Saxon building, and the dedication was later changed to Holy Trinity.[23] In Wiltshire, the thirteenth-century church of Sherrington in the Wylye valley was dedicated to the two third-century physicians, St Cosmos and St Damien, who are also commemorated in carvings on the west front of Salisbury cathedral. By the sixteenth century, however, the observance of their festival on 27 September each year had been abandoned in favour of the much more popular feast of St Michael and All Angels on 29 September, and soon all memory of the former dedication had been forgotten. The original dedication was restored in the twentieth century after the discovery of the will of John Carter, rector of Sherrington, dated 1553, in which he asked to be buried in 'the chauncell of Cosmos and Damien of Sherryton'.

The clergy

About the parish clergy and other officials, it is impossible to generalise, since they varied so much in origins and background, learning, wealth, ability and efficiency. Again, the prime source of information is the bishop's register, since this will record ordinations, inductions, patrons, changes of benefices, clerical delinquency and other details about the diocesan clergy. The ranks of the clergy included wealthy pluralists and non-residents, many of them important church administrators or royal servants; the beneficed rectors residing in their parishes; and the vicars, chaplains and host of unbeneficed clergy as well as deacons and others in minor orders?[24] It is important to beware of the false impression created by bishops' registers concerning the conduct of the clergy, for evil-doers naturally figure much more prominently than the multitude of conscientious clergy living peaceably in their parishes and doing nothing to attract the adverse attention of their bishop or his officials. Bishops' registers certainly contain plenty of evidence of clerical lapses. The energetic bishop of Salisbury, Simon of Ghent (1297-1315), visited the Dorset part of his diocese in 1302 and noted a host of human failings: missing books and ornaments, dilapidated churches, failure to provide all the services, unreasonable fees, neglect of parochial duties and similar faults. Several churches or newly-built parts of churches had not been consecrated; at Shaftesbury, rough games were played in the churchyard; elsewhere, animals grazed among the graves; and at Winterbourne Stickland, the rector was a foreigner who could speak no English and had to be ordered to find a chaplain to instruct him. As well as in bishops' registers, similar informative visitations of appropriated parish churches are also found in monastic cartularies and in the records of cathedral chapters. The records of the Dean and Chapter of Wells, for example, contain much information about their churches and the doings of the clergy, as well as about various offences of the laity and the enforcement of ecclesiastical law. The courts sat in the parish churches to hear cases against both clergy and laity and to impose penalties ranging from admonition and public penance to excommunication. For example, the bishop's commissionary sitting in the parish church of Banwell (Somerset) in 1338 heard charges of fornication against Alice Manschupe of Blackford and Christina Cokes of Wedmore; both confessed to the offences and were ordered to go barefoot twice round the church of Banwell.[25] In 1249-52, and again in 1297, the Dean and Chapter of St Paul's held visitations of their appropriated churches in London and the neighbouring counties, and these give us an enormous amount of detail about the fabric of the churches, the decoration, furnishings, images, equipment, books, and about the clergy; they provide a superb source of information on many aspects of church life and of local history.[26]

In educational attainments the clergy also differed greatly one from another. The bishops' registers contain many complaints about lack of education among the clergy, like the priest whom Bishop Grosseteste of Lincoln refused to institute, on the grounds that he was *'Insufficienter literatus, ne dicam fere omnino illiteratus'* (insufficiently educated, not to say almost completely illiterate); or the seven priests who served the parish church and numerous chapelries of Sonning in Berkshire in 1220: each was examined by William de Wanda, Dean of Salisbury, but only one was able to understand even simple Latin or give any account of the Christian faith.[27] Not all were ill-educated, however, and there are numerous examples of schools kept by parish clergy, and of men who later rose to great prominence in church and state whose early education was obtained from the local priest.[28] From the evidence of the bishops' registers and from their own wills, however, many of the parish clergy seem to have been local men, who probably differed little from their parishioners in education or outlook. Their interests may have been a little wider, and their aspirations a little higher, but most of them were only a little better off than their flock and they were equally dependent upon agricultural uncertainties for their livelihood. The evidence also suggests that their houses differed little from the others in the village and reflected the same farming interests. For example, the rectory at Glentham in Lincolnshire in 1305 included an ox-house, a cart-house, a hay-house and a sheep-fold, all thatched with reed; and a vicarage newly built at Theddlethorpe in the same county in the late fourteenth century had a hall, two chambers, a kitchen, bake-house and brew-house, as well as a stable for three horses, a hay-store, and other farming buildings including a sty for twelve pigs. All was roofed with straw, and the surrounding glebe land was enclosed with dikes *'juxta morem patrie'* (according to the custom of the district).[29]

There were many like Richard Fanellor, the rector of Chilton Foliat (Wilts), during the fourteenth century. He was a local man who kept in touch with his family, farmed his own glebe land, and when he died in 1397 directed that he should be buried in his own church, and that £5 10s 0d should be spent on his funeral. He left gifts and legacies to his three sisters, to his shepherd and other servants, to the fabric of the cathedral of Salisbury and to his own church at Chilton Foliat.[30] Of very few of the parish clergy do we get any intimate picture or detailed biography. An exception is the Life of St Wulfstan, a parish priest who became bishop of Worcester (1062-1107), written by William of Malmesbury.[31] The twelfth-century life of the anchorite Wulfric of Haselbury in Somerset contains a vivid picture of the parish priest of Haselbury as well as of Wulfric himself. Wulfric lived in a cell beside the church of Haselbury from 1125 until his death in 1155. His reputation for sanctity, miracles and wisdom spread far and wide, and a stream of penitents, supplicants and sufferers came to his window and sought his help, advice and prayers. Among his visitors were the kings Henry I and Stephen, and even the great St Bernard of Clairvaux, hearing of his sanctity, is said to have asked for his prayers. Wulfric maintained a close friendship with the priest Brichtric and with his successor, Osbern. Brichtric was evidently a devout, hard-working and dedicated priest, and is described as follows:

> He was a man whose simplicity and humility were very like those of the Blessed Wulfric, for he busied himself in the same way with psalms and prayers by day and by night, and, so far as his ministry allowed him, gave himself up to perpetual watchings in his church.

Brichtric evidently lacked formal education, and could only speak in English, for on one occasion he complained to Wulfric that he was compelled to remain silent before the bishop and the archdeacon for he could not speak the French which was the language of the educated class; Brichtric understandably felt unfairly treated on another occasion when Wulfric not only cured a dumb man but enabled him to speak in several different languages.[32] In the twelfth century the Church had not yet completely enforced the rule of clerical celibacy, and there are many examples of married priests. It comes as no surprise therefore to find that Britchric was married; his wife was named Godida, and their son, Osbern, became Wulfric's attendant and acolyte, and eventually succeeded his father as the parish priest of Haselbury. Another neighbouring priest named Segar is also mentioned; he was married and had four sons, all of whom entered the Cistercian monastery at Forde, three as monks and one as a lay-brother. The Life of Wulfric of Haselbury shows the parish priests as unlearned but dedicated men, full of simple piety, and deeply immersed in the pastoral care of their parishes. They also seem to have had a fund of simple common sense, for when Wulfric confessed to one of them that he was greatly distressed because in a moment of ill-temper he had cursed a mouse for nibbling at his clothing and that the creature had immediately fallen dead at his feet, the priest replied that he wished Wulfric would curse all the mice in the district in the same way.[33] Equally informative is the biography of Gilbert, rector of Sempringham (Lincolnshire) and founder of the order of Gilbertine Canons. He was the son of a Norman knight, Gocelin, who was patron of the church of Sempringham, and after an education in France, Gilbert became rector of the parish in c.1120. At Sempringham he kept a school for the village children, and the fifteenth-century English version of his biography describes his teaching as follows:

> For first was he a maystir of lernyng to the smale petites, swech as lerne to rede, spelle and synge. Tho childryn that were undyr his disciplyne he taute not only her lessones on the book, but beside this, he taute for to pley in dew tyme, and here playes taute he that thei shuld be honest and mery with-outen clamour or grete noyse.[34]

Later, Gilbert joined the household of the bishop of Lincoln; he retained the rectory of Sempringham and in c.1131 returned to the village and established on his own estate a joint house of nuns and canons which was the beginning of the Gilbertine houses in England. He also resumed his parochial duties and became greatly venerated for his personal sanctity, charity and successful insistence upon a strictly religious life throughout his parish.[35]

Perhaps most interesting of all the early-medieval clergy of whose lives we know more than the bare outline was William of Pagula, a highly-educated Englishman who spent much of his career in the lowly position of vicar of Winkfield near Windsor. After a distinguished career at Oxford where he became a Doctor of Canon Law, he became vicar of Winkfield in 1314 and remained there until his death in c.1332. While there he wrote a number of theological treatises, and also produced the *Oculus Sacerdotis*, a practical guide for parish priests. The *Oculus Sacerdotis* deals with all the duties of the priest, from the conduct of services, to the administration of all the sacraments. All this is presented in English and in a simple practical style, as is his discussion of the arguments for and against marriage, setting out the reasons for entering into marriage and all its drawbacks, including the fact that anything else, such as a horse, an ass, an ox, a dog can be tried out before purchase; only a wife has to be taken on trust; and a beautiful wife will have other men running after her, while it is irksome to have an ugly wife whom no one else wants.[36]

Evidence for liturgy and ritual

One other development of the early Middle Ages emerges from a study of the structure of English parish churches, and will be evident to local historians in many places. This is the common practice of lengthening and enlarging the chancel in order to accommodate increasing ritual and more priests, deacons and acolytes, as well as adding an aisle or aisles to the nave, thus making it possible to have processions around the church. Chancels were generally extended eastwards rather than widened, and such extensions are frequently out of alignment with the rest of the church, a feature which, during the nineteenth century, was thought to be an intentional piece of symbolism, but which is much more likely to be the result of various medieval extensions and rebuildings of both nave and chancel.[37]

An elaborate ritual or liturgical use demanding more than a single priest would have been impossible in most Saxon or Norman chancels, and changing fashion in the conduct of services was the main motive in the building of the numerous thirteenth-century chancels which can be seen in all parts of the country.

Evidence of increasing ritual and drama in the services can be seen too in the elaborately-carved Easter sepulchres, which survive in some chancels; *sedilia*, or seats where the priest and attendants sat during sermons, and during the singing of anthems or other ceremonies, were also commonly installed on the south sides of chancels during the thirteenth and fourteenth centuries and indicate the increasing ritual and the growing number of persons involved in the conduct of the services. Highly-decorated examples of *sedilia* can be seen at Weston Longville (Norfolk), Hawton (Notts), Ilkeston (Derbys), Cliffe (Kent), Patrington (Yorks), Castle Hedingham (Essex), Luton (Beds), Nantwich (Cheshire) and in other churches throughout the country. Many side-altars have been demolished but the evidence for them often remains in the piscina or shallow recess with a drain set in the wall generally on the south side of the altar, where the priest washed the sacred vessels. These also give some indication of the increasing number of priests and services, even in small parish churches. Further evidence of the increasing elaboration in ritual, processions, music, lights, banners and other features of the service is also provided by the surviving inventories listing churches' possessions. The endeavour to relate the changing plan and architectural features of a church to the developments in liturgical ideas and ritual throughout the Middle Ages, though difficult, can be a profitable line of enquiry. The extent of new building in chancels, altars, naves, and aisles, and the addition of towers, is reflected in the bishops' registers since new work had to be consecrated by the bishop. Thus in a tour through the Cornish part of his diocese in 1259, Bishop Walter Bronescombe of Exeter conducted consecrations at 21 churches, and in 1326 Robert Petit, suffragan to Bishop Roger Martival of Salisbury, consecrated no fewer than 53 churches in the diocese after recent building work had been carried out. At Urchfont (Wilts) in the Salisbury diocese, the chancel had been found to be insufficient and unsatisfactory during a visitation by Bishop Simon of Ghent in 1301, and both the rector and the archdeacon of Wiltshire had been reproved. The effect was dramatic, for within the next few years the church was provided with a remarkably fine vaulted chancel, obviously a very ambitious and expensive undertaking for a parish church. The earliest surviving building contract for part of a parish church is for Sandon (Herts) in 1348, and is concerned with the rebuilding of the chancel; it was made between the mason Thomas Rikelyng and the Dean and Chapter of St Paul's Cathedral, who were the patrons.[38]

Parishioners, patrons and private oratories

During the thirteenth century the convention grew up that the parishioners were responsible for the upkeep of the nave, while the patron or rector was charged with the duty of maintaining the chancel. This convention was formalised at the Synod of Exeter in 1287 when parishioners were ordered under pain of penalties in the Church courts to contribute to the repair of their churches *'secundum portionem terrae quam possident in eadem parochia'* (according to the quality of land they possess in each parish). An early example of parochial collections, gifts and voluntary contributions towards the parish church comes from Bridgwater (Somerset) in 1318; collections of money and of brass and lead vessels raised eleven pounds for re-casting the church bells, and later in the century larger sums were raised to build the elegant spire which still dominates the town.[39]

Another common development of the twelfth and thirteenth centuries was the building of private chapelries and oratories in distant parts of parishes. Again, the bishops' registers or monastic cartularies are the prime source of evidence for the date, the names of the builders and the reasons for these chapels, for they had to be licensed and consecrated by the diocesan bishop, while conditions were frequently laid down concerning their use and in order to preserve the rights and dues payable to the parish church. Thus the Cartulary of Cirencester Abbey records that Walter de Brussels was allowed by the abbey to found a chapel at Arle and to have Mass said there on three days of the week, and that this was confirmed by the bishop of Worcester who consecrated the chapel and a graveyard there in c.1141. Likewise, at Shriveham in 1233 the men of the hamlet of Longcot were allowed to have a chapel with a graveyard because of their distance from the mother church. Frequently conditions were attached to such grants, insisting on dues being paid to the parish church or on attendance there during the great festivals. At Cookham (Berks) in 1237, Sir William of Culworth was allowed to have a private oratory, provided its dimensions did not exceed 24 feet by 16 feet.[40] Such private oratories and chapels of ease were especially common in the large moorland parishes of the north of England and in Devon and Cornwall. By the end of the Middle Ages, the large parish of Hartland in Devon, for example, had ten subsidiary chapels as well as the stately parish church of St Nectan; Tiverton had six and most large parishes had one or more chapels, some of which gradually acquired parochial status.

Priests and people

An interesting source of information about the way in which parish churches were used by the community can be found in the *Inquisitions Post Mortem* on behalf of the Crown to establish the age of an heir to property; these can be found in the printed *Calendars of Miscellanous Inquisitions*. If a child inherited property before attaining the age of 21, he or she became a Ward of the Crown. Occasionally therefore, enquiries had to be made to establish proofs of age and this was done by enquiring about the date of the child's baptism, which normally took place on the day of birth or very soon after. For children who might eventually inherit substantial property, efforts were made to ensure that the day of the baptism should be remembered by local people, since in the days before parish registers, this was the only way of ensuring that the true age of the child could be established. Often, such enquiries give considerable detail about the scene in the church on the day of baptism. For example, John de Welle was born at Bonthorpe (Lincs) in 1334 and was baptised in the church of St Helen at Willoughby on the day of his birth. An enquiry 21 years later produced testimony as follows:

> John Musters, Knight, aged forty-five years said that he came on the said Tuesday to do Fealty to Sir John de Wilughby, Knight, for his lands in Somercotes, and saw the godmother of the said John, Margaret, Prioress of Greenfield, carrying him from the said church wrapped in swaddling clothes. Robert de Alford agrees, and says that on the said Tuesday an agreement was made between him and John Jolyf of Willoughby in the said church touching divers trespasses, when the said John, son of Adam, came to be baptised.[41]

At Lytchett Matravers (Dorset) the baptism of John Arundell, who was to become lord of the manor, took place in 1408, and when the villagers were questioned about it at an enquiry held at Blandford Forum (Chipping Blandford) 21 years later, they could remember a wealth of detail about the eventful day. Walter Russell remembered that he carried two pots full of wine into the church for the refreshment of the godfathers and the godmother at the baptism. Perhaps others also had some of the wine, for John Hekford stated that one Robert Roo had died suddenly in the church, and Richard Pylke remembered that his father was seized with paralysis on that day, while John Garland recalled that he had broken his right arm by falling in the road on his way from the baptism.[42] Such baptisms were of course exceptional, but every baby was brought to the church to be baptised. The priest thus came into close personal contact with every family, and the font was an important symbol of the pastoral authority of the parish church. It was for this reason that in countless churches the ancient font was preserved even when all the rest of the church was rebuilt or renewed, so that today the font often provides a clearer indication of the age of the church than almost any other single part of its structure. The priest was also brought into close contact with the people through the sacraments of marriage and extreme unction, and we can end this chapter by examining briefly the enormous clerical mortality during the Black Death of 1348-9, which illustrates very clearly how many of the clergy were in their parishes and in contact with the sick and dying during the horrific onslaught of the plague. Again, the bishops' registers which record the institutions to benefices are the prime source, and local historians should not neglect to work out the figures of institutions during the Black Death and subsequent fourteenth-century plagues for their own and surrounding parishes. For example, in Wiltshire the bishops' registers show that in the decade before 1349 the annual number of new institutions of the parish clergy was never higher than forty in a single year; in 1349 it rose to over one hundred. Similarly in Cornwall, the average number before 1349 was five; during 1349-50 it rose to eighty-five. In Dorset, where the Black Death started and the plague was particularly virulent, the incumbents of almost half the parishes died during 1349-50. Likewise, in the diocese of Bath and Wells the average number of institutions to benefices during the 1340s was about nine per month. During the height of the plague the figures were as follows:

November	1348	9
December	1348	32
January	1349	47
February	1349	43
March	1349	36
April	1349	40
May	1349	21
June	1349	7[43]

Similarly figures can be extracted from bishops' registers all over the country, and are impressive evidence of the diligence of the clergy in carrying out the requirements of their office. In most English parishes the local historian has to accept that until the later Middle Ages the written sources of information are few, and that there will inevitably be large gaps in knowledge and many questions which cannot be answered. Nonetheless, careful research and observation will establish some details of the incumbents, the patrons and the financial position of the parish, while the church building itself may throw some light on the spiritual life of the parish. The sites and structure, and survivals such as an early font, stone-carving, decoration, or evidence of former chapels, altars, screens and doorways can provide evidence of ecclesiastical development, the increase or decline of wealth and population, or clues to religious life and beliefs.

Chapter Three

THE LATER MIDDLE AGES

Although detailed documentary evidence concerning parish life, community activities and the part played by the parishoners in the building, decoration and furnishing of their churches is not abundant for the early Middle Ages, there is no lack of detailed material for the fourteenth and fifteenth centuries, for this was a period when the Church's involvement in all aspects of community affairs was at its height. The survival of medieval records has of course, been uneven, and while some dioceses are rich in material, others have very little, but even for those parishes where medieval documentary sources such as diocesan records or churchwardens' accounts are sparse or completely lacking, the local historian can still find useful information about the parish community and religious life during the later Middle Ages from a careful examination of the church building and from the evidence of extensions and alterations, or the remains of former altars, screens, colour, decoration and furnishings which a thorough inspection of the building may reveal.

This chapter will discuss these various sources in more detail, and will examine the sort of evidence which they provide concerning the central rôle of the parish churches in all aspects of community life, and the questions which should be asked about the church and the parish community.

Bishops' registers

From the early thirteenth century, and especially from the pontificate and reforms of one of the greatest of the medieval popes, Innocent III (1198-1216), the Church began to pay more attention to the systematic preservation of its records. The great series of papal registers which are an invaluable source for English ecclesiastical history begin in 1198; at the same time royal records were more carefully kept, and bishops' registers for many English dioceses begin during the thirteenth century, for example, York (1225), Exeter (1257), Bath and Wells (1264), Worcester (1268), Hereford (1275) and Canterbury (1279). By the later Middle Ages, diocesan administration by bishops, suffragans, archdeacons and rural deans, with visitations, ecclesiastical courts and all the various church officials and institutions, formed the essential framework for everyday life and ensured that the influence of the Church touched almost every sphere of a parishoner's life, from his baptism to beyond the grave.

Because the concerns of the Church were so comprehensive and far-reaching, there are few aspects of medieval life which are not reflected in the bishops' registers, and they provide information on secular as well as religious life in the parishes. Many registers have been published by local record societies, or by societies such as the Canterbury and York Society which was founded for that purpose. Details of all the episcopal registers can be found in D. M. Smith, *Guide to Bishops' Registers of England and Wales,* 1981, and a list of those which have been printed is in E. D. Graves, *A Bibliography of English History to 1485,* 1975, 758-90. A useful brief guide to the background and content of the registers is D. M. Owen, *Medieval Records in Print: Bishops' Registers,* Historical Association, 1982. Most of the earlier printed registers were produced in the original Latin with English headings, but later volumes are generally in English translation, have English summaries or have been calendared in English. But even for those many local historians who do not find Latin easy, the material in the registers relating to individual parishes is often so useful and informative that it is well worth the labour of translating those parts which the index lists as relating to the parish or parishes being studied. The laws and officials of the Church, its spiritual influence and financial demands, touched every sphere of secular life; it was the Church which provided the king with advisers and civil servants, which produced educated men as household priests for gentry families, and kept an army of parish clergy, guild chaplains and chantry priests whose influence was felt in the remotest corners of the land. As a landowner, the Church had a dominant economic influence in many parishes, the Church courts enforced the canon law and the financial obligations of parishoners and, above all, it was the clergy who possessed the unique power to hear confessions, to give absolution and to celebrate the supreme mystery of the Mass!

The bishops' registers are an indispensable source for the names of patrons and incumbents, and for priests ordained or instituted to parochial chapelries, chantries, private oratories or free chapels—they, incidentally, provide the only evidence for the former existence of some of these short-lived estblishments. Generally, such institutions were quite straight-forward. A typical example from the register of Robert Hallum, Bishop of Salisbury (1407-17), records the following:

> Institution of Nicholas Coventre, priest, to the church of Upton Lovell, vacant by the resignation of Robert Hayward. Patron John Lovell, lord of Lovell and Holland. 16 July 1408[2]

Occasionally, a little more human detail is given, as for example in the case of Henry Vyller, priest, instituted to the vicarage of West Hendred (Berks) by Bishop Robert Hallum in July 1408; not only are we told that the patrons were Prior Richard and the convent of the Holy Trinity at Wallingford, but also that the former vicar, Peter Grene, had resigned on account of old age, and that his successor had sworn an oath on the gospels to pay him ten marks (£6 13s 4d) annually as a pension[3]

At the same time, Bishop Hallum ordered an inquiry into the state of affairs at Castle Combe (Wilts). It emerged that Adam de Uske, rector of

Castle Combe, had been living in Rome as an official at the papal court, and that in 1406 he had left Rome and joined the rival papal court at Avignon. For this he had been excommunicated by the Roman Pope, Gregory XI. Meanwhile, the church at Castle Combe had been grossly neglected, and the parishioners had been obliged to pay for a chaplain to administer the sacraments to them. The bishop ordered that a new rector, Ralph de Derham, priest, should be instituted.[4] Parishioners who in such circumstances used their initiative to hire a priest to minister to them, without the licence of the bishop, could likewise find themselves in trouble. Thomas Bekynton, Bishop of Bath and Wells (1443-65) imposed an interdict on the chapelry of Pensford in 1448 and suspended the priest, Thomas Northion.

> who calls himself chaplain of Pensford, on account of the said Thomas
> having been admitted by the people of Pensford to preach in the said Chapel
> and having done so without the bishop's licence.[5]

For those clergy who were graduates, biographical details can be found in A. B. Emden, *A Biographical Register of the University of Oxford to 1500;* 3 vols., 1957-9; and *A Biographical Register of the University of Cambridge to 1500,* 1963.

Bishops' registers record licences granted to clergy to leave their parishes for study, royal service, pilgrimage, because of infirmity, or for some other reason. For example, in 1401 Archbishop Gray granted a licence to William Morewyk, rector of Lokynton, to be absent from his parish for one year, providing in the meantime a sufficient deputy to minister to the spiritual needs of the parish. Such licences could mean that a parish was left in the care of chaplains or curates for very long periods. At Crowcombe in west Somerset, Geoffrey Lavington, rector, was licensed to be absent to study in 1320, and his successor, John de Shiplake, was licensed to be absent in Hugh Audley's service; in 1335 the rector, John Cam, had leave to study at Oxford, and in 1343 James de Molton was allowed to hold the parish in plurality with the prebend of Howden in Yorkshire.[6]

In 1330 the Archbishop of York, William Melton, (1317-40) granted a licence to Master William de Burton, vicar of Kirby Moorside, to go on pilgrimage to Compostella in performance of a vow. Likewise, in 1328 he granted a licence to Simon ·de Munketon, rector of Escrick, to be absent from his parish for three years in order to go on pilgrimage to the shrine of St James of Compostella, and also in order to study at a university. There are many similar examples which provide unique evidence concerning the parish clergy, their concerns and interests.

Bishops' registers also provide information about alterations in the dedications and patronal festivals of parish churches, illustrating changes in the popularity and cult of different saints. For example, in 1408 Bishop Hallum of Salisbury granted a licence to the vicar and parishioners of Sparsholt (Berks) at their petition, to change the dedication of their church from the obscure and probably original dedication to St Tecla, to the much more popular St Martin; later the dedication was changed to Holy Cross.[7] Sadly, we are seldom told the reasons for such changes, nor why parishioners chose particular saints. One factor leading to change was that, as the dedication feast of each parish was a public holiday and was celebrated in style, parishioners were at pains to avoid harvest periods or days which clashed with some greater ecclesiastical festival or one which might already have a holiday. In 1445 Bishop Edmund Lacy of Exeter (1420-55) granted a licence to the parishioners of St Dominic in Cornwall to change the date on which they celebrated their patronal festival from 30 August to 9 May, because the parishioners complained that essential work on the harvest interfered with the festivities during August.[8]

Canon law required that new or enlarged churches, and newly-built chapels or altars, should be consecrated by a bishop, and the bishops' registers contain unique evidence for the rebuilding and extension of churches, the division or union of parishes, the foundation of chantries and the growth of private oratories or chapels in castles or manor houses, or at places far distant from parish churches. This sort of evidence often provides the only surviving information about the development or decline of communities, movements of population, the building of bridges and roads, and the growth or decay of industries; it is thus of great value for local historians, especially for the Middle Ages when other sources are scarce, and well worth the effort to locate and translate it. Bishop Brantyngham of Exeter (1370-94), for example, licensed over 130 private oratories or chapels of ease in the large parishes of Devon and Cornwall, and his successor, Bishop Stafford (1395-1421), licensed more than 100 more. In 1437 Bishop Edmund Lacy of Exeter granted the inhabitants of Laneast the right to have a parochial chapel and churchyard dedicated to the popular west country saint, St Sidwell, because they were more than five miles from the mother church of St Stephen's-by-Launceston; it was difficult to carry bodies over the rough hilly roads for burial, and tradesmen and husbandmen were kept from their work for long periods in order to bury the dead. At the other end of the country, the inhabitants of Eskdale in Cumbria complained in 1445 that they lived ten miles from the mother church of St Bees, and that they were separated from it by two broad stretches of water and by three streams 'which swell in rainy and wintry weather so that they cannot conveniently go thither for christenings, burials, divine offices, sacraments and sacramentals.' They were, therefore, given episcopal licence to elevate their chapel to the status of a parish church, with rights of baptism and burial. The church at Ashwick in the diocese of Bath and Wells was a subsidiary chapel of the ancient minster at Kilmersdon nearly five miles away; in 1413 it was granted the right by the bishop to have a churchyard and to baptise children and bury the dead at Ashwick instead of at Kilmersdon because of 'the difficulties of the ways, deep with water at many times of the year and covered with snow', but Ashwick was not made into a separate parish, for the bishop also ordered that each year all the inhabitants of Ashwick should attend at the mother church of Kilmersdon on the patronal festival, and should make an offering there. Not until 1826 did Ashwick attain complete parochial status.[9] Such divisions of parishes and the gradual acquisition of rights by daughter churches were a continuation and completion of the long process whereby the huge areas once subject to minster churches were eventually broken up into separate parishes.

Incidental evidence can also be found in the bishops' registers for road and bridge building, the supply of water or similar benevolent and charitable works. For example, in 1486 Thomas Rotheram, Archbishop of York (1480-1500) granted an indulgence of 40 days to those who helped in any way in the rebuilding of the wooden bridge across the Trent at Kelham near Newark which had been carried away by floods. In 1445 Bishop Thomas Bekynton granted 40 days' indulgence to all who contributed to the repair of the road from Bristol towards Wells which was dangerous to travellers; and when in 1458 the harbour at Watchet was destroyed by a storm all the parishes in the diocese were exhorted by the bishop to send money for its reconstruction.[10] In 1488, an indulgence of 40 days was granted to all who contributed to the repair of the church of St Mary-le-Strand outside Temple Bar in London, which had been despoiled by thieves and its books and ornaments stolen.[11]

Occasionally, disputes over the rights of a chapelry to receive tithes and other offerings led to a decision by the bishop; the lands liable to pay tithes to a chapelry or chaplain are recorded in great detail and provide a unique picture of the agricultural arrangements. For example, in the late-thirteenth century Nicholas Longspee, Bishop of Salisbury (1291-7), granted to Geoffrey de Turberville, knight, and Isabel his wife, the right to have a chapel dedicated to St John the Baptist, and a chaplain, on the manor of East Hendred for the use of their household, on the grounds that the house was so far from the mother parish church that, particularly in winter, they could not conveniently attend it to hear the divine offices and receive the sacraments. The chaplain was to be supported by the tithes of the manor, and only members of the family were to be admitted to the sacraments. More than a century later, in 1412, when a dispute arose between the rector of the parish of East Hendred and the chaplain of St John the Baptist concerning their respective rights to tithes and offerings, the bishop of Salisbury, Robert Hallum, laid down in great detail all the lands and properties which were to pay tithe to the chapel, specifying the lands and furlongs in the common fields with their names and situations, the meadow land, and the rights to tithes on sheep, cows and milk, together with offerings. The whole provides a remarkably early and detailed description of the manor and is a valuable source of local history.

Visitations

An informative section of some bishops' registers is the record of parochial visitations conducted by the bishop, either in person or by deputy; some bishops kept separate records of their findings but few of these have survived. Groups of laymen from each parish, known as Questmen, were summoned to answer questions about the parish, the fabric of the church, the books and equipment, the lives and conduct of the clergy and the morals of the laity. Inevitably, the answers to such wide-ranging enquiries are of the greatest interest and throw light on many otherwise hidden aspects of local life, customs, belief and conduct.

The sort of detail to be found can be seen in the register of Simon of Ghent, Bishop of Salisbury (1297-1315), who was much occupied with attempts to reform the religious life in his large diocese, and conducted several visitations.[12] Archdeacons also carried out visitations of the churches in their area, particularly to ensure that the church buildings were in good repair and that they possessed all the necessary vestments, books and equipment for the proper conduct of the services. The archdeacon was also concerned with the conduct of the clergy and with the behaviour and morals of the laity, and any offenders could be brought before the archdeacon's court. The account of a visitation carried out by the Archdeacon of Norwich in 1368 has been printed by the Norfolk Record Society, and shows how informative and useful for local history and church life such records can be.[13] It is material of this sort which lends colour and detail to local history and illustrates the wide spectrum of belief, practice and custom which existed in medieval England, making all generalisation hazardous.

> We have constantly to be turning back to the sources and raw materials of our history if we are to avoid the dangers of trying to swamp the particular in the general, and to fit upon the infinite diversity of human life a systematic pattern which it will not endure![14]

The depositions made by witnesses in the ecclesiastical courts offer detailed information about many topics—social customs, occupations, topography, farming and parochial life, as well as about Church affairs.

Records of cathedral chapters

The records of the deans and chapters of cathedrals are similarly informative about the affairs of those parishes which were within their own exempt or 'peculiar' jurisdictions. Many of these records have also been published by record societies and are an extremely useful source of local history. For example, the visitations of the churches under the jurisdiction of the Dean and Chapter of York during the years from 1362 to 1481 reveal many defects in the church buildings, inadequate provision of service books, and numerous offences by clergy and laity, including non-residence, failure to attend church, adultery, superstition, witchcraft and heresy. At Bishopshill in 1481, the tower and bells needed attention and

> The church windows are also broken and birds come in and foul all the church. The church is not well kept in paving and stalling. The font has no lock. The said churchwardens do not wash the albs, altar-cloths and surplices once in a year. Much chattering and talking within the said church and specially in the service time. When the word of God is declared in the said church and the parishioners have warning to come to hear it, most of them do not come at all..![15]

With all records of courts and visitations it has to be remembered that the ecclesiastical officials were concerned only with reporting what was wrong, and with recording offenders and evildoers; they make no mention of churches which were in good repair, which had all necessary books, where the clergy were conscientious or where the laity gave no cause for adverse comment. The wide range of subjects with which the church authorities were concerned can also be seen from the record of visitations of those parishes which were 'peculiars' of the Dean of Salisbury during 1404-17. These were conducted by the Dean, John Chandler, who kept a register in which he recorded his findings. As Dean of Salisbury, he had jurisdiction over more than 60 parishes. As well as defects in churches and their equipment, the dean dealt with numerous irregularities among the clergy, ranging from negligence to sexual incontinence; and among the laity the offences included heresy, perhaps induced by the activity of Lollard preachers, the use of magic and witchcraft, absence from church, attendance at fairs and revels during service time, irreverence in church, fighting and violence in churchyards, sexual irregularities, slander, and failure to pay tithes and other church dues.[16] Offenders who were reported at visitations were brought before one of the various ecclesiastical courts whose normal penalties ranged from a fine to excommunication. Most common was the sentence of public penance, a punishment which must have been a daunting prospect in a small community where each person was well-known to all others. In 1491 John Edward of Newbury (Berks) was sentenced to perform public penance in the market places and in the churches of Newbury, Salisbury, Devizes and Abingdon, at times when the maximum number of people would be present. His offence was that he had supported the Lollard belief:

> that in the sacramente of the Auter (Altar) is not the very body of Criste but a thing confecte in commemoracion of the same and a signe of a better thinge[17]

At Grantham in 1469, a tanner, Thomas Wortley, was sentenced to read aloud a confession in the market place at the time when the market was fullest. His offence was described as follows:

> ...the said Thomas Wortley in the nyghte tyme smote violently oon Edward Syngar, a minister of the churche of Grantham and drewe blood of him within the churcheyerd of Grantham whereby the said churcheyerd was poluted and of the administration of all sacramentalles suspendyd, to the grete displeasure of God, contempt to our moder Holy Churche and grete noyance and offense to all this paryshe..[18]

Likewise, in 1412 Richard Edward, chaplain of the prebendal church of Heytesbury, appeared before the Bishop of Salisbury in Sonning parish church and confessed to charges of disobedience to the bishop and of heretical wickedness. For this offence and for disrespect to the bishop, an interdict had been imposed on Heytesbury church. In spite of the interdict, some of the clergy and parishioners had broken down the door of the church and celebrated mass and other divine offices there in contempt of the bishop. Richard Edward was ordered that on the first day after the interdict on Heytesbury church was lifted, when the greatest number of people were present,

> ...he should take off his priestly vestments, except his chasuble, and in the presence of the people, should genuflect to the font and say the seven penitential psalms with the litany; he should then rise and say in a loud and intelligible voice that he had erred and acted wrongly in not obeying the bishop...[19]

The evidence of wills

An important aspect of medieval wills was the donations which were made for religious and charitable purposes; the record of such gifts is a significant source for assessing the opinions of those who have left no other indication of their deeper thoughts. Bequests to parish churches are very frequent, and are informative about the work on the church which was then in progress, or about the date of furnishings, altars, chapels, aisles or other additions, and wills can be an essential source in reconstructing the medieval appearance or furnishings of a church. For example, much of the dating for the great western towers of Norfolk, Suffolk and Somerset, which were such a popular addition to parish churches during the late Middle Ages, comes from the surviving wills in which money or goods are bequeathed to the project. Late-medieval wills also provide a good indication of the richness of the colouring, lights, statues, stained glass and decoration of the parish churches, and of the furnishings which were destroyed during the Reformation and later. In Bristol, for example, to take only three of the early-sixteenth century wills, Thomas Norton, who died in 1513, left money for 'the gilding of the image of St Jamys at the High Auter of St Peter's', Joanna Thorne left vestments and a pair of silver candlesticks to St Nicholas church in 1525 'to honour God and Seynt Nicholas withal, and that she myght therefore be prayed for every Sunday', and Thomas Harte, a Bristol merchant, who died in 1540 when the Reformation was already under way, left sums of money to various churches for enriching the furnishing and decoration of their altars[20] Wills can also provide evidence for the furnishings, statues, altars and lights in parish churches, and for the existence of separate chapels and oratories; and they can give information about annual customs and ceremonies. For example, the will of John Cole of Thelnetham (Suffolk), who died in 1527, ordered 'a new crosse to be made and sett upp where the gospell is saide upon Ascension Even'. He also left three acres of land to provide bread and ale for the parishioners at the cross during the procession?[21] There are other equally informative examples, and collections of late-medieval wills have been printed?[22] The medieval church never ceased to emphasise the importance of almsgiving and charitable works and accordingly wills also supply evidence about almshouses, hospitals, friaries, hermitages and other similar institutions which may have existed in a parish, as well as about tithes and offerings, social concern, religious attitudes and funeral customs. Occasionally, they provide information on the services and officials of the parish church. For example, in 1480 a London mercer left a bequest in his will to maintain a parish clerk in the church of Moulton (Lincs), and this, incidentally, sets out the duties of this important but often somewhat shadowy figure in church life. The clerk's duties were as follows:

> ...to helpe to synge or saye divine service, and also to go with the priest when he shall be called to housel folkes (i.e. to administer the Sacrament) in the said parishe...to ringe belles and take charge of suche goodes as belongen to the saide cherche and keepe the keys of the same by the discretion of thrifty men of the same parishe[23]

The object of most bequests of this sort was to ensure that prayers were said for the soul of the testator after death, just as the wealthy founded chantries and the less well-off joined guilds which arranged both elaborate funerals and perpetual prayers for their members. Likewise, those who could afford to do so built large monuments to remind the living to pray for them after death, or erected brass memorials, always with the prominent exhortation to pray for the repose of their soul.

It was because a will was concerned with pious and charitable objects and with the good of the testator's soul, as well as with the disposal of his earthly goods, that the Church constantly urged the clergy to ensure that their parishioners did not die without making a will, that the names of the parish clergy are so often found either as scribes or witnesses of wills, and that the whole business of 'probate', i.e. the official registration and validation of a will—became a matter for the Church authorities and took up so much time in the ecclesiastical courts.

Services in the parish church

Apart from the complaints and irregularities reported at visitations, there is little firm evidence about the conduct of services, the normal behaviour of parishioners in church or their deeper feelings and beliefs. The most important indication of their regard for the church is the remarkable way in which money was raised to enlarge, rebuild or beautify the church buildings, and the fact that few churches, even in the smallest communities, did not have a new aisle, side chapel, western tower or expensive furnishings during the later Middle Ages. There were generally three services for the laity on Sundays and Holy Days, Matins followed by Mass during the morning and Evensong during the afternoon. Langland in *Piers Plowman* wrote that:

> Upon Sundays to cease, God's service to hear
> Both Mattins and Mass, and after meat, in churches,
> To hear their Evensong every man ought.

But few parishioners seem to have attained to this ideal. In many parish churches there were several services each day, and often several celebrations of Mass, as the number of clergy, curates, chaplains and chantry priests multiplied during the later Middle Ages. As early as 1377, the poll-tax returns reveal that there were 1,315 clergy in Devon, or one priest to every

55 of the laity; in Wiltshire before the Reformation, even the smallest and most remote churches had at least one priest in addition to the rector or vicar, and most had two or three. In 1432 St Thomas's church in Salisbury, which served a population of between 2,000 and 3,000 parishioners, had the following staff:

21 priest vicars

16 deacons

11 sub-deacons

9 chantry priests[24]

Many other similar examples might be cited, especially from towns or in churches where numerous chantries or a collegiate foundation had been established. Medieval congregations took little part in the services; the major parts were in Latin and were conducted beyond the rood screen, there were no hymns and only occasional sermons, and until the fifteenth century there were few seats. Churches were unheated and must have been very cold in winter in spite of the straw or rushes that were spread on the floor. It is small wonder that there were complaints of inattention, talking and unseemly behaviour. John Myrc, a canon of Lilleshall in Shropshire, in his *Instructions for Parish Priests* written about 1400, urges the clergy to insist on reverent behaviour and to teach their congregations to avoid talking and gazing about, and to:

> …put away alle vanity,
> And say their Pater Noster and their Ave,
> Nor none in churche stonde schall,
> Nor leane to pylar nor to wall,
> But fayre on knees they schalle them sette,
> Kneeling down upon the flatte,
> And pray to God wyth hearte meeke,
> To give them grace and Mercy eke?[25]

The regular round of festivals, processions and ceremonies—ashes on Ash Wednesday, palms on Palm Sunday, candles at Candlemas, the rituals of Holy Week and the Easter Sepulchre, and the procession with the Sacred Host at Corpus Christi—all served to reinforce the central belief of the congregation.

It is clear from the surviving records, and the decoration of late-medieval churches, that it was, above all, the sacraments and the regular performance of elaborate ritual which provided medieval congregations with a sense of security and created an intense attachment to the parish church. The doctrines of the church were no doubt inadequately comprehended and the commandments were frequently broken, but the daily Mass and the ordered sequence of annual ceremonies offered the possibility of an escape from the fires of Hell, and the hope of a life in Heaven far removed from the earthly wretchedness which was the portion of most people during the Middle Ages. For the conduct of the services, many parish churches, even the smallest, were richly equipped. It is true that visitation records show that some churches lacked necessary books or equipment, and it is not difficult to find examples of poverty-stricken churches in bad repair or with inadequate furnishings, but surviving late-medieval inventories often reveal remarkable collections of silver and gilt crosses, chalices, censers, candlesticks, as well as rich vestments, altar hangings, and service books.

Chantry chapels

The most characteristic religious foundations of the later Middle Ages were the chantry chapels. Chantries were endowments made either by individuals or by groups and fraternities, whereby a priest was employed to sing masses for the souls of the founders or others. By the fifteenth century, most large churches had at least one chantry and many were also established in the smaller parish churches. In the west country, for example, two chantries were established in St Mary Redcliffe, Bristol by the wealthy and pious merchant William Canynges in 1466 and 1467; likewise, a chantry was founded in St Mary's, Southampton by Joan Holmhegge, widow of Nicholas Holmhegge, a prosperous merchant and former mayor of Southampton. Many churches have elaborately constructed aisles or side chapels which were built as chantries, like the Beauchamp chapel at St John's, Devizes or the Tocotes chapel at Bromham (Wilts), the Morton chapel at Bere Regis (Dorset) or the Brocas chapel at Sherborne St John near Basingstoke. The Hungerford family amassed a huge fortune and acquired widespread estates during the later Middle Ages; successive members of the family spent large sums on bequests to the church, and by the end of the fifteenth century they had founded twelve chantries, seven 'obits' or anniversary masses, two almshouses and a school, as well as rebuilding the parish churches at Wellow and Farleigh Hungerford and making numerous other gifts to cathedrals and parish churches. Walter, Lord Hungerford, for example, founded a chantry at Heytesbury with an almshouse for twelve bedesmen, and a school. The *Magister scolarum* was expected to manage the almshouse, to say mass daily, and to teach in the school except on Sundays and feast days, when he was to join in matins, high mass and evensong in the parish church.[26]

Guilds and fraternities vied with each other in the opulence of their chantry chapels. The chantry of the wealthy guild of Merchant Tailors in Bristol, for example, occupied the whole of the south aisle of St Ewen's church. It was separated from the nave by carved wooden screens, and an inventory of 1401 shows that the chapel was decorated with tapestries showing scenes from the life of St John the Baptist, their patron saint, and that it possessed valuable vestments and hangings for the altar, chalices, crosses, plate and processional banners or pageants?[27] During the later Middle Ages there are references to nearly 200 religious fraternities in the 107 parishes in and around London, and as well as masses, many provided lights, vestments or sermons in their parish churches, others arranged feasts, pilgrimages or processions, while some provided for the care of sick or needy members. Fraternity chantries enabled even the poorer members of society to share in the benefits of a constant succession of masses, and to have their names on the bede roll. Typical was the instruction in the bede roll of the Confraternity of Jesus Mass at St Edmund's, Salisbury:

> Also ye shall pray for all the soulis of all the brethern and susterne beinge quicke and dede, and in speciall good doers in ther lyves. Also yowe shall praye for the soules that ar departede owt of this worlde?[28]

Chapter Four

CHURCHWARDENS' ACCOUNTS AND OTHER LATE-MEDIEVAL SOURCES

Churchwardens' accounts

The churchwardens were the most important lay officials in each parish; as their title suggests they were concerned with the maintenance of the fabric of the church and with the provision of the necessary materials, books, vestments, furnishings and equipment for the conduct of the services. Not until the sixteenth century were they burdened by the Tudors with other duties such as poor relief, highway maintenance, the punishment of vagabonds or the destruction of vermin. The practice in most parishes was for two churchwardens to be appointed annually, generally at the Easter Vestry meeting; during the Middle Ages it is not clear how or why particular individuals were chosen, nor is there any evidence of the later custom that one warden was chosen by the incumbent and the other by the parishioners. The earliest surviving churchwardens' accounts are those of St Michael's, Bath, which begin in 1349, and it is clear from these that already the churchwardens were concerned with all aspects of the life of the Church in the parish, from raising money, administering the property, caring for the church building and paying for memorial masses to be celebrated for the benefactors of the church, to providing books, lights, furnishings and equipment. Enough churchwardens' accounts survive from the fifteenth century and from all over the country, to give a good indication of parochial life, and to answer the question of how the money was raised to pay for the ever-more lavish architecture of English parish churches, with their expensive western towers, high clerestories, aisles, chapels, screens, carving, painting, lights and stained glass. The surviving accounts also show how the building work was organised and directed by the churchwardens on behalf of the parishioners!

Since the churchwardens were accountable to their fellow parishioners for the often large sums of money with which they were entrusted, their accounts were no doubt kept with care in all parishes, but sadly, only a small number has survived from the Middle Ages. Those that do survive, however, are worth careful study, since much the same procedures for fund-raising were followed in all parishes, and everywhere the churchwardens had the same responsibilities and concerns. Occasionally, inventories of church goods made by the churchwardens can be found, and, more rarely, informative contracts made with masons, carpenters, carvers and other workmen for extensions or decorative work on the church.

The surviving accounts of Louth (Lincs) illustrate the major features. An inventory survives for 1486 and shows that the church possessed several crosses of silver, seven chalices, several censers, pyxes, and other sacred vessels for use in the services; there were no less than 47 manuscript service books of all kinds, and larger quantities of vestments, hangings for the altar, towels, beads and other equipment. The churchwardens' income came from gifts, bequests, fees for burials in the church, ringing the bells at weddings and funerals, and large contributions from the several religious guilds established in the parish. In 1501, the Louth churchwardens began a major project to build a lofty spire on their church; the spire set on top of an already lofty tower was finally to reach a height of 295 feet, and remains as one of the most graceful of English spires. The project cost £305 7s 5d. It was built between 1501 and 1515, and was entirely due to the enthusiasm and money-raising zeal of the parishioners. The Louth accounts for this period reveal the passionate concern of the churchwardens and parishioners for the adornment of their church, for they did not scruple to get themselves heavily into debt, borrowing money from various sources so that the work of building could continue. The accounts also show the difficulties which they had with their master mason. In 1505 Christopher Scune was appointed to the post, but as he was also in charge of major works at Ripon and Durham, he came to Louth very seldom. The resident mason at Louth, in charge of day-to-day affairs, was a local man, Laurence Lemying. As the work proceeded, the churchwardens found it increasingly difficult to get Scune to come to Louth, and at last, after many urgent appeals had been sent to him, he was sacked and replaced by a master mason from Boston, John Tempas, Finally, in 1515 the spire was finished and the churchwardens triumphantly recorded the occasion in their accounts:

> The 15th Sunday after Holy Trinity of the year (1515) the weathercock was set upon the broach of the Holy Rood Eve after, there being William Ayleby parish priest, with many of his brethren priests there present, hallowing the said weathercock and the stone that it stands upon, and so conveyed upon the said broach; and the said priests singing Te Deum Laudamus, with organs, and then the kirkwardens garred ring all the bells, and caused all the people there being to have bread and ale; and all to the loving of God, our Lady and All Saints?

The main feature that emerges from any examination of the late-medieval evidence is how frequently the rebuilding or enlargement of the parish church was entirely due to the enthusiasm and generosity of the whole community in the parish. Whatever their motives—and these no doubt ranged from simple enthusiasm for the project, through local rivalry with neighbouring parishes over the size and splendour of the parish churches or the height and magnificence of their towers, to sheer concern for personal salvation and an understandable desire to avoid the torments of the sort of hell so frequently and vividly depicted in late-medieval imagery—there is no doubt that incredibly large sums of money were raised from poor and thinly-populated parishes. Perhaps the best surviving evidence of this comes from Bodmin in Cornwall. During the second half of the fifteenth century, much of the church in the little town was rebuilt, the old Norman structure was ruthlessly demolished and replaced by a grand new church in the latest style; similar rebuildings and enlargements occurred throughout the country, but what makes the events at Bodmin so important is the fact that the complete building-account survives, covering the years 1469 to 1472. Money was raised by the sale of parts of the old church; for example windows, presumably stained-glass windows, were sold to nearby parishes, St Kew and Helland; gifts of both money and goods were received; house-to-house collections were organised; and, above all, money came in from parish functions and especially from fund-raising carried out by the local guilds during their annual Whitsuntide celebrations. The money was carefully stored by the churchwardens until there was sufficient for rebuilding to commence. Stone was obtained from the nearby moorland, and higher quality granite from Pentewan on the coast near St Austell. The way in which the stone was brought to Bodmin from the quarries at Pentewan illustrates some of the difficulties which medieval builders faced in the transport of their materials, for in order to avoid the hard overland journey across the high moorland of mid-Cornwall, the Bodmin churchwardens arranged for the stone to be transported by barge across St Austell bay to Fowey and thence up the river Fowey to Lostwithiel; there it was loaded on to waggons and wains for the final part of the journey to Bodmin. Timber, both for the church itself and for all the necessary scaffolding, was obtained locally, some of it being given by local landowners. Much of the building work was also done by local workmen, but for the roof and the doorways and windows, masons and carpenters were obtained from as far away as Exeter, and accommodation had to be provided for them in Bodmin while they worked on the new church. Large numbers of workmen were employed on the project, for there was little mechanical assistance apart from a crane and a bucket.

From the detailed Bodmin accounts, we can calculate that the total cost of the work amounted to £268 17s 9½d, excluding all the materials and labour contributed by local people, for which no charge was made. It cannot be too often emphasised that, whatever the motives of the donors, the raising of such large sums for parish churches in so many parishes was an immense achievement, and it is impressive evidence of the communal desire to make their churches as large and opulent as possible, and of the strength of religious faith which could lead such relatively poor communities to devote so much of their material wealth to the greater glory of God.[3]

The Church and the community

Documentary sources such as bishops' registers, churchwardens' accounts and presentments or reports provide ample evidence .for the close involvement of the parish church in all aspects of community life. Churchwardens' accounts show that the principal fund-raising activity was the church ale, a parish gathering at which food and drink were supplied by the churchwardens, and which was accompanied by sports, dancing, drama and other festivities. Church ales regularly raised amazingly large sums for the parish church, and the proceeds financed many projects of building work and decoration. The close involvement of the community with the parish church can also be observed in some manorial accounts. There were many places where fines imposed for minor infringements of manorial regulations went, not to the lord, but to the upkeep of the parish church.[4] At Landbeach (Cambs) in 1498, the manorial custom stated that if any tenant allowed his sheep to stray into the meadows or corn fields, he should pay 12d to the parish church.[5] The churchwardens' accounts of Totnes (Devon) show how the wooden tower of the parish church was demolished during the 1440s, and collections known as 'Sunday pence' were organised to replace it by a stone tower. The parishioners themselves worked in a nearby quarry, digging stone for the project, and brought the stone by barge up the Dart to the town quay, and there carried it to the church. Before work started, the churchwardens travelled to Tavistock, Callington and elsewhere, to 'view divers bell towers in the country' to get ideas as to the sort of tower they would like. Roger Growdone, master mason, was then appointed to supervise the work of the building. Here again, however, as at Bodmin and scores of other places, it is clear that the whole project was a community effort, and that whatever motives or pressures were involved, it was paid for by the parishioners themselves.[6] The cost (£40) of building the tower of Eye church in Suffolk in 1470 was:

> gatheryd yere partly with the plough, (i.e. Plough-Monday collections), partly in church ales, partly in legacies given in that way, but chiefly of the frank and devoute hartes of the people.

Carved along the gallery at Cawston church (Norfolk) are the words:

> Gode spede the plow, and send us ale corn enow, our purpose to mak, at crow of cok of the plowlete of Sygate. Be merry and glade, Wat Goodale this work mad.

Whatever the precise meaning of this curious inscription, its general message is clear enough, that it was from the profits of church ales and merry-making that the church was built and furnished. Many building accounts and contracts have been collected as an appendix in L.F. Salzman, *Building in England*, 1967, 413-584. They give details of how the work was carried out, how the whole community was frequently involved, how in some places rivalry between parishes provided a powerful motive, and how, as at Bodmin and Louth, so many large-scale projects involving great sums of money were supervised by the churchwardens. Above all, the contracts and the churchwardens' accounts show clearly the way in which the great surge of late-medieval church building and furnishing, which has left so many parishes with vast, ornate churches far beyond the capacity of their twentieth-century congregations to maintain, was organised and financed.

The contract for building a tower at Walberswick church in Suffolk in 1425 specifies that the general design was to be like that of Tunstall, while the windows were to be like those in the tower at Halesworth. In the same way, a contract for building a tower at Helmingham in Suffolk, made in 1487, specified that it should have the best features of two neighbouring towers, 'a sufficient newe stepyll of Framsden...so that it be mayd after the facion of the stepyll of Bramston...' An agreement with a mason to make battlements around the church at Orby, Lincs, in 1529 stipulated that they should be similar to those at Weston Admeals, while those around the tower were to be like the ones at East Keal?

When the parishioners of Dunster in west Somerset decided to add a tower to their parish church in 1442, the project was a communal enterprise arranged by the churchwardens on behalf of the entire parish. The contract survives for the Dunster tower, and this shows that while the actual building was to be carried out by a local mason, John Marys of Stogursey, the materials, stone and wood, were to be provided by the parish and brought to the churchyard. Other points of interest emerge from the Dunster contract. John Marys was evidently allowed considerable latitude in the manner of construction so long as it was done 'after reason and good proportion'; apparently only the design of the tower-windows was precisely stipulated and these were to be according to the pattern or design made by one Richard Pope, freemason or architect. According to the terms of the contract John Marys was to be paid for his work on the tower at the rate of 13s 4d per foot, excluding the materials.[8]

The records of the many trade and religious guilds also provide evidence of the appearance, furnishings and decoration of the parish churches and of their part in community life, for most guilds were active in raising money for the churches and many had their own guild chapels or aisles in churches. In the towns, there was commonly a vital overlap between the ruling oligarchy and a religious guild. In Bristol, for example, the Church was totally involved in civic life; the annual round of ceremonies and processions established by custom for the mayor and carefully recorded by the town clerk, Robert Ricart, towards the end of the fifteenth century, emphasises the essential link between the civic authority and the parish churches in Bristol. From the time of his oath-taking in September the mayor embarked upon an ordered round of visits to the parish churches. At Michaelmas he and the council assembled at the High Cross and went in procession to St Michael's church. During the next few months, the programme laid down by custom for the mayor involved regular visits to the parish churches of Bristol, religious processions through the streets, listening to sermons and attendance at many 'obits' or masses on the anniversaries of the deaths of benefactors.

Perhaps the most interesting of all the ceremonies occurred on 6 December, the feast of St Nicholas, patron saint of children, when the mayor and council walked to St Nicholas's church to join in the ceremony of the boy bishop, to hear mass and to listen to the boy bishop's sermon and receive his blessing. Later they returned to St Nicholas's church for the boy bishop's evensong. This ancient ceremony, in which a choirboy played the part of the bishop for a day, was not unique to Bristol and in many places it formed part of the revels of the Christmas season. These, and other ceremonies which regularly marked the progress of each year, were evidently regarded as contributing to the well-being of all citizens and as

> laudable customs…to the honour and comen wele of this worshipful towne and all th'inhabitants of the same.

Other annual ceremonies in Bristol included the hocktide games, the Rogationtide processions and the St George's day celebrations, all of which served to give formal expression to the social groupings in the town, and there were other occasions which provided an outlet and release for the inevitable tensions which built up in such a tightly packed yet rigidly structured society as Bristol, where there were great differences in wealth and social status. An occasion when the accepted order was turned upside down, with licensed misrule, was on May Day when there are references in several Bristol churchwardens' accounts to Robin Hood and Little John, to the payment of minstrels and to the purchase of meat and drink for 'the King and Queen and all theyr company' who took part in the revels. Here again, there is a link between these revels and the parish churches? A similar close bond and affinity of interests between church and civic authorities can be seen in many other places. At Rye (Kent), the chamberlain's accounts for the town during the 1470s include frequent payments for players in church and churchyards, contributions to the church, and references to town meetings held in the church and town armaments stored there. For example:

> 1474-76
>
> Payed to the players of Romeney, the which played in the chirche   16d
>
> Paid for bread and ale in the church when John Trego and John Estone made their account   3d
>
> By consent of the Mayer and his bretherne given to the pleyers of Lede (Lydd), the whiche pleyed here the Sunday after Cristemas holidayes   16d
>
> Payed to the pleyers of Wynchilsea, the whiche pleyed in the churche yarde uppone the day of the Purificacion of oure Ladye   16d

Likewise at nearby Lydd the corporation records, kept by the town clerk, record payments to groups of players and to the boy bishop who came every year from Romney on St Nicholas's day and preached a sermon in the church; there were also regular payments for repairs to the church, lights, minstrels and players at the feast of the dedication. In times of danger, the church tower was used as a lookout in case of invasion by the French![10]

Architectural evidence

Even in the great majority of parishes which have no medieval churchwardens' accounts, or where other medieval sources are sparse or uninformative, the local historian can often find evidence for late-medieval church life from a careful, systematic study of the parish church. Recent work on church archaeology and architecture, notably by Dr Warwick Rodwell, has shown just how much can be learnt from the church building even without the additional evidence of archaeological excavation![11]

Changes in population or wealth and in religious ideas and ritual can be observed in enlarged chancels, subsidiary chapels, chantries, side altars and western towers. Some evidence of the late-medieval appearance of the church and of services, rituals and processions can be gathered from the surviving fragments of colour, wall-paintings and stained glass or of former altars, screens, statues, carvings and seating arrangements.[12] A piscina often survives to show the site of a former altar, while further evidence is sometimes provided by a 'squint' which once enabled the priest at a side altar to observe the progress of mass at the high altar. In a few churches evidence remains of the Easter Sepulchre, generally situated on the north side of the altar; here the Sacred Host was placed on Good Friday and watched over until Easter Sunday, when it was ceremonially restored to the high altar with the dramatic *Quem Quaeritis* ritual. Richly carved sepulchres remain at Hawton (Notts), Patrington (Yorks), Navenby and Heckington (Lincs), while at Tarrrant Hinton (Dorset), the sepulchre is inscribed with the words of the angel to the women at the empty tomb *Venire et Videte Locum Ubi Positus erat Dominus* (come and see the place where the Lord lay). There are also many documentary references to this ceremony. William Canynges, the Bristol merchant, gave to St Mary Redcliffe an Easter Sepulchre, which included a representation of Heaven 'made of Stained clothes' and Hell 'made of timber and iron-work thereto, with Divels to the number of 13'.[13] The churchwardens' accounts of All Hallows, Sherborne, show that there was a richly-carved Easter Sepulchre and that watch was kept over it each year; the watchmen were paid for their task as well as being given ale and a fire of coals to keep them warm.[14]

No opportunity was missed to increase the sense of awe and mystery in churches, with stained glass, paintings, lights and statues, and, most spectacular of all, the great rood screen dividing nave from chancel and surmounted by the figures of the crucified Christ, the Blessed Virgin and St John. Most of these magnificently-carved and painted screens were swept away during the Reformation changes, but examples survive, although without their rood or crucifix, in East Anglia and the West Country, and many late-medieval churchwardens' accounts contain much information on how the funds were raised and the work of building the screens was organised. Few parish churches contain more than a few fragments of their medieval stained glass, but the effect which this had on the atmosphere of the churches can be appreciated at St Neots (Cornwall), where each window was provided by a different section of the local community, and at Fairford (Glos) where the whole church was rebuilt and the glass installed in c. 1490 by the Tame family whose wealth was derived from the wool trade.

The existence of so many late-medieval pulpits is evidence for the growing popularity of sermons, just as the lecterns indicate the practice of public reading to the congregation. It was sermons and readings which created the need for seats in the nave; many examples of pre-Reformation seating survive. The churchwardens' accounts supply evidence of many others, since the practice of charging rents for pews developed very rapidly and soon became a major source of income; the pew ends quickly began to display fine examples of wood-carving and, especially in the West Country, were decorated with a variety of secular and sacred subjects, with folklore, grotesques, fertility symbols, mermaids, ships, windmills and hunting scenes standing next to figures of the saints or Instruments of the Passion![5]

The fact that, by the late Middle Ages, the nave had become the responsibility of the parishioners while the duty of maintaining the chancel rested with the rector or patron, means that there is often quite a startling discrepancy between the size and workmanship of the two parts of some parish churches. At Yatton (Avon), where the patron was one of the prebendaries of Wells cathedral, the churchwardens' accounts show that very large sums of money were raised by the parishioners to rebuild and beautify the nave of the church, while the chancel remains small and quite out of scale with the splendid nave. At Methwold (Norfolk), the fourteenth-century chancel is quite overshadowed by the fine nave and by the great tower and spire erected by the parishioners. In some places, however, parishioners and patron combined in a complete rebuilding programme. St Mary's, Ecclesfield, in the West Riding of Yorkshire, was lavishly reconstructed and enlarged during the period 1480-1520 as the result of collaboration between the parishioners and the Carthusian monks of the distant priory of St Anne in Coventry, who were the rectors of the parish. The fine Perpendicular church of Lowick (Northants), was rebuilt through the joint efforts of the parishioners and the Greene family whose alabaster monuments dominate the chancel.

While evidence for expansion and the enlargement of churches, both by individuals or by the concerted efforts of parishioners, is everywhere to be found, widespread examples of decline, poverty and contraction can also be discovered. In Wiltshire, the present village of Shrewton originally consisted of several medieval settlements, among them Shrewton, Elston, Maddington and Rollestone, each with its own church. Today, the Victorian church at Shrewton serves as the parish church for the greatly reduced area of settlement, Elston has lost its church, Maddington church survives as a chapelry and is much reduced in size, Rollestone church has been declared redundant![6] The large number of ruined or vanished churches in Norfolk, Suffolk and parts of Yorkshire and Herefordshire is an indication of the late-medieval economic changes in those areas. An example of the way even a well-established parish church could fall into disuse and disappear so completely that even its site is uncertain, is Wittenham *alias* Rowley on the borders of Wiltshire and Somerset. The village was situated along the Wiltshire side of the river Frome, and is referred to in a charter of 987, in Domesday Book when it was assessed for five hides, and in various early-medieval records. The first definite reference to a parish church occurs in 1299, but no doubt a church had existed to serve the spiritual needs of the parishioners for long before that date. The church was dedicated to St Nicholas, and consisted of a nave and chancel; it also possessed a churchyard. It was an independent parish church with its own rector and two churchwardens. By the late fourteenth century, the village was in decline, possibly because of the Black Death, or perhaps because part of the village had been destroyed to make a park for the Hungerford family of Farleigh Hungerford castle, which is situated just across the River Frome. In 1428 Walter, Lord Hungerford, secured the agreement of the bishop to unite the parishes of Farleigh Hungerford and Wittenham on the grounds that the latter parish was depopulated, and:

> hath been so impoverished, and the fruits, profits and emoluments thereof have become so poor and scanty, that, for a long time there hath been found no secular chaplain willing to undertake or to occupy the church.

Elaborate arrangements were made in the Act of Union and Annexation, in order that the church of Wittenham should be kept in good repair, that the books, ornaments and vestments should remain in the church, that Mass should be said there on certain specified days each year, and that memorial masses for the Hungerford family should continue to be celebrated there annually. On all other occasions, the parishioners were to attend the church at Farleigh Hungerford, just across the river. In spite of the safeguards, Wittenham church seems rapidly to have fallen into decay. There is an entry in the *Valor Ecclesiasticus* of 1535 that the sum of 8 pence was due from the church at Wittenham, but no subsequent references. The church must have fallen down or have been demolished, and by the nineteenth century all memory of its situation had been lost, although the most likely location, a piece of open common, was still known as Holy Green. Apart from this, no clue survives, either in documents nor in earthworks, to indicate where precisely the church or village lay![17]

Secular use of church and churchyard

Not only did the medieval parish churches serve their communities through services and prayers; they were also the centres of community life. Barochial festivities were held regularly during the summer, especially at Whitsun, Midsummer, Michaelmas or on the patronal festival of the church; ale and food were sold and entertainment was provided by minstrels, players, bearwards, Robin Hood and Little John, or by dancing, bowling, archery and other diversions; churchwardens' accounts from all over the country bear witness to the effectiveness of these church ales as money-raisers. Such activities may originally have been held in the naves of the churches, uncluttered as these were by pews, but by the fifteenth century, when the survival of churchwardens' accounts becomes more common, parishes in some parts of the country had built church houses for their church ales![18] The parishioners of St Ewen's, in Bristol, built a church house beside the church in 1493; sixteen people contributed money towards the work, including a woman who paid 2d a week, and dozens of other townsfolk gave wood, stone, sand, time and labour![19] At Landbeach (Cambs), a church house was built 'at the common charge of the Townshippe' in 1527 and thereafter was used for church ales and parish meetings of all sorts.[20] Even after the building of church houses, some festivities continued to be held in churches. In 1506 the churchwardens' accounts of St Lawrence, Reading, record the following expenditure:

To Macrell for makying clene of the church against the day of drinking
in the said church   4d

For flesh, spyce and bakying of pasteys agaynst the said drynking   2s 9½d

For ale at the same drynking   1s 5d

For mete and drynke to the Taberer   9d?[21]

The churchwardens of St Michael's, Bath, staged a play in the church in
1482, and at Ashburton (Devon) the churchwardens kept a stock of players'
costumes and other stage properties which they occasionally hired out to
neighbouring parishes. The Ashburton accounts, like those of St John's,
Peterborough; St Margaret's, Southwark; St Michael's, Braintree (Essex); St
Mary's, Taunton, and others, show that the plays, which were apparently
religious dramas and mystery plays, were performed inside the church.[22]
Mystery plays were also performed in the church at Dunstable, and at
Eversholt (Beds) the church possessed 'playing coats' as well as 'playbooks
and garments'.[23] The churchwardens' accounts of Yatton (Somerset), record
regular payments to minstrels who played in the church, and at Launceston
there was a regular guild of minstrels attached to the church of St Mary
Magdalene. At Croscombe (Somerset), the money collected each year in the
parish by 'Robin Hood' was an important source of income for the church.[24]
The regular annual ceremonies associated with Palm Sunday, Corpus
Christi and Rogationtide, or well-dressing, rush-bearing and other rituals,
all helped to preserve the integrated fabric of medieval life, and the fact that
so much of it perished at the Reformation greatly impoverished communal
activities. Markets and fairs, as well as sports and games, were frequently
held in churchyards in spite of episcopal condemnation of the practice. At
Yeovil (Somerset), the churchwardens derived a large part of their income
from the stallkeepers who paid to erect their booths against the churchyard
wall, and from renting out the weights and measures belonging to the
church for use at the weekly market. St Edmund's, Salisbury, also had a
regular income from the stallholders. Churches were used as schools and
meeting places for the conduct of civic and secular business. Chambers over
porches, such as the fine examples at Cirencester (Glos); St Nicholas, Kings
Lynn; Burford (Oxon); Thaxted (Essex) and Warmington (Warwickshire)
were used for meetings, business and the storage of valuables and
documents.[25] Since most parishioners assembled for Mass each Sunday, that
was the obvious time for proclamations to be made.[26]

The medieval congregation

Whether the evidence is archaeological, architectural or documentary, the
local historian should above all be concerned with what it can reveal about
the local community, about the clergy and laity who built, enlarged,
decorated and cared for the church, who worshipped within it, whose
social life centred upon it, and who are buried in its churchyard. From their
wills and from the evidence of the many chantry foundations, guild
endowments and bequests, we can appreciate their strong and literal belief

in purgatory, hell and eternal damnation. We can also attempt to reconstruct from the archives and the architecture something of the atmosphere of medieval worship. For this purpose, the surviving fragments of wall-paintings, stained glass and carving are particularly useful. Carvings frequently reveal a whole subculture of belief in demons, monsters and pagan forces of evil in the world, while surviving fragments of wall-painting give an indication of popular theology, and reveal much about the basic teaching of the medieval Church.[27] The carvings and paintings in medieval churches were by far the commonest art forms available to the majority of people, and the walls of even the smallest parish churches were liberally decorated with mural paintings. The commonest subjects were scenes from the life of Christ or the Virgin, legends of the saints or moralistic teaching on the vanity of human life and vivid warnings of the effect of sinfulness and the neglect of the Church's teaching. One popular subject was the Three Living and the Three Dead, where three young men or three princes in the prime of their youth are shown meeting with three skeletons, a subject which was evidently useful to late-medieval preachers who were at pains to emphasise the transitory nature of this world and of wordly wealth, an attitude neatly summed up in the lines inscribed on the fly-leaf of a medieval manuscript by an anonymous writer:

> For under the sunne a man may se
> Thys world ys butte a vanyte.
> Grace passeth gollde
> And precyous stoon,
> And god schal be god
> When goolde ys goon?[28]

The same theme was expressed in the Dance of Death or the *Danse Macabre* to which references can be found in late-medieval churchwardens' accounts. This was a subject with a particular appeal in the late-Middle Ages and was often painted on a large canvas and hung up in churches during Holy Week; it depicted the figure of Death as a dancing skeleton inviting various classes of contemporary society to join him in the dance. An early and very famous example of this painting was displayed from 1430, in St Paul's cathedral, and it was often referred to as the 'Dance of Pauls' or occasionally as the 'Dance of Powles' and this has sometimes led to misunderstanding and to confusion with maypole dancing.[29] In the churchwardens' accounts of St Edmund's, Salisbury, for 1490-91, payments are recorded as follows:

> To William Belrynger for clensinge of the churche at the Dawnse of
> Powles 8d

> Also for a pece of Tymber of a ynner grounselle (i.e. framework) of Powlis
> Daunce and bordes for other necessaries 3s 1d

> To Will Joynour for workmanship of the seid Powlis Daunce 10s 2d

> To John Lokyar for xxiii grete nailes for the Daunce of Powlis 4d[30]

The underlying concepts of the Christian religion such as the incarnation, atonement, redemption and the continuing sacrifice of the

1 Knowlton church, near Cranborne, Dorset
This is an excellent example of a parish church situated within an important pagan religious monument. The present structure dates from the twelfth century, and no doubt replaced an earlier building; it is situated away from the village and inside the bank and ditch of a circular prehistoric 'henge' or ritual site. the building survived as a parish church until the eighteenth century, when it fell into ruin. (*J.E. Hancock*)

2 Saxon arch at Breamore, Hampshire
The massive tenth-century arch of this former minster church leads into a 'porticus' or side-chapel, and the deeply-cut inscription HER SPUTELAD SEO GECPYDRAEDNES DE (Here the covenant is revealed to thee) illustrates something of the zeal and energy of the Saxon priests.

3 Friendly Society banner,
Stogursey, Somerset
One of the heavy wooden 'banners' which
are still kept in the parish church at
Stogursey. They were carried around the
village in the annual procession which
ended with a church service, followed by a
feast. Other banners in the church show
figures and inscriptions such as 'Britannia',
'Ceres' and 'Success to Trade'. They are a
reminder of the continuing close
involvement of the Church with charity
and poor relief.

4 Norman font from Lullington church
near Frome, Somerset
The elaborate decoration and symbolism
of such fonts gives some indication of the
attitudes of twelfth-century worshippers.
Only through the sacraments of the
Church can the evil power of the horned
god and his sinister companions be
overcome and the flower-strewn heavenly
mansions be reached. The prominent
Latin inscription adds further emphasis
Hoc fontis sacro pereunt delicta lavacro (In the
washing of this sacred font are sins
cleansed).

5 The Green Man,
Crowcombe church, Somerset
This late-medieval bench-end
shows the remarkable way in
which pagan symbols
continued to be prominently
displayed in parish churches,
and the attraction which pagan
gods, fertility symbols,
monsters, grotesques and
hideous creatures continued to
possess for medieval
congregations.

6 The rood screen at
Attleborough, Norfolk
This late-fifteenth century
wooden screen completely
divides the nave from the
chancel and is richly carved and
painted with figures of saints
and the arms of the English
dioceses. Originally nave altars
stood in front of the screen.

7 Wall-painting, St Thomas, Salisbury

One of a series of late-medieval wall-paintings in the church. They include a great 'doom' or Last Judgement over the chancel arch, and a series in the south chapel illustrating scenes from the life of the Virgin. This painting shows the incident following the Annunciation when the Virgin meets her cousin Elizabeth who is also with child.

8 Martyrdom of St Edmund, Pickering, North Yorkshire

This fifteenth-century painting, which is one of several survivals in Pickering church, is a good example of the vivid and explicit scenes of martyrdom so beloved of medieval congregations. Like the representations of the Last Judgement and the horrifying scenes in Hell, the purpose was to admonish, warn and edify the congregation, and no doubt such paintings were an admirable aid to preachers. The surviving paintings at Pickering and the many fragments elsewhere give a good idea of the colour and imagery which were to be found in most medieval churches. St Edmund (841 – 870) became king of East Anglia in 855. He was allegedly martyred by the Danes for his refusal to deny Christ; they tied him naked to a tree and riddled his body with arrows.

9 Massive parish chest from
Hook Norton, Oxfordshire
From as early as the thirteenth century,
parish churches were required to have a
chest for books, vestments and
valuables, and during the sixteenth
century parishioners were ordered to
provide a chest with three locks for
receiving alms given to the poor.

10 Hawkesbury church,
Gloucestershire (now Avon)
A good example of a church which
provides evidence of continuous
architectural development and lavish
expenditure throughout the Middle
Ages. The chancel was the responsiblity
of Pershore abbey and is dwarfed by the
nave and tower, which the parishioners
rebuilt and furnished on a grand scale.
The village has moved to a new site
more than a mile from the church, but
the tombstones and memorials provide
evidence of the parishioners' continuing
prosperity, as do the eighteenth and
nineteenth century pews, chandeliers,
stained glass and church plate.

11 The Church House, Crowcombe, Somerset
This was built as a parish hall for church ales and other fund raising activities in 1515, and is still used for its original purpose. The meeting hall is on the first floor and the lower rooms were used for storage and as a kitchen. During the seventeenth century the building was used to accommodate the parish poor.

12 Dole cupboard, Sleaford, Lincolnshire
This seventeenth-century cupboard was used to contain bread and other food for distribution to the poor. Such cupboards are often to be found in churches, as are the lists of parochial charities and bequests; they illustrate the continuing involvement of the Church with charity and poor relief.

13 Crowded pews at Rycote, Oxfordshire

The interior of this small medieval church is dominated by the seventeenth-century pews, and in particular by those on each side of the chancel steps. These elaborate pews are ornately carved and domed, and are placed on the cut-down rood screen, totally obscuring the view of the altar for the rest of the congregation. The one on the right was the family pew of the Norreys family and is surmounted by the musicians' gallery; the pew on the left is said to have been erected for Charles I when he visited Rycote in 1625.

14 The interior of Old Dilton, near Westbury, Wiltshire

The medieval church has a complete set of eighteenth-century fittings, including a fine 'three-decker' pulpit towering over the box pews. The west gallery, above the medieval font, was used by the musicians; the other gallery, which occupies the north-east corner of the church and has a separate entrance, was for long used as the village school. (*M.J. Lansdown*)

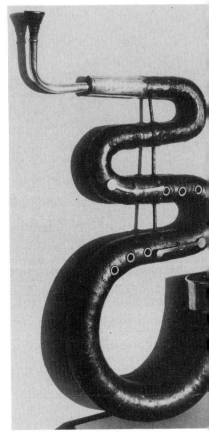

15 Monument of 1791 at Sherborne, Gloucestershire
This striking monument depicting a buxom angel and a grinning skeleton commemorates a member of the Dutton family and is situated on the north side of the altar. There is another large monument on the south side, and together they completely dominate the chancel. The Duttons had owned Sherborne since the sixteenth century, and the church is attached to their large mansion. At Sherborne, as in so many other places, the huge monuments demonstrate the wealth, and total power over the parish church, of the landed families during the eighteenth century.

16 Serpent from Chew Stoke, Somerset (now Avon)
This was a popular instrument with church musicians and serves as a reminder of the important part they played in church life and in the services before the almost universal adoption of the organ. This instrument remained in use until the 1850s.

Mass are not easy to comprehend, and were doubly difficult when the worshippers did not understand the language in which the ceremonies of the Church were conducted. Thus, symbols, painting, stained glass, statues and drama were an essential adjunct to instruction. Good examples of what can be learnt from glass painting are the Last Judgement scenes depicted in the west window at Fairford (Glos), or over the chancel arch at Clayton (Sussex). At St Thomas's, Salisbury, the fifteenth-century Doom over the chancel arch shows Christ surrounded by the apostles, judging the crowded hosts of naked souls, who have been called forth from their graves by the last trumpet. The just are led away to the eternal peace and tranquillity of heaven, while the wicked are hauled off by terrible devils, into the gaping jaws of a hideous, fiery hell:

> Here is a medieval guidebook to heaven and hell, more vivid and direct than any theological treatise; as we gaze at it and try to understand we find that for once we are on an equal footing with the congregation for whom it was made 500 years ago.[31]

The contemplation, each Sunday, of the detailed realistic hell which is so graphically shown in St Thomas' church, cannot have failed to make a profound impression upon the parishioners. To avoid the perils there portrayed would justify any expense on chantries, obits, lights or other benefactions, especially for men who were constantly at the mercy of plague, famine, fire or other natural disasters, from

> ...the arrow that flieth by day,
> From the pestilence that walketh in darkness
> (And)...the sickness that destroyeth in the noon-day.

and whose only refuge was in the church:

> For thou Lord, art my hope:
> Thou hast set thine house of defence very high
> There shall no evil happen unto thee:
> Neither shall any plague come nigh thy dwelling.

The decoration and appearance of late-medieval parish churches

From the evidence that survives in the parish churches themselves, as well as from documentary sources, it is possible to make the difficult imaginative leap which is necessary if we are to recreate a picture of the decoration and furnishing of a typical late-medieval parish church. Perhaps the most difficult aspect to imagine is the colour, since many parish churches must have been a riot of different colours, with painted stone and woodwork, wall-paintings and stained glass. Enough survives in a few churches, as for example at Copford in Essex and Pickering in Yorkshire, or from the painted screens of East Anglia or Devon, and the wall-paintings at Kempley in Gloucestershire, Torbryan in Devon, St Neot in Cornwall, Tarrant Crawford in Dorset or Sutton Bingham in Somerset, to show, albeit in a faded and partial way, what many church interiors must have been like; and late-medieval churchwardens' accounts show frequent payments to painters for decorating all parts of the church. The profusion of lights, altars, screens and statues is also clear from surviving examples and from a few written sources. Occasionally, inventories of church goods survive for the later-Middle Ages and give an excellent indication of just how much was lost in the destruction and confiscations of the sixteenth century. For example, an inventory dated 1508 exists of the goods in All Hallows church at Sherborne in Dorset, a church formerly attached to the great abbey church there, and which was demolished after the Reformation, when the parish obtained the former abbey church. All Hallows possessed numerous crosses, candlesticks, pyxes for the Blessed Sacrament, a silver pax for the kiss of peace ceremony during Mass, statues, precious stones, rosaries, beads and other valuable items which had been acquired as gifts over the years, as well as numerous sets of vestments and needlework for the altars etc. At Pilton in Somerset, an inventory made in 1509 lists a similar variety of valuable objects, including 15 suits of vestments and more than a dozen mass-books, processionaries, books of chants, etc., some printed and some in manuscript.

A remarkable account exists of the appearance of Long Melford church in Suffolk, just before the Reformation. It was made by Roger Martyn of Melford Place in c.1580 and describes the church as it was in his youth, before all the changes of the Reformation period. He remembers, first, the spectacular glory of the chancel, with its painted statues, the elaborate reredos to the high altar and the gilt tabernacle reaching up to the roof. The side altars were also lavishly decorated and furnished with statues. A fine rood screen ran across the whole building, surmounted by the figure of the crucified Christ:

> ...A fair Rood Loft, with the Rood, Mary and John, of every side, and with a fair pair of Organs standing thereby...the side thereof towards the body of the church, in twelve partitions in boards, was fair painted with the images of the twelve apostles.

He remembers also the roof of the church 'beautified with fair guilt stars'. The church also possessed 'many rich Copes and Suites of vestments'... Other things which had evidently impressed him as a boy included the Easter Sepulchre, an elaborate wooden structure, which was set up in the chancel on Maundy Thursday; the processions on Palm Sunday, Corpus Christi and Rogationtide week, and the bonfires and celebrations held to mark St James's Eve, Midsummer Eve, the Eve of St Peter and St Paul and finally St Thomas's Eve when there was bread and ale and 'some long pyes of mutton and peascods'[32]

Much of this regular round of ceremonial and festivals, together with most of the decoration and valuable possessions of parish churches, disappeared or were confiscated by the Crown during the upheavals of the Reformation, and the dramatic effects of this revolution, both upon the appearance of parish churches and upon the life of the parish, will be described in the next chapter.

Chapter Five

THE REFORMATION CHANGES AND THEIR EFFECT ON THE CHURCH LIFE OF LOCAL COMMUNITIES

The manifold religious changes of the Reformation ensured that the sixteenth century was the most stressful and disturbing period of upheaval which most parishes were to witness in their religious life, with dramatic alterations in doctrine and services, in the appearance, furnishings and decoration of the parish church, and in the part which the Church played in the social life of the community. The twists and turns of government policy presented both clergy and parishioners with acute problems of belief and conduct, and led, as never before, to sharp divisions of opinion and violent debate about religious matters among all classes of society. The changes in religion and the destruction of many long-established rituals of community life which had been centred upon the parish churches, represent a more abrupt break with the past than anything which was to be witnessed in most parishes until the coming of industrialisation and the massive increase of population of the nineteenth century. Many parish histories, however, devote little space to the impact of the religious changes and often make only a few broad generalisations about it. It is true that for many places parochial sources of documentary information do not survive, and other sources are scattered and not easy to use, but it is generally possible for the local historian to give at least some indication of the controversies and of the impact of the religious changes upon the clergy and parishioners and on the appearance of the parish church. The interesting material which can be found, especially among the diocesan records, and the light which this can shed on the crucial issues which parishioners faced and on their response to the upheavals of the times, is likely to repay the trouble of the search.

Above all, the local historian should try to trace the various stages in the remarkable revolution which occurred during the sixteenth century in the workship, atmosphere and appearance of the English parish church. He or she should attempt to find evidence of the attitude of the clergy and parishioners to these changes and to explain the remarkable process whereby the majority of parishioners, who in 1530 were apparently still strongly attached to the Church and to the Catholic faith, had by 1570 become, outwardly at least, staunch in their adherence to Protestantism. These changes also had a profound effect upon local rituals, processions and other ceremonies in town and country alike, and the local historian should try to trace the disruption of the ancient customs and local ceremonies. This is not, by any means, to suggest that the task is easy. Few parishioners were articulate enough to record their views on contemporary changes, and most conformed to, without openly questioning, the successive alterations in doctrine and services which were now imposed with all the authority of both Church and State and enforced by the dramatic punishment of protesters. But evidence of popular attitudes can occasionally be found and should be sought, for the impact of changes such as the introduction of the vernacular bible and of new services, the destruction of relics and images, the obliteration of wall-paintings and stained glass, and the prohibition of many ancient, popular rituals, festivals and observances can hardly be exaggerated. Even in the twentieth century liturgical changes have caused great uneasiness in many congregations, and in the sixteenth century the effect must have been very much greater among conservative villagers, all of whose religious beliefs centred upon the Latin Mass. The reaction of congregations on Whitsunday 1549, when the Holy Communion service in English was first celebrated and became the only legally-permitted form of worship, must have been profound, and can hardly be ignored by local historians. In towns such as Bristol, York, Coventry, Norwich, Lincoln and many others, the destruction or secularisation of the rich annual pattern of religious festivals, ceremonies, processions, drinkings, bonfires and plays, which accompanied the Reformation, had a tremendous impact on the character of community and civic life.

In the decades before the Reformation there is, in most parishes, little evidence of any hostility to the Church or disagreement with its doctrines. In a few places, notably in the West Midlands, Bristol and the Chilterns, the Lollard tradition of opposition to some aspects of the Church's teaching and practice remained alive, but such places were the exception, and the surviving sources indicate that most people continued to hold their parish churches in high regard. In wills, the commonest bequest was to the parish church, and gifts of vestments, ornaments, books or furnishings remained common; chantries and guild chapels, both of which were frequently housed within the parish churches, also continued to attract offerings, gifts and the bequests of testators. Churchwardens' accounts also reveal frequent gifts from parishioners and contributions to building work or other projects, such as the provision of seats. The accounts of the remote Devonshire parish of Morebath, situated on Exmoor, are typical in the sort of gifts they record during the 1520s, and although the splendidly-told story of the theft of a chalice is highly unusual, the response of the parishioners is an eloquent tribute to their attachment to the church.

Churchwardens' Accounts of Morebath, Devon

1520 James Radnyche gave a cope to this church for which was received 1s 9d

1521 Alison Huely gave to this churche   8d

1522 W. Rumbelow gave to the Store of St George a sheep for which was
      received   1s 0d
      Thomas Trymwell gave to the Store of Our Lady a sheep   1s 0d

1523 Margaret Lake gave to this Church in wax   5s 0d
      She also gave an Altar cloth to St Sidwell's altar, and a basin of
      Latyn to set light on afore St Sidwell   2s 0d

1526 We made of our Church ale   £2 13s 4d

1528 William atte Pole gave a sheep to the store of St Anthony   1s 0d
      He did bequeath again a new image of our Lady   6s 0d

1529 Thomas Tricky of Culmstock gave unto the store of St John
      a swarm of bees—the which now resteth in John Morse's
      keeping at the Half Moon
      Elnor Nicoll gave her wedding ring, the which did helppe make
      Saint Sidwell's shoes   8d
      Christina Trymell gave her best gown to help buy a new image   4s 0d

1534 Ye Stelying of ye chalys of ye Churche
      Memorandum that in this forsayd yere ye xx day of November...a
      theff with a ladder got up a pon this churche and pullyd up the ladder
      after him and sett the ladder to the tower wyndow and broke uppe that
      window and so got in to the bells and from the bells came a downe in
      to the churche and with a fyre box strake fyre and to proffe this he lefth
      his iron that he strake fyre with all by hynd him: and was fownd: and
      then bruke oppe the stok coffer: and the wother grett coffer: and tok a
      way the challis that was in the stok sent Sydwyll this schow of sylver
      and no nother thyng: and so got owt to the quire dore: and pullyd the
      quyre dore after him: So a pon this yong men and maydyns of this
      parysse dru them selffe togethers and with there gifts and provysyon
      they bought in a nother challis with out ony chargis of the parysse: as it
      is here after expressed and schowyd by a cownt: bothe of the value of
      the challis and also of there gefts.

Then follow the names and contributions—81 in number—the total
amount collected being £1 10s 0½d. In the same year, 1534, while the
parliament at Westminster was passing the Act of Supremacy which
effectively abolished the Pope's power in England and brought to an end the
thousand year-old link with the Catholic Church, the parishioners at
Morebath were engaged in reseating their church, all the timber for the
work being given by members of the little congregation!

There are many general accounts of the Reformation changes, which
trace all the convolutions of government policy and provide the essential
background information for any local study of this complex period.
Among the most useful national accounts for the local historian are G.R.
Elton, *England Under the Tudors*, 1955, and the same author's collection of
national documents, including crucial Acts of Parliament and government
edicts, in *The Tudor Constitution*, 1965. Probably the best of all of the many
accounts of the Reformation is A.G. Dickens, *The English Reformation*,
Batsford, 1964 and subsequent editions.

At the local level, an indispensable source is the formal account of all
ecclesiastical property provided by the monumental *Valor Ecclesiasticus* of
1535. This great survey of clerical wealth and revenues was produced under
the energetic and efficient administration of Thomas Cromwell; it was
published in six large volumes by the Record Commission, during the
nineteenth century, J. Caley and J. Hunter, eds., *Valor Ecclesiaticas temp.
Henrici VIII Auctoritate Regia Institus*, Record Commission 1810-34. The
Valor Ecclesiasticus provides a comprehensive account of the Church on the
eve of the Reformation, the dioceses, archdeaconries, rural deaneries and

parishes, as well as of the monastic houses and their widespread properties. It includes details of all rectories, vicarages and chapelries, of their lands and income, and the names of the incumbent and chantry chaplains. Its six large folio volumes have been described as 'by far the most informative single source on the economic history of the Tudor Church, and...worthy in its fashion to be placed alongside Domesday Book'? The Record Commission volumes also include maps showing the extent of dioceses, archdeaconries and deaneries.

The progress of the Reformation

The dissolution of the monasteries between 1536 and 1539 had a considerable impact upon many parishes, providing new parish churches for some, and lay rectors or *impropriators* for others; while few parishes were unaffected by the great transfer of lands and property which followed the destruction of the abbeys. By the Annates Act of 1534 the Crown, as successor to the Pope, claimed the *annates* or *first fruits* of each benefice, that is, the first year's income and a tenth of the income in all succeeding years. This was to continue until 1703, when the income was assigned by the Crown to the Governors of Queen Anne's Bounty for the augmentation of poor livings. From 1534 therefore, the Crown had a financial interest in all ecclesiastical benefices, their changes in value and the names of incumbents and patrons, now in the Public Record Office, provide useful alternatives to the bishops' registers for tracing details of income and the names of clergy?

Parish churches were also affected in 1547 by the dissolution of chantries and the confiscation by the Crown of that part of the funds of guilds and corporations assigned to so-called 'superstitious objects'. This measure had a greater impact on the life of most parishes than the more spectacular dissolution of the monasteries, for there was a large number of chantry foundations designed to provide perpetual masses for the souls of the founders and their families, or for the souls of all members of guilds and religious societies. Some chantries were in separate chapels, others were founded at side altars in parish churches; many were in towns and were closely connected with civic life, while others provided schools, almshouses and hospitals; a few were situated in outlying parts of remote communities. In addition, there were many smaller endowments for lamps and lights in churches, occasional masses, and various charitable functions. In Somerset, there were 108 chantries, 53 chapels, 4 hospitals, one chantry school, 19 guilds, one college and 258 endowments for lights and 'obits' or anniversary masses. York possessed nearly a hundred chantries and religious guilds, many of them having an important role in religious and civic life, the care of the old and the sick, or in education, and it was the York Corpus Christi guild which produced the popular mystery plays there each year. In Bristol, the guilds of merchants, the craft fellowships and the religious societies had established numerous chantries in the 18 parish churches which were crowded into the small area within and around the medieval walls. The Guild of Kalendars, an ancient association of clergy and laity, which

existed to offer masses and intercessions for their brethren living and dead,
and to carry out various charitable works, had a chapel in All Saints' church.
The Fraternity of Mariners maintained the hospital of St Bartholomew with
a priest and twelve poor seamen; another religious guild endowed the
Chapel of the Assumption on Bristol bridge with a priest to say daily
masses, and also undertook

> to keep and repair the Bridge of Bristol, piers, arches and walls, for the
> defence thereof against the ravages of the sea ebbing and flowing daily under
> the same.

The Weavers' Guild had a chantry in the Temple church; the Bakers' Guild
maintained a chantry priest in the Black Friars' church; the wealthy Guild of
Merchant Tailors had a chapel in St Ewen's church, richly decorated with
paintings, tapestries, screens, opulent furnishings and expensive plate.[5]
Official disapproval of the doctrine of purgatory and of masses for the dead,
described in the Chantry Act of 1547 as 'vain opinions of purgatory and
masses satisfactory to be done for them which be departed', combined with
the pressing financial needs of the Crown, made the dissolution of the
chantries inevitable, and the Act became law on 25 December 1547,
transferring all their endowments, goods and valuables to the King. The
Chantry Certificates, which were produced in 1548 as part of the process of
suppression, give a picture of the chantries, guilds and other endowments at
the end of their existence, with valuable local, architectural and
topographical information and details of charities, hospitals, schools and
almshouses. The manuscripts are in the Public Record Office. (See P.R.O.
Guide, i, 80-88; many county societies have issued printed editions).

A further confiscation of church goods occurred in 1552. The new, simple
form of worship ordered by the Act of Uniformity of 1549, and contained
in the first English Prayer Book, made much of the medieval plate,
vestments and other valuables belonging to parish churches unnecessary.
Moreover, as the Privy Council frankly announced in March 1551:

> that for as much as the King's Majesty had need presently of a mass of money,
> therefore commissions should be addressed unto all shires of England to take
> into the King's hands such church plate as remaineth, to be employed unto
> his Highness' use.

The confiscations were made during 1552, when inventories of plate were
produced for each parish church, and many of these have also been printed
by local societies. The originals are in the Public Record Office.[6] Parish
churches were left with only the bare minimum required for the conduct of
the new services. For example, in the following three Dorset parishes which
possessed only small amounts of plate, the commissioners were quick to
seize the best:

> The Parish of Porestocke—Two Chalices of Silver, parcel gilt. To the
> church's use there is appointed the worst chalice.

> The Parish of Loders—Two chalices of silver, one all gilt, the other parcel
> gilt. To the church's use there is appointed one chalice parcel gilt.

The Parish of Evershute—Two chalices of silver, parcel gilt. To the church's use there is appointed the least chalice.

Churchwardens' accounts

From the sixteenth century, many more churchwardens' accounts survive; they are an invaluable guide to the way in which the reforms, changes and reversals of government policy were followed in the parish, how the churches were stripped of statues, screens, paintings and ornaments, and how community life was profoundly affected by the religious changes and suppressions. In Bristol, for example, the early-sixteenth century churchwardens' accounts, with the inventories of church goods which accompany them, show the richness and splendour of the churches; and the payments made by the wardens illustrate the rôle which the churches played in the life of the town?

For those parishes where sixteenth-century churchwardens' accounts survive, the progress of the Reformation can be followed in detail from the recorded expenditure. The early changes of the Reformation—the break with Rome, the elevation of the monarch to the position of supreme head of the Church, the dissolution of the monasteries—had comparatively little effect upon the parish churches. The first change which affected the ordinary parishioner came with the the Royal Injunctions of 1538 which ordered, among other things, that parish registers of baptisms, marriages and burials should be kept, and that every church should have an English bible. A large number of wooden chests in parish churches, in which records of all sorts as well as the parish registers were stored, date from this period, since the Injunction of 1538 ordered that each parish was to provide 'a sure coffer' with two locks for the safekeeping of the registers[8]

From all over the country, churchwardens' accounts reveal that these orders were immediately complied with, and churchwardens purchased register books and coffers or chests in which the registers could be kept, as well as copies of the bible in English. For example, at Yatton in north Somerset in 1538 the churchwardens recorded:

Payd for a bybyll	ixs vid
Payd for making a chayne to the bybyll	viiid
Payd for bords to make the church coffur	iiiis viiid

At Houghton Conquest (Beds), the churchwardens paid £1 4s 0d 'for a Bible when the parish were commanded to have one'. This was the Great Bible which is familiar as the source of the psalms in the Book of Common Prayer of 1662.[9] A few parishes heeded the official warnings against idolatry during the later years of Henry VIII, and there was some destruction of images and wall-paintings, but for the most part traditional ceremonies and services continued unchanged, and the interior appearance of most parish churches was little altered. With the accession of the young Edward VI in 1547, however, sweeping changes began and are closely reflected in churchwardens' accounts![10] In May 1548 the Privy Council formally abolished and forbade many ancient and colourful rituals, such as the ceremony of the boy bishop, candles at Candlemas, palms and processions around the churchyard on Palm Sunday, ashes on Ash Wednesday, creeping to the cross on Good Friday, the Easter Sepulchre and the *Quem Quaeritis* ritual, the use of the 'holy loaf' after Mass on Sundays and of holy water. The Council also ordered the destruction of all images, while in 1550, the Act against Superstitious Books and Images ordered the destruction of all Latin service books and the complete defacement of all images, tombs or monuments except those erected in memory of

> any King, prince, nobleman or other dead person, which hath not been commonly reputed or taken for a saint.[1]

The Yatton accounts record expenses in taking down images in 1548, and in 1549 they contain the entry:

> This yere the sylver crosse of our church was sold and the money of the sayd crosse was bestowed upon the making of a sirton sklusse or yere (certain sluice or weir) against the rage of the salte water.

Clearly, the churchwardens could foresee the likelihood that their cross would be confiscated by the Crown, just as chantry possessions had been in the previous year. In 1549 the purchase of the first English Prayer Book is recorded, 7s 10d was paid to men who knocked down the stone altars and a wooden communion table was purchased. At the same time, a painter was paid the large sum of £5 for white-washing the whole of the Church interior in order to obliterate the wall-paintings which were now regarded as idolatrous. In 1552 the second English Prayer Book was purchased. Then in 1553 Edward VI died and the Yatton accounts record the accession of his Catholic half-sister Mary:

> To the ryngers at the proclamation of our soverayn lady quene Mary   vi d

Almost immediately, the churchwardens were obliged to spend large sums to replace all the church goods, ornaments, books and vestments which had been destroyed only a few years before. They record expenditure on missals, processionals, a censer, a container for holy oil, vestments, images and for rebuilding the stone altars.

In November 1558, the ringers at Yatton were again paid for welcoming a new sovereign, and the Elizabethan Settlement involved the churchwardens there in further expenses. They purchased the new Book of Common Prayer, and paid once more for the images and stone altars to be removed from the church; this time the great rood screen, which divided the nave from the chancel and which had managed to survive the earlier onslaughts, fell victim to reforming zeal, and the accounts record:

> For takyng down the rood   vd

Later in the reign of Elizabeth, the whitewashed walls of the church were adorned with scriptural texts. The marked constrast in the appearance of the parish churches before and after the Reformation can be seen from two inventories of the possessions of St Werburgh's, Bristol. In the 1520s the church contained a large quantity of plate, crosses, jewels, numerous vestments, paintings, a large number of service books of all kinds, hangings for the altars, candlesticks, censers and receptacles for the Blessed Sacrament, while the church itself was ablaze with lights, wall-paintings, stained glass, decorated altars and the painted rood screen. In 1567 an inventory of the church goods shows that the remaining possessions were:

> a communion cup, a quart pot, a pewter pot of a pynt, a bible, the paraphrases of Erasmus, the homilies, a cope, a pall of velvet, a white cloth for the communion table, a surplice, carpet, prayer book and a chest.

Another example of an informative series of churchwardens' accounts is that of Boxford (Suffolk) for the years 1530-61. During the 1530s, the major part of the churchwardens' income came from church ales and entertainments. 'Gatherings' or collections were made at various annual celebrations, and the church ales were enlivened by games, musicians, Morris dancing and stage plays. The money was spent by churchwardens on the upkeep of the church and on wax, incense, vestments, books and furniture for the church, and on the maintenance of the church bells. At Boxford, as in so many other places, the churchwardens obeyed promptly the orders of successive governments. A bible was purchased in 1538 and parish registers begun; the boy bishop ceremonies were brought to an end in 1541; the tabernacles, images, rood-loft and wall-paintings were destroyed early in the reign of Edward VI, and the Book of Common Prayer was purchased![14]

In the course of her reign, Queen Mary renounced all the changes in religion and in the services and appearance of the churches which had been made during the previous two decades, and returned to the situation as it had been before Henry VIII had begun the religious upheaval. For those who had regretted or resented the changes of the reign of Edward VI it must have been a great joy to see the Latin mass and the old round of familiar feasts and saints' days restored once more. There were, however, many others who did not welcolme the restoration of the old ways, and who steadfastly refused to obey the edicts of the government. The story of the martyrs of Mary's reign, of the horrific tally of burnings and persecution, is too well known to need retelling here, but what must be emphasised is that the changes which were ordered were apparently carried out in the parish churches without question or delay. With a few notable exceptions, most of those who suffered for their adherence to Protestantism under Mary were drawn from the lower orders of society, shopkeepers, tradesmen, craftsmen; the wealthier sections of the community, the leaders of society in rural parishes from whom the churchwardens were generally chosen, conformed, or at least, concealed any open opposition to the Marian regime, as to all other Tudor governments. No hostile reaction was apparently provoked even though the restorations of Mary's reign cost the parishes a great deal of money. For whereas the destruction of furnishings and decorations under Edward had not involved much expenditure, the replacement of rood-screens, vestments, stone altars, plate, Latin service books, censers and other necessary equipment under Mary was extremely expensive. But again, churchwardens' accounts from all over the country show that parish churches were rapidly re-equipped with all the things necessary for the conduct of the services in the Catholic tradition, the stone altars were rebuilt, the rood-screens and their figures repaced, and new vestments, service books, candlesticks, censers, containers for holy oil and images of the saints were purchased. The wardens at St James's, Garlickhythe in London paid £4 13s 8d for a new rood and a new Easter Sepulchre to replace those torn out only a few years before; at Stamford (Berks), some idea that the restoration of the old order was welcomed comes through the accounts, for a new stone altar was built and the wooden communion table 'which served in ye churche for ye communion in the wycked tyme of sysme (schism)' was sold for 5s 0d. The sentences of scripture were removed from the walls of churches and a start was made upon restoring the old decorations, pictures of the saints, statues and stained glass. But the five years of Mary's reign ended with her death in November 1558, and Elizabeth's accession and subsequent decision to restore the religious legislation of her father's later years, the break with Rome and the position of the Church of England, led to a further orgy of destruction. Roods, statues, screens, vestments, stone altars and Latin service books were once more swept away, and wooden communion tables, English bibles and service books and walls adorned with biblical texts were restored. Commissioners toured the country to see that the work of destruction was carried out, and few rood-screens or stone altars survived their visits. The following extracts from the wardens' accounts of St Mary's, Devizes, covering the decade 1551-61, tell their own tale of the bewildering rapidity of change in the church:

1551 (Ed. VI)	Paid for…plucking down of the (stone) Altars	1s 2d
1553 (Mary)	Paid for…setting up the great Altar	8d
1555 (Mary)	Paid for defacing the Scriptures on the walls	2s 4d
	Paid for…putting in the Roodloft	6s 0d
1557 (Mary)	Paid for tymber to make the pyctor (picture) that standeth by the Rode named Mary and John	2s 0d
1561 (Eliz.)	Paid for taking down of the Roodloft	6s 0d.[15]

Similarly at Ashburton (Devon), 3s 4d was paid in 1549 'for takyng down the Rood and other images'; later these were all burnt. Under Mary, the rood and the stone altars were restored, only to be taken down again and destroyed early in the reign of Elizabeth.[16]

Churchwardens' accounts were designed to record income and expenditure, and cannot be expected to provide comments on the successive changes. We cannot tell from them whether the orders of the government were carried out grudgingly or willingly; whether the churchwardens and the congregations welcomed the changes or resented the disruption and expense; or if they were saddened at the destruction and loss of so many things of great beauty and craftsmanship, although there are occasional references to plate, vestments, statues and other items being hidden so that they might be used again if the religious climate should change. A rare exception of this kind is found in the parish register of Landbeach (Cambs) following the entries of 1562 (although bearing the date 1594) together with the name of the vicar, Nicholas Nemo; this seems to suggest that there were many in the parish who disliked the changes, would have welcomed the return of the Pope and the Latin services, and had still not removed the rood-loft and other Catholic ornaments from their church:

> Pope the fox will eat no grapes, and whi he can not git them; so at this towne thei love inglish servis because thei can have none other, as apperith bi the candilbeme and rodlofte as I think: judge you by me![7]

Another example occurs in the churchwardens' accounts of Morebath on the borders of Devon and Someset. In this remote moorland parish the vicar, Christopher Trychay, continued to hold his office throughout all the changes of the Reformation from 1520-73, making each successive change as it was ordered by the government, without protest or comment. In 1551, however, when the church goods which had been hidden by the parishioners during Edward's reign were brought back to the church, he at last betrayed his true feeling:

> Item, of John Williams of Bery we received again an image of Mary and the king and the queen concerning St George.
> And of William Morsse at Lauton was received an image of John.
> And of the widow Jurdyn trails and knots.
> And of divers others persons here was rescued pageants and books and divers other things concerning our rood-loft.
> Like true and faithfull Christian people this was restored to this church, by the which doings it showeth that they did like good Catholic men.

Expressions of feeling are rare; for most parishes there is no indication of the general opinion, and all that we can say is that clergy and laity were too cowed to resist the instructions of successive governments and obeyed promptly, without public protest![8] For any indication of popular attitudes and for the evidence of the effect of all the religious changes in particular parishes we must turn to other sources.

Diocesan records

From the sixteenth century onwards, it becomes essential for the local historian to make use of the diocesan sources, although their bulk, complexity and the difficulties of language and palaeography remain, and deter many from consulting material which can be uniquely informative about church activities, religious beliefs, community life and the activities and attitudes of parishioners. The best guide to this material is J.S. Purvis, *Introduction to Ecclesiastical Records*, 1953, which explains the origin and purpose of the records and provides examples and transcripts.

(a) Visitations and churchwardens' presentments

A rich source of information about parish life can be found in the records of the visitations conducted by archbishops, bishops and archdeacons. The practice of formal visitations, which was inherited from the Middle Ages, became an extremely important means of enforcing religious change and conformity to new ways during the sixteenth century. Archdeacons' visitations were often held annually and bishops' visitations at intervals of three or four years, though not all officials were so conscientious and not all dioceses have preserved the records of these visitations. It is well worth looking for surviving material, since it may well contain the list of all the rectors and vicars, licensed preachers, chaplains, curates and schoolmasters, surgeons and midwives summoned to appear before the churchwardens from each parish who were charged to bring *presentments* or reports on the church fabric, furnishings, churchyard, the services, the conduct of the clergy and the moral state and religious attitudes of the parishioners. To guide the churchwardens in making their presentments, Elizabethan bishops began to issue *articles of enquiry* or lists of questions concerning the religious affairs and spiritual state of the parishes on which they required answers and information. Elizabethan visitation records can therefore supply details of church fabrics, furnishings, the progress of the Reformation in each parish and the extent to which government orders on such matters as images, wall-paintings or rood-screens were being complied with, on the conduct of the clergy, on the growth of Puritanism, on 'schismatics', or those who refused to attend church services, and Catholic recusants. There may also be information on the spiritual life of the parish, the services and the number of communicants, on the glebe and parsonage house, on parochial charities, and on the survival of old customs, revels and festivals. One result of all the Reformation changes was a great reduction in the number of clergy in each parish. On the eve of the Reformation, the West Riding of Yorkshire had nearly 900 clergymen, but the changes under Henry VIII and Edward VI, especially the dissolution of chantries, colleges and hospitals, meant that by the accession of Mary in 1553 there were only 250. At Pontefract in 1553, a parishioner complained that whereas there had formerly been

> one abbey, two colleges, a house of friars, preachers, one ancress, one hermit, four chantry priests, one guild priest,

the town was now left with only 'an unlearned vicar' and two curates![19]

It should be emphasised that details of sixteenth-century visitations do not survive for all dioceses, and that where they do exist they do not invariably provide useful information about each parish, since some places had nothing significant to report, or the clergy and churchwardens avoided further enquiry by simply stating that all was well (*omnia bene*).

The following examples of episcopal visitations of Gloucester diocese during the mid-sixteenth century give some indication of the range of material which may be found concerning the state of the church, the life of the parishioners, the progress of reform and the reaction to change among both clergy and laity. In 1548 several persons were reported for adultery and fornication or for slander, drunkenness and other moral offences; most of these were subsequently sentenced by the Ecclesiastical Court to perform public penance and make an announcement of their contrition. In the uncertainty and upheaval of the times and following the dissolution of the chantries in the previous year, many parish churches were in a bad state of repair, and several chancels, which were the responsibility of the clergy, had been allowed to fall into decay. At Thornbury, the chancel was 'sore in decaye and there can be no masse said in the same whan it raynethe'; at Oldbury-on-Severn

> the highe chaucell there is in such ruine and decaye that masse and other divine service can not be celebrate therein.

The various reforms already imposed by the government and the uncertainty about the future had led several parishes to sell their plate and other valuables. At Staunton, the chalice had been sold to pay for church repairs; Longhope had sold a chalice, pyx and cross to pay for soldiers going to Scotland 'and also for th'amendyng of the highe waye betwixt the said parisshe and Huntleye'. In other places, laymen had taken away the church valuables, perhaps for safekeeping. At Hill, John Byrd

> toke owte of the chapel there one vestiment, ii cruettes and oon banner.

At Frampton-on-Severn plate and jewels worth £1 13s 6½d had

> byn conveyed awey by oon Stanley.

Some were obviously unhappy at the new ideas and doctrines which were being introduced, others evidently wished for a faster pace of change, while many were apathetic. The bishop was told that at Slimbridge

> in the tyme of divine service William Bowre and William Cloterboke doo reade openly in the churche and doo trouble the people.

At Dymock, there were many in the congregation who

> do use them self whan they be at Goddes service to talke and babbull in the churche yard.

At Tidenham, the vicar had already broken the stained glass windows in his church, overthrown the churchyard cross and was refusing to say Mass, while at Woolaston, the curate would not say the Ave Maria.

In 1551 the zealous reformer John Hooper became Bishop of Gloucester and immediately conducted a visitation of his diocese. This uncovered many deficiencies, especially among the clergy, for as well as the usual crop of moral failures, absentees and other complaints, the bishop found that out of 331 clergy he examined, 9 did not know how many commandments there were and 168 could not repeat them; 10 could not repeat the Lord's Prayer, 39 did not know where it appeared in the bible and 34 could not say who was its author. In some parishes Catholic practices and rituals continued, in others it seems likely that clergy and laity had combined in delay over carrying out the government's commands. In parish after parish, we can observe in these visitation records the uneven progress of reform, and the gradual change under the combined pressure of government edict and episcopal power.[20]

A series of churchwardens' presentments for parishes in the diocese of Gloucester during 1563 reveals a great deal about the progress of the Reformation and the state of each parish. In almost every place there were reports of persons who absented themselves from church, possibly because they disliked the new doctrines and services. John Berkeley was said to have 'certain images decked with roses set up in his chamber' and some old service books. At Hinton-on-the-Green, the youth of the parish

> will not tarry in their church at the time of service, but will go out of the church before it is done.

Again, they may have objected to the new liturgy, but we are not told. On the other hand, at Minsterworth, the parson was already displaying two Puritan characteristics. He refused to wear the vestments

> and says no man shall make him use any such like superstitions. . . . Further, on Sundays he doth weary the parish with over-long preaching.

The failings of a few parishioners are described in detail. At Barnsley, one Alice Pinbury was thought to be a witch because she treated human diseases and also

> horses and all other beasts she takes upon her to help by way of charming, and in such way that she will have nobody privy of her sayings.

Eleanor Polle of Ruardean in the Forest of Dean typified an age-old problem and had clearly exasperated the churchwardens. She was

> a common scold and a distruber of the whole parish both in church and out, and if we have not a reformation, she will cause manslaughter in our parish..[21]

A visitation of Sussex in 1569 found that many roods and rood-lofts remained in place, 'and those taken down still lie in many churches ready to be put up again'; while where the rood itself had been taken down, parishioners had painted a cross upon the chancel arch. Many people were also reported to have images concealed and hidden away ready to be brought back into the churches if times should change.[21]

The large diocese of Salisbury, covering the counties of Wiltshire, Dorset and Berkshire, included many peculiars where ecclesiastical control was exercised by the Dean of Salisbury or by one of the prebendaries. For these peculiars, the churchwardens' presentments for the later-seventeenth centuries provide dramatic, first-hand evidence of the state of the Church in each parish. Many people were reported for moral offences or for failing to attend church, and for working or playing games on Sundays; others habitually slept through the church services. In many places, the church was said to be in urgent need of repair, or to lack a bible or other essentials; this is hardly surprising in view of the heavy cost of all liturgical changes since the 1540s. In 1562 Bishop Jewel of Salisbury complained of the bad state into which many churches in the diocese had been allowed to fall, and wrote:

> It is a sin and shame to see so many churches so ruinous and so foully decayed in almost every corner.

At Alton Pancras (Dorset), the vicar was said to go to nearby Cheselbourne 'to footeball upon the sabbothe day'. At Lyme Regis, the ancient Easter and Whitsuntide customs of a procession, with musical instruments and bearing spring foliage, around the town and on to the Cobb or quay, is described in detail and with obvious disapproval 'which wee take to be a profane use contrary to the Ryght Sanctity of the lord's day'. At Upton Scudamore near Warminster (Wilts) in 1585, the vicar, Thomas Hickman, had already adopted many Puritan views and the churchwardens reported these in great detail:

> He commandeth that we shall not bowe our knees at the name of Jesus, neyther put off our hats and capps, neyther to do any more Reverence at thie tyme than we doe at any other tyme, and the sayd parson sayeth yt is playne ydolatrice.

He insisted that his parishioners stood to receive the Communion; he refused to wear a surplice or to use the baptism service in the Prayer Book; he would not teach the Catechism, and so on ; a list of some fifteen similar complaints was included. Hickman had evidently found an effective way of preventing sports and games from being played in the churchyard, for the churchwardens complained that

> He grazes his sheep in the churchyard whereby the porch is filled with dung and the parishioners do carry the same on their shoes into the church, which is a greate smell, and doth much grudge the parishioners conscience.

At Preston near Weymouth (Dorset), one parishioner had built a pew which

> is offensive to curtayne persons sitting behinde yt, by reason of the height of yt, yt standinge a greate deale higher than any seate in the sayde church soe that those persons there neither see nor well heare the minister reading divine service.

Eight persons from Fordington (Dorset) were reported

> for that they have played at a game with a Ball called fives in the Churchyard, and thereby have broken the glasse of one of the windows of the church, the reparacion whereof is unto the value of 5s 0d.

At Ryme Intrinseca (Dorset) and several other places, the Rogationide processions around the parish bounds had been abandoned, and two women of the parish continually interrupted the services with their quarrelling:

> Shusan the wief of Robert Husway and Agnes the wief of John Plowman be contendinge and sterringe in the church and the one thrustinge and pullinge out the other.

The services at Sherborne (Dorset) were frequently upset by children crying and misbehaving, or by persons who played bowls in the churchyard. Thomas Tyher of Charminster (Dorset) was reported for

> usinge witchcraft and performing publicklie physicke by unlawful meanes contrarie unto authoritie...
> ...also for saying that Joane Blick of Charminster had seven devilles in her and undertaking to cast them out of her...[23]

As with all sources, it is necessary to beware of malice or exaggeration and not all visitation records or churchwardens' presentments will contain good local material, but the possibility of finding such details and the occasional glimpses they give of the thoughts, attitudes and actions of ordinary parishioners make the search well worthwhile.

(b) Ecclesiastical court records

Like the visitation records, the documentary evidence produced by the Church courts is an excellent and often quite untapped source for the local historian; the records also present quite formidable problems. Many people are understandably deterred by the difficulties from tackling this source. The methods of the courts were complex and tedious, and the records are often overwhelming in quantity, unsorted, unindexed and difficult to read. Professor G.R. Elton has warned researchers that

> The act books of Church courts are among the more strikingly repulsive of all the relics of the past—written in cramped and hurried hands, in very abbreviated and technical Latin, often preserved (if that is the right word) in fairly noisome conditions, ill-sorted and mostly unlisted, unindexed and sometimes broken in pieces...
>   On the other hand they offer a most promising field to research because they illumine the history of the Church and people in ways that no other source can. They take one to the realities?[24]

In spite of all the difficulties, these records are worth careful study because of the many aspects of daily life, morals, religious beliefs, conduct, and personal relationships which fell within the jurisdiction of the Church courts. Their concerns range from the moral and spiritual state of the clergy to heresy, moral offences, slander, non-payment of tithes, witchcraft and non-attendance at church. Only through the detailed study of this material by local researchers can the repeated generalisations of national historians about the state of the church or the progress of religious change in the parishes be checked, verified or amended. The records of the Church courts bring us closely into contact with daily lives of all classes of society, and since the evidence of witnesses was recorded in English and often apparently in the witnesses' own words, we can, as in no other source, hear the authentic voice of individual people?[25] Witnesses' depositions show very clearly the total lack of privacy in sixteeth-century life; someone was always passing by, or happened to be peering through a window or a crack in a door, and there always seemed to be witnesses, even to the most intimate scenes. Some examples from the records of the Church courts relating to

Bristol and district will serve to illustrate the material that can be found.

We can read the sort of pleasantries which were exchanged in the streets, such as the case tried in St Mary Redcliffe in 1540 when Elizabeth Corford was accused of brawling in the street at Bedminster with Agnes Morgan, and of saying to her:

> Thou art an arrant hore, a common hore, and every man knoweth thou art a naughtie harlott. I will tear thy hore's coat that all other hores shall be ware by thee.

Elizabeth was duly sentenced to perform public penance. There were several similar cases, and others which involved testamentary disputes, immorality, drunkenness, non-attendance at church, working on Sundays, or the survival of 'relics of popery' in parish churches. William Wilkins of Redcliffe was sentenced to public penance in St Mary Redcliffe in1560 for adultery with Joanna Thomas, and was ordered to

> ...repayer to the parish of Redclif, haveinge a sheet about him, barefoot and barelegged, with a white rodd in his hande, and to kneel penetently before the communion table all the time of morning prayer and the communyon, and at the time of the reading of the homily against adultry to stande before the pulpit while the curate declare the cause of his penance doing.

Such public penance was commonly imposed by the Church courts and must have been a daunting prospect in a small community[26]

The fact that the parish churches were little used on weekdays when the old round of daily services was abandoned, is illustrated by the case of Matilda Davis, a common harlot, in 1558. She told the court that she had met with a Mr Perks at the Sign of the Pelican in Bristol, and that

> on...about midsomer last past he wold com unto the sexton's house window in St Thomas's parish where she dwelt...and wold entice her to go with him to the churche wheare he used her, and theare, when he had shutt the church dore he used her as she saithe most ungodly and abominably in a pew within the body of the church there,...and at every time he gave her as she saithe xiid at a time?[27]

Seating arrangements and the right to sit in particular pews were a fruitful source of dispute. In 1575 Edward Arden and Alice Haynes of Mangotsfield were accused of entering the church and

> there with yron barres, pickaxes and other such like tooles did break down a pew in the church there in which Eliz. Springall the wyffe of Thomas Springall hath alwaies used to sitt, to the great disturbance of the parishe...

The clergy were also disciplined by the courts, like Maurice Durrand, curate of St Werbergh's, and Thomas Tyson, curate of St Peter's, who in 1592 were solemnly warned by the court that

> they have been dyvers times drunken and that hereafter they doe not frequente alehouses or taverns, but behave themselves in such honest and decente sorte as becometh the estate and profession of a minister.

Other cases illustrate the ferment of religious ideas and the discussion of religious matters among all classes of society during the reign of Mary. In 1555 two men of Chew Magna appeared before the court for openly declaring that 'they will not believe the preacher, let him do what he will'; three others were accused of abusing the Sacrament and of saying that it was no better than ordinary bread. At Yatton, Joan Slytche 'openly did say that she set not a poynte by the Pope's holiness nor by her curate'; two other people refused to acknowledge that 'in the Sacrament there is really the naturall body of our Lord Jesus Christ that was borne of the Virgin'. A servant girl from Cameley would not hold up her hands nor kneel down at the elevation of the Host, and was forced to run away to avoid being brought before the church court. In 1556 William Saxton, a weaver, was condemned to be burnt for steadfastly maintaining that 'the Sacrament of the Eucharist is nought else but material bread, and not the Body or Blood of Christ'. He was executed on St Michael's Hill on 18 September 1556.[28]

Particularly full and interesting is the evidence given in the case of Margery Northoll in 1539. Margery had been left a widow at the age of 26, and came to Bristol in August 1539 with the declared intention that in the town she would find another husband. She stayed first with a friend, Matilda Blagdon, in Bedminster, and later moved to a house in Temple Street. Wherever she went, however, there were always witnesses who could later testify to the court concerning her words and actions. All the witnesses agreed that she arrived in Bristol bringing with her bottles of sack, and that she had announced that in Bristol she could easily find three or four new husbands. Her first attempt was on an elderly, wealthy clothier, Thomas Butler, who lived in Redcliffe Street. But her attempt to interest him obviously failed, and Margery was heard to declare that she would rather have a young man even if he had but one shirt to his back. Her friend Matilda Blagdon then suggested that she should try

an honest young man whose name is Thomas Jones, servant of Mr Gorges

They therefore sent for Thomas Jones to come to the house. When he arrived Margery produced a bottle of sack and witnesses reported that

they sat at the table drinking sack merrily together.

After a time Thomas Jones announced that he must go, for said he:

'I must goo home for I have harvest folks at home and therefore I am sorry.'

Margery however refused to let him go and insisted that he should stay the night so they might talk further. Witnesses then saw Margery produce another bottle of sack. The next day witnesses saw Margery and Thomas walking hand in hand in the garden, and then sitting on a seat under a woodbine. They then heard Margery say to Thomas:

'Let us not goo yn, here ys a good place, for there are many folks within'.
And then she sett a clothe there a-redy and sett afore them wyne and ale and there they dranke and were merry together.

After some time Thomas again protested that he was sorry but he must go home to attend to his master's affairs, and witnesses heard Margery say to him:

> 'What nede you to be sorry, go ye home Thomas to your harvest, for I am your wife and you be my husband, and by my faith and trothe we wyll never be departed tyll Godd departe us.'

The witnesses, watching through the parlour window, saw that Thomas likewise took Margery by the hand and said:

> 'By my faith and trothe I take you to be my wyffe'.

Thomas then went home, but a few days later he sent a messenger with an expensive present of a string of corall beads with gaudys of silver to Margery. In the meantime, however, Margery had met someone else and refused to accept the beads, saying:

> 'God make him a good man, I will never have his tokens.'

The new man in her life was a weaver from the parish of Temple called Thomas Hayward to whom Margery also solemnly plighted her troth. Following a complaint from Thomas Jones, Margery found herself before the ecclesiastical court, and was ordered totally to renounce the company of Thomas Hayward.[29]

The common point of these examples of proceedings before the Church courts, and there are many hundreds of similar ones which might be quoted, is that they all illustrate very clearly the close involvement of the Church with all aspects of community life and the careful control exercised by the Church courts over the thoughts, speech and actions of individuals.

Evidence for individual responses to the religious changes

The most difficult problem in any local study of the Reformation is to assess the impact of the changes on the religious attitudes of ordinary parishioners. One source which does offer an opportunity of at least a glimpse of the religious opinions of ordinary men and women may be found in the wills which they left. Wills and their accompanying probate inventories are an important source for many aspects of local history, from genealogy, domestic architecture and household furnishings to farming history, crafts, trades and economic changes; the wills can also provide an unique insight into religious attitudes. The first bequest in a sixteenth-century will was the soul of the testator to God, and the phrases which are employed in bequeathing the soul may afford some glimpse of the religious opinions of the person making the will. This was probably the only time in his life that an ordinary person had occasion to set down on paper any hint of his religious beliefs, and wills from various parts of the country have recently been carefully studied with this in mind. The will may, of course, have been written by a scribe who employed a common form for this part or merely copied from some other will; but nevertheless a devout Catholic would bequeath his soul not only to God but also 'to the blessed Virgin Mary and the whole Company of Heaven', while a Protestant testator would use a phrase such as 'to Almighty God and his only son our Lord Jesus Christ, by whose precious death and passion I hope to be saved'. There are many thousands of wills surviving from the sixteenth century, and it is clear from those that have so far been analysed that there was a steady growth of Protestant belief during the middle decades of the sixteenth century. For example, Professor A.G. Dickens has analysed wills from Yorkshire and Nottinghamshire and shows that whereas in the late 1530s only 14 per cent of wills contained Protestant phraseology, by the early 1550s the proportion omitting all reference to the Virgin and the saints had risen to more than 60 per cent. Similar studies have been made of Nottinghamshire, Kent and Cambridgeshire villages; and in Kings Langley (Herts) of 42 sixteenth-century wills the clear change over the sixteenth century was as follows:

	Traditional wills in Catholic form	Wills with non-traditional wording
1521-30	7	0
1531-40	4	3
1541-50	4	4
1551-60	7	2
1561-70	0	3
1571-80	0	3
1581-90	0	2
1591-1600	0	3[30]

But whether they were Catholic or Protestant, few men during the sixteenth century doubted that God was intimately concerned with the minutest details of their daily lives. Likewise plagues, disease and natural disasters were attributed to the direct intervention of the Almighty in punishing some wickedness, just as good fortune was regarded as a sign of divine favour. A hard-headed and highly successful sixteenth-century Bristol merchant, when sending valuable cargoes abroad, was careful to note against each entry in his ledger 'God send hit saff'; and it was more than common form that sixteenth- and seventeenth-century letter-writers ended their correspondence with phrases such as 'May God send you long life and good fortune', 'Our Lord Jesus Christ preserve you in grace', or 'I pray God to send you as well as your heart desireth'.[31] Typical also of the feeling that the controlling hand of the Almighty touched every aspect of life was the Berkshire farmer Robert Loder who, when making up his accounts for the year 1616, wrote:

This year sowing too early I lost (The Lord being the cause thereof, but that the instrument wherewith it pleased him to work)...the sum of £10 at least, so exceeding full was my barley with charlock, in all likelihood by means of that instrumental cause, the Lord my God ... being without doubt the efficient cause thereof.[32]

An inevitable result of a period of such far-reaching and contradictory changes was to produce among some people, both clergy and laity, a degree of apathy and indifference. A remarkable number of the clergy adapted themselves to each new order of service and each change of theology, and continued to minister to their congregations. A few no doubt were openly or privately cynical, or put the maintenance of their accustomed income before all else, or simply wished to avoid trouble. The best-known of all such men was Simon Aleyn, vicar of Bray in Berkshire 1540-88, who retained his benefice through all the changes of the sixteenth century, and according to Thomas Fuller's famous account thus effectively silenced a critic who complained that he was prepared to accept any theological change:

> ... being taxed by one for being a turncoat and an unconstant changeling,
> Not so, said he, for I always kept my principle, which is this, to live and die
> the vicar of Bray.[33]

Many other clergy were simply perplexed by the changes they were witnessing and by their involvement in controversies which they scarcely comprehended, like William Herne who was the vicar of St Petrock's Exeter, from 1528 until his death in 1566, and who continued to serve his parishioners there through all the religious changes. During the reign of Edward VI, Herne had declared to his friend John Midwinter, who was Mayor of Exeter and a staunch Protestant, that he would be torn apart by wild horses rather than say Mass again. Nevertheless, when Edward VI died and Mary came to the throne, Herne conformed to the Catholic order once more. When Midwinter saw him robed for Mass he 'poynted unto him with his fynger remembringe as it were his old protestations that he would never singe masse agayne; but parson Herne openly yn the churche spak alowd unto hym. "It is no remedye man, it is no remedye".' Another example of an incumbent who, although very reluctant and much disturbed in his conscience eventually conformed to all the changes, is Robert Parkyn who was curate of Adwick-le-Street near Doncaster (Yorkshire) during the middle years of the sixteenth-century. His 'commonplace book' compiled about 1555 gives an intimate glimpse of the feelings of a conservatively-minded north-countryman who conformed with great reluctance to the changes of Edward VI's reign and rejoiced when Catholicism was restored under 'the gratius Quene Marie'. Parkyn, however, continued to hold his benefice in spite of his misgivings until his death in 1570.[34]

Two further examples, one a priest, the other a layman, will suffice to illustrate the completeness of the revolution through which such men had lived. The first is John Chetmill, who was ordained as a priest early in the 1520s. In 1538 he became vicar of Sherborne, Dorset, and the parish priest of the church of All Hallows which was actually built up against the walls of the great Benedictine Abbey of St Mary's. Here he must have been quite overshadowed in every sense by the wealthy and ancient abbey with its extensive landed estates and superb church, under its powerful abbot, 16 monks and numerous retainers. In 1539 the monastery was suppressed and the abbot and monks departed; a year later the town acquired the great abbey church as its parish and All Hallows was demolished. It must have been almost overwhelming for John Chetmill to find himself in charge of this enormous church with its outstanding architectural features; but he apparently accepted this change as he accepted the new English service book, the changes in the vestments and ritual and the new theology of Edward VI's reign—and as he also came to terms with the reversal of all these changes under Mary when once more he said the Latin mass and observed all the old feasts and fasts. Likewise, in 1558-59 Chetmill accepted the new regime imposed by the Elizabethan government, and he remained as vicar of Sherborne until his death in 1566. It would be quite wrong to think of such a man necessarily as a turncoat or time-server. John Chetmill was evidently concerned for the well-being of his people and there is ample evidence of his dedicated work amongst them. For example, there are few wills made in the town during his incumbency which do not bear either his handwriting as the scribe or his signature as a witness, evidence of his regular attendance upon the sick and dying. It is difficult to believe that he would have served their interests better by resignation.[35]

The second example is a layman, Roger Martyn of Long Melford in Suffolk, who has been referred to earlier. He recalled that the high altar had been dismantled under Edward VI, set up again in Queen Mary's time and finally demolished early in Elizabeth's reign. He recollected the 'rich Copes and suits of vestments', the Easter Sepulchre and the organs upon the rood-loft. These organs had been brought into his house, and he obviously kept them to await a further change in religious fashion when they might be required once more. Three times a year the choir had dined at Melford Hall, and

> on St James' Even there was a bonefire and a tub of ale and bread given to the poor, and before my doore there were made three other bonefires, viz., on Midsummer Even, on the Even of St Peter and Paul when they had the like drinkings, and on St Thomas' Even, on which, if it fell not the fish day, they had some long pyes of mutton and peasecods set out upon boards with the aforesaid quantity of bread and ale;...and my Grandfather...had, at the lighting of the bonefires, wax tapers with balls of wax, yellow and green, set up all the Breadth of the Hall, lighted them and burning there, before the image of St John the Baptist; and after they were put out, a watch candle was lighted and sit in the midst of the said Hall, upon the pavement burning all night.[36]

The memories flow out with all the freshness and jumbled recollection of an old man recalling his youth; but through it comes the realisation that the world he remembers has disappeared. The differences which he described in the appearance of the church, the services, the ceremonies and the doctrine are a measure of the total revolution in parochial life which men like he and John Chetmill had witnessed in their lifetimes.

The effects of the Reformation

No adequate account of parochial history can avoid making some attempt to assess the impact of a movement so all-embracing in its effects and so pervasive in its consequences as the Reformation. The changes greatly diminished the role of the Church in the community life, and instead loaded upon clergy and churchwardens a mass of new secular duties, turning the parish into a basic unit of local government. The results of the changes will be apparent in the appearance of the parish church, in the remains or evidence of former altars, screens, furnishings, decoration, paintings or stained glass, in the disfigured statues and sculpture, empty niches or traces of former colouring. In those parishes for which the sort of documentary evidence which has been discussed in the foregoing pages survives, the upheaval can be traced through the destruction of chantries, shrines and relics and the confiscations of church valuables, through the parochial response to successive government orders, and in the religious attitudes of the parishioners and the spiritual life of the parish.

In many ways the most dramatic effect was on popular culture, communal recreations, games, processions and annual ceremonies. As already shown, the dissolution of the chantries in 1547 led to a break-up of many fraternities and guilds which in towns such as York, Bristol, Coventry, Hereford, Canterbury, Norwich and many others, and in the villages, had been responsible for popular enactments of mystery plays, pilgrimages, religious processions and many other rituals, some of them very ancient, which were popular with all classes of society. The growth of Puritanism during the reign of Elizabeth brought further criticism of communal activities such as church ales, parish revels, play-acting, and pageants; in most counties religious drama had ceased by the 1580s, and other traditional festivities were under increasing attack. In Gloucestershire, John Smyth reported that parish wakes and fairs 'diminish and grow sickly'; and Edmund Grindall, Archbishop of York, enquired of all his parishes in the diocese of York in 1576 whether they had allowed in their churches or churchyards

> ...any lords of misrule or summer lords or ladies, or any disguised persons, or others, in Christmas or at May-Games, or any morris dancers...

In the York diocese several pre-Reformation traditions and ceremonies continued during the reign of Elizabeth. An attempt was made to revive the Wakefield Corpus Christi play during the 1570s, and rituals such as burning candles and bell-ringing for the dead on All Souls' Eve, rush-bearing, May games and the erection of May-poles continued in many parishes, as well as superstitions, witchcraft, magic and sorcery.[37] In Somerset, the Puritan landowner Sir Francis Hastings left sums of money in his will of 1596 to several parish churches

> upon condition that they never use againe theyr churchales, to the pro-phaning of the Lorde's Sabboathe, the abusing of his creatures in drunkness and ryott, and the corrupting of their youth by tryning them up in gaminge and lascivious wantoness and sundry other disorders.[38]

In place of these cermonies and games, the Puritans pushed preaching and attendance at sermons into the forefront of community life. As early as 1547, the Injunctions of Edward VI had ordered that each parish should provide 'a comely and honest pulpit', and this was repeated in the Elizabethan Injunctions of 1559. The Puritan insistence upon the importance of preaching and a preaching ministry explains why in North America, which has largely taken its religion from the Puritans, the term 'preacher' is so widely used as a synonym for minister or clergyman.

In some parts of the country, medieval rituals lingered on much longer than in others. In Lancashire, Sussex, Devon and Cornwall, for example, older beliefs and customs survived well into the seventeenth century. And in 1579 Bishop Cox of Ely found that at Horseheath (Cambs) there was

> a stone in the church yard there, with images uppon it, which...the Towne there, when they come by it to the church there, do make great reverence.

A year later however, it was reported that 'the cross and ymages are deformed quite'.[39] At St Edmund's, Salisbury, in 1630 a Puritan lawyer, Henry Sherfield, was enraged by the fact that many worshippers venerated a stained glass window 'wherein God is painted in many places, as if he were there creating the world', and many of the congregation continued to bow before the figure of God portrayed in the window as 'a little old Man in a blue and red coat'. Sherfield therefore, took a pickstaff, climbed up to the window and completely destroyed it; having completed his work he fell heavily to the ground and 'lay there a quarter of an Hour groaning (and) afterwards kept his House for a Month'[40]

In every parish the clergy and church wardens found a mass of new secular duties imposed upon them as a result of the Reformation changes. Tudor legislation required the incumbent of each parish to be active in exhorting his parishioners to contribute to poor relief; he was required to be present when rogues and vagabonds were whipped in his parish; he was obliged to lead the rogationtide processions around the parish bounds—the one procession which survived the Reformation; he superintended public confessions, which were required by Quarter Sessions as well as by the ecclesiastical courts, and with the churchwardens he was responsible for prosecuting recusants. But, above all, it was upon the churchwardens that the principal secular burdens were imposed, as the parish ceased to be a purely ecclesiastical unit and came to play a crucial, administrative role in local government. Under the Tudors, the churchwardens in each parish were charged with responsibility for the care of the poor, the assessment and collection of church rates, the maintenance of highways and bridges, the destruction of vermin, the organisation of musters and the care of the parish weapons and armour. All this was, of course, in addition to their traditional duties of care for the parish church, the provision of the essentials for the conduct of its services and the enforcement of ecclesiastical law.[41]

Chapter Six

THE CHURCH AND PARISH LIFE IN THE SEVENTEENTH CENTURY

Although the Elizabethan Settlement of 1559 had brought England once more to the side of the Protestant Reformation in Europe, and had stripped the parish churches of most of their statues, screens, wall-paintings, stained glass and other reminders of the former Catholic traditions, and although congregations no longer lavished their wealth upon the church buildings, furnishings or decoration as they had formerly done, nonetheless the parish churches continued to be the social and cultural, as well as the religious, centres of each community. Attendance at church was compulsory and was enforced by the Church courts, and the Sunday services were the only occasions when the whole parish, men and women alike, met together, so that these weekly gatherings assumed great importance in the social life of the community.

The Act of Uniformity of 1559 had ordered that everyone should regularly attend their parish church

> ...all and every person and persons inhabiting within this realm or any other the Queen's Majesty's dominions shall resort to their parish church...upon every Sunday and other days ordained and used to be kept as Holy Days, and then and there to abide orderly and soberly during the time of Common Prayer, preachings or other service of God there to be used and ministered.

Failure to attend was punished by the Church courts, although in very large parishes or among the poor in towns, enforcement was always difficult, and many were the excuses offered for non-attendance, ranging from old-age, sickness or infirmity, to the care of infants, the demands of particular trades or the lack of suitable clothing. In 1675 the churchwardens of Christ Church, Bristol, presented to the bishop a list of parishioners who had failed to attend church, but added that there were 'several others, very inconsiderable people, which we thought fit purposely to omit by reason of their poverty'! All parishioners were obliged to attend their own parish church even though other churches might be closer, and many people had to walk long distances each Sunday. Some evidence of this occasionally remains in the hat and coat pegs which still adorn the walls of some parish churches, where they have escaped the hand of the restorer, or in the notices which exhort women to remove their 'pattens' or over-shoes before entering the church. At Hawkesbury (Avon), there is still a notice in the porch which reads:

> It is Desired that all Persons that come to this Church would be Careful to

leave their Dogs at home and that Women would not walk in with their Pattens on.

Similar notices can be seen in the porches at Walpole St Peter (Norfolk), Trent (Dorset) and Wanborough (Wilts). The pattens were left on the stone benches which remain on either side of most church porches. Further evidence of the long distances which people had to travel to church occurs in the Somerset Quarter Sessions' accounts for 1627. Ellis Pawley of the large parish of Martock petitioned for a renewal of the licence to sell beer at his house near the church, and was supported by numerous parishioners who stated that

> ...he hath a convenient clenly house for the parishioners sometimes to refresh themselves in, (they) being so far from the parish church that often times on the Sabbath day and other hollydaies they cannot go home and come again to church the same day; and that for the women of the parish when they bring theire young children to be christened do often stay to warm their babes, coming sometimes a mile, sometimes two from home in the cold?

From the standpoint of the twentieth century, it is difficult to visualise the scene in the parish churches on Sundays during the seventeenth century, when all parishioners were required to attend. The crowded benches, the shuffling, talking and ill-behaviour, the quarrels which had begun earlier over some secular matter and which broke out again in church when the parties found themselves in close proximity, are all attested by the charges brought in the Church courts against the worst offenders. The necessity which many parishes felt to employ a beadle or 'waker' to keep order and to ensure attention during the services provides further evidence. For example, at Cirencester during the seventeenth century, a beadle was employed to keep order during the services, and to prevent parents bringing to church 'such of their children as either by crying or other noise shall be any disturbance in divine service'. In 1620 the churchwardens of Carlton-in-Lindrick (Notts) reported that

> the wife of George Minall of Carlton broughte a most unquiet childe to the churche to the greate offence of the whole congregation, who although she was entreated by Mr Benson to sende away the childe, yet she would not do, so that he was enforced to give over prayers because he coulde not be hearde for the offensive noyse?[3]

Puritan divines constantly complained of congregations who were inattentive or somnolent, or who came to church only to gaze around upon their neighbours and to exchange gossip. Even George Herbert, the saintly rector of Bemerton (Wilts) during the 1630s, had to exhort his congregation to attend carefully to the service and to say the responses clearly, 'not in a hudling or slubbering fashion, gaping, or scratching the head, or spitting even in the midst of their answer'[4] Church attendance was often uncomfortable: in summer many churches were crowded, hot and stuffy, while the practice of burial inside the churches and the decomposing bodies in the vaults of gentry families did nothing to improve the atmosphere; in winter, the unheated buildings must have been very cold and long Puritan sermons must have tried the patience of many congregations. The hour glasses which are still attached to pulpits, for example at Amberley (Sussex), Compton Basset (Wilts), Earl Stonham (Suffolk) and Stoke-sub-Hamdon (Somerset), are a reminder of the long sermons and cold feet endured by many seventeenth-century congregations.

Inevitably, complete attendance by every parishioner was never achieved, nor was it a realistic expectation, especially in the very large parishes of the north and west of England. Nonetheless it remained the ideal, and when Richard Gough of Myddle in Shropshire wrote his account of the families in the parish at the end of the seventeenth century, he did so by taking each pew in the church in turn and describing the family which occupied it, thus covering almost all the parishioners[5] The lists of pews and plans of seating arrangements which survive among parish records can provide information about all the families, farms and cottages in a parish. At Brompton Regis on Exmoor a list of 1629, headed 'A note of the seats in the church and to what estates they doe belong', is of great value since it records several farms which have since disappeared. As with many other similar lists, it is clear that each pew was regarded as belonging to a particular farm or estate, that the church was packed with seats and pews, and that the men and women sat in separate parts of the church. The seating arrangements mirrored the rigid social structure of the parish, with the wealthy farmers and farmers' wives occupying the pews at the front, and the poor crowded uncomfortably into the seats at the back. Some of the pews had evidently been built by those who occupied them, and for the very poor with no property rights there was 'a plank for the use of the parish'[6]

The right to a particular seat in the parish church was an important sign of social status; pew-rights were frequently mentioned in property leases, any attempt to alter seating arrangements was strenuously resisted, and the right to a specific seat was a fruitful cause of disputes before the Church courts. In 1632 Richard Neile, archbishop of York, recalled that 'whilst he was Bishop of Winchester, noe causes perteyninge to the ecclesiastical jurisdiction under him were more frequent than Broyles about seats'. There were also many disputes about private pews which had been rebuilt or enlarged by their occupants, so that persons sitting behind could neither see nor hear the parson. At South Leverton, Nottinghamshire in 1638 it was alleged that Alexander Sampson

> hath made a seate in our church that is not uniforme. It is higher than any other that is neare unto to it, and it continues still so high that it hideth the sight of the deske and the Altar from all them that sitt behinde itt[7]

Churchwardens' presentments and the records of the Church courts are full of similar complaints. The seventeenth century also saw a great increase in large ornate pews or even whole aisles erected for the use of the lord of the manor and his family. At Ryecote in Oxfordshire the church is presided over by two elaborately enclosed pews on either side of the entrance to the chancel; one was the Norreys' family pew and the other is said to have been erected for Charles I when he visited Ryecote in 1625. Lord Ashburnham's pew at Ampthill in Bedfordshire was designed by Wren and occupied a whole gallery. It was decorated with green silk sprinkled with gold, and furnished with easy chairs covered with green taffeta and equipped with velvet cushions. Melton Constable, Norfolk is almost overwhelmed by the Hastings family pew of 1681, as is Croft in north Yorkshire by the Milbanke family pew of c.1680, while at Whitby, the Cholmley pew occupies the position of a medieval rood screen, dividing nave from chancel and raised on four huge columns, adding a final touch of confusion to the mass of galleries, balconies and crowded box pews in this interesting church. The impact of local gentry families was even more dramatic in their huge tombs and arrogant memorials, often completely out of scale with the rest of the church, so that for example Lydiard Tregoze, Wiltshire is entirely dominated by the monuments of the St John family; Bisham, Berkshire by the Hoby tombs; Swinbrook, Oxfordshire by the Fettiplaces; and Hucclecote, Bedfordshire by the Chernock family who had rebuilt the church; throughout the country large parts of parish churches were taken up by similar enormous memorials.[8]

From the mid-seventeenth century it also became increasingly common for those who could afford to do so to erect tombs, headstones or other memorials in the churchyard, and the decoration, symbolism and elegant lettering of these are worthy of close study and recording since many were produced by local craftsmen and are genuine examples of local art. They also provide valuable details about the person commemorated and his family; while many include emblems of the deceased's trade, and elaborate symbolism representing death, judgement, resurrection, the inexorable passage of Time and the brevity of human life. An invaluable guide to the symbolism which can be found and to the whole subject of churchyards is F. Burgess, *English Churchyard Memorials*, 1963. The recording of these tomb-stones and other memorials is an important and useful task for local historians or for local history societies, and a useful guide on methods which can be used and the information which should be collected is J. Jones, *How To Record Graveyards*, C.B.A., 3rd edn., 1984.

Church services continued to be occasionally enlivened by the performance of public penance, for this remained a common sentence of the Church courts, especially for fornication and adultery. One example out of many which survive in the records of the courts comes from an instruction sent by the Dean of Salisbury to Richard Dike, the curate of Charminster (Dorset) in June 1631:

> Ursula Greene of your parish is injoined on Sunday next to come to your parish church porch at the second peale to morning prayer with a white sheete loose about her, her face uncovered and with a white rod in her hand of an ell longe where she shall stand until you begin service at which time your parish clarke shall lead the said penitent by the hand and place her in the middle alley of the church or against the pulpit where she shall stand until the second lesson be ended at the end whereof she shall in penitent manner make this confession following: Vizt.

I doe before almighty god and you his church and congregation here present acknowledge and confess that I have most greviously offended his heavenly Majestie in committing the wicked and detestable offence of fornicacion with Christopher Harbyn for which offence I am hartily sorrey and doe unfaynedly repent me of the same. And doe desire you here present not only to pray to god for the forgiveness of my offence but that it may be an example to you all to avoyd the like and I faythfully promise by gods assistance never to offend in the like againe.

The following note is appended to the document:

Ursula Greene of the parish of Charminster did performe the 19th day of June 1631 all those things that are enjoyne her to performe by the right of Dr Mason Dean of Sarum.

It is signed by Richard Dike, curate of Charminster.[9]

The men involved in these cases appear to have got off more lightly and were obliged only to pay a fine, or in some cases could commute their penance by a fine. Men did not always escape public penance however, and from many examples that survive in the records of the Church courts, we can quote the case of William Robson of Humshaugh (Northumberland) in 1635. He was charged before the church court with having committed adultery with two women and was sentenced to perform public penance 'once in Hexham church, another tyme in Symondburne Church, and the third tyme at the market crosse at Hexham'. He was also imprisoned in the common gaol 'until he shall have Learned the catechisme'. Public penance was a very real punishment, an humiliation and a great public ordeal, and those who could afford it were prepared to pay considerable sums to commute the penance if the judge would so allow. In 1634 George Butterfield of Wycombe (Bucks) paid the very large sum of £25 in lieu of public penance in a white sheet for adultery; and, in 1640, a Dorset man paid £40 to the Church court rather than perform penance in various churches 'to save himself from publique shame amongst his neighbours'. But few could afford this and most were compelled to undergo the penance.[10] Lesser offences such as non-attendance at church, quarrelling or ill-behaviour during services, working or tippling on Sundays, were punished by fines or by confession before the minister and churchwardens, with possibly some parishioners present but not in full view of the whole congregation.

Throughout the seventeenth century, and especially during the decades before the Civil War, parish churches and churchyards continued to be used for all sorts of secular purposes and to serve as the social centres for each community. People living in remote parts of rural parishes could generally only meet with their neighbours and friends on Sundays, and naturally stayed to talk after the service was ended. The incumbent at Rossendale (Lancs) described in 1603 how 'the congregation of people, men and women, which do daily assemble and come to the church of Rossendale, do use after evening prayers on Sundays and holy days is ended to stay in the church conferring or talking one with another by the space of an hour at least, except it be in the cold of winter'. Ralph Josselin, who was later vicar of Earls Colne (Essex), described how as a young man at Steeple Bumpstead during the 1630s he used to walk off alone after services in order to meditate upon the sermon, and did not stay with the rest of the congregation talking in the churchyard. Richard Baxter, who was later to be one of the foremost nonconformist ministers, described how during his boyhood in the village of Eaton Constantine (Shropshire) in the 1620s the parishioners attended the service in the parish church and then

> the rest of the day even till dark almost, except eating-time was spent in dancing under a maypole and a great tree ... where all the town did meet together.

Signs of approaching change were already apparent, however, for Baxter's family did not join in the festivities, spending the day in meditation and Bible study, and suffering in consequence 'the derision of the vulgar rabble under the odious name of a Puritan'![1]

The naves of parish churches also continued to be used for many secular purposes. In Easter Week, some churches were used for parish meetings to choose churchwardens, overseers of the poor, parish constables and other officials. Handbills were posted in the porch or public announcements were made from the pulpit, as at Gillingham (Dorset), where in 1624 a meeting of the whole parish to discuss proposals to enclose the royal forest was held in the parish church after notice had been given by the vicar on three previous Sundays. Manorial and other courts were also held in some churches, and at Tetbury (Glos), the Quarter Sessions court was held in the parish church when an outbreak of plague made the regular meeting in Gloucester impossible. Manorial and other documents were often left in the parish chest for safe-keeping. The danger of fire in many houses, especially those which were thatched, and the lack of security, meant that the parish church provided a useful repository for important documents. The manorial court rolls of Alrewas (Staffs), were kept in the parish church, as were those of Fordington (Dorset). An inventory of the contents of the parish chest at Bridport (Dorset), made during the early seventeenth century shows that it contained personal papers belonging to several local families. Parish armour and weapons were kept in the churches and the churchyards were frequently used for musters of the trained bands. Fire-fighting equipment was lodged in the parish churches: in 1628, there were 190 fire buckets in the four churches of Northampton, and other churches had hoses and pumps or 'engines'. Fire-fighting equipment, including huge hooks to pull thatch from burning roofs, can still be seen at Puddletown and Bere Regis (Dorset), at Eaton Bray (Beds), Iver (Bucks) and Hook Norton (Oxon)![2]

The church bells were used as warnings, to call men to work, as a curfew, to celebrate anniversaries such as the monarch's birthday or the Gunpowder Plot, to rejoice at victories or to announce a death, as well as to summon the congregation to church. The continuing popularity of bell-ringing as a pastime is attested by the heavy expenditure on bells which is to be found in all seventeenth- and eighteenth-century churchwardens' accounts, for large sums had constantly to be spent on ropes, frames, oil, re-casting of bells, and especially on 'baldrics' which were the leather thongs by which the clapper was attached to the bell.[13] For example, the churchwardens' accounts of Crewkerne (Somerset) for 1665, contain the following items of expenditure on the bells:

Two bell-ropes, the great bell and the 4th bell	6-0
Paid the ringers the 29th May (Oak Apple Day, which commemorated the King's escape after the battle of Worcester in 1651, and his restoration in 1660)	5-0
In beere to the Ringers at the over throw of the Dutch (i.e. the beginning of the Second Dutch War 1665-67)	5-0
A pint of oyle about the bells, clock and chimes	7
To the Ringers in beere at the rejoycing at the Dutch over throw	2-0
More to the Ringers at the same time	1-0
To the ringers the 5th of November	6-0[14]

Churches were occasionally used as prisons. Parliamentarian prisoners were locked up in Cirencester church by Prince Rupert in 1642 and the stained glass windows were broken by their relatives who brought food to them. The Dorset Clubmen, captured by Cromwell in 1645, were imprisoned in the church at Iwerne Courtney where Cromwell himself lectured to them from the pulpit and made them all promise to be well behaved in future, reporting to Fairfax that

they are poor silly creatures, whom if you please to let me send home, they promise to be very dutiful for time to come, and will be hanged before they come out again.[15]

After the battle of Sedgemoor in 1685, more than 500 of Monmouth's supporters were locked up in Westonzoyland church, from where 22 were taken to be hanged and several others died from their wounds, and the churchwardens' accounts show the large sums later spent on burying the dead and cleaning the church.[16] The dreadful results of the Monmouth Rebellion and the Bloody Assize are also reflected in numerous west-country churchwardens' accounts. For example, at Wyke Regis in 1685 the churchwardens recorded:

Paid for two polles and spars for hanging the rebels quarters	9-0
Paid for Beer expended about hanging the Dead quarters	2-0[17]

The one procession which survived the Reformation was the annual Rogationtide perambulation of the parish boundaries, and this ancient practice continued to be observed in many parishes during the seventeenth century, although increasingly churchwardens' presentments show that, as enclosures made the boundaries definite and perambulation difficult, it ceased to be carried out. At Netherbury (Dorset) in 1631 the churchwardens reported that:

The inclosures have made the waies difficult and the bounds so certaine that
we held it fitt to be omitted![18]

Householders at places where the processions had a traditional right to food
and drink were not sorry to see an end to the custom, for in many places it
had become a public holiday with free refreshments, although few were as
open as the men of Uffington (Berks) who suggested to the vicar:

> Lette us not liefe (leave) our custome, but goe to those places which of right
> are to make us a drinkinge![19]

Churchwardens' accounts frequently contain many references to expenses
incurred in the perambulation, as for example at St Martin's, Leicester in
1639 'for bread and beere at the Perambulacion 3s 6d. For poynts and ribbon
given to the children 3s 0d.' At Deptford (Kent) in 1684 the very large sum
of £9 1s 0d was spent by the churchwardens on the perambulation, as
follows:

Paid Mr Douse for a processioning dinner	£4 7s 0d
Paid Mr Cox at the halfway house for meat, bread, beer, and cakes at the processioning	£2 16s 0d
Paid to the widow Spett for cakes	£1 0s 0d
Paid Rob. Phipps for bread and beer at ye Black-Jack and Shovel	4s 0d
Paid for 2 bottles of Canary which we had in Peckham Lane	4s 0d
Paid to make ye boys drink when we came home	1s 0d
Paid more ye same day with ye gentlemen of ye parish at Mr Douse's after dinner	8s 6d[20]

Even regular processions, however, did not always avoid disputes between
neighbouring parishes over their respective boundaries, particularly in areas
without any natural features which could be used for demarcation. For
example, two neighbouring parishes on the chalk downlands in Dorset,
Stratton and Charminster, engaged in a long and expensive dispute over
their mutual boundary during the early seventeenth century and the case
eventually reached the Exchequer Court in 1616. All the witnesses agreed
that the practice of beating the bounds had been carried out each year, but
the difficulty had arisen because each party had followed a different route.
The Stratton witnesses alleged that

> the inhabitants of Charminster within this eight and thirty yeares have
> altered theyr course of procession…and at the first cominge of the now
> curatt…in his first perambulation in procession dyd forsake their old and
> wonted way and course…and did appoynt the said Curatt to goe farther in
> upon Stratton by Fifty acres or thereabout than they did before, which is the
> land in variance…

They also stated that the oldest inhabitants of Charminster 'who were men
when the others were boys' and who knew that the Stratton allegations
were true, had been prevented by threats from attending and giving
evidence. The curate was in the difficult position of having to rely on local

knowledge of the bounds along which he had to lead the Rogationtide procession, particularly in his first years; and the whole dispute illustrates the importance of the topic and the strength of feeling aroused by it[21]

In many parishes the church housed the only available library. The *Injunctions* of 1559 and other orders to clergy and churchwardens required the addition of Erasmus's *Paraphrases*, Foxe's *Book of Martyrs* and Bishop English', and that it should be set up in the church where the 'parishioners may most commodiously resort to the same and read it'. Queen Elizabeth's *Injunctions* of 1559 and other orders to clergy and churchwardens required the addition of Erasmus's Paraphrases, Foxe's *Book of Martyrs* and Bishop Jewel's *Apology*. In many parishes benevolent donors added to these basic requirements and supplied other books for public use; such books were obviously highly valued, for they are lovingly listed year after year by churchwardens in their accounts and inventories. The fine church of St Wulfram at Grantham was presented with a library of 300 books in 1598 by Francis Trigge, rector of the nearby parish of Welbourn, and the leatherbound volumes remain in the library over the south porch, each secured by a metal chain just long enough to allow them to be placed on a shelf for reading. At Langley Marish (Bucks) a library was bequeathed to the church by Sir John Kederminster in 1623 and housed in a transept beside the Kederminster chapel. The parish of Cheltenham (Glos) was presented with a three-volume set of Foxe's *Book of Martyrs* by a London grocer, who had once lived in the town, and the books were set on a revolving stand 'to the end that the same may be free in common for all to read at convenient times'. In 1635 the churchwardens of St Mary's, Devizes, bought a three-volume copy of Foxe's *Book of Martyrs* and chained the volumes to a reading desk in the church so that the parishioners could read it to remind themselves of the perils and consequences of popery[22] By the end of the seventeenth century many parish churches, especially in towns, had notable libraries, such as those at All Saints, Bristol; St Botolph's, Boston; All Saint's, Northampton; or St John's Bedford.

Any business of more than ordinary importance was often conducted in the church or churchyard, no doubt in the belief that the hallowed surroundings lent a greater solemnity to the agreements made there. At Crowcombe (Som), a marriage portion of £200 was to be paid 'upon the font stone of the church of Crowcombe', and at Isham (Northants) in 1634 the price of various lands and houses was paid 'upon the communion table of the parish church'. Justices of the Peace often specified that regular payments should be made at the parish church, as in 1627, when the Somerset justices ordered the father of an illegitimate child 'to pay weekly every sabboth day immediately after evening prayer in the church porch of Bruham (Brewham) aforesaid unto the overseas of the poor 9d'. At Catterick (Yorks) in 1625, the father of an illegitimate child was ordered to pay 4d a week to the parish until the child was seven years old, and the money was paid each Sunday in Catterick church?[23]

Schools were often kept in churches, emphasising the close link between the Church and education, for the Canons of 1571 laid down that no one was to teach unless licensed by the diocesan bishop. Many seventeenth-century schools were short-lived or intermittent, depending upon the enthusiasm of an incumbent or curate, or the temporary residence of an educated man in need of an income or a recently-ordained cleric awaiting a benefice. An episcopal visitation of the diocese of Carlisle in 1702 revealed that schools were being kept in 21 out of the 101 churches visited, and at Westward near Wigton, for example, the bishop noted that the boys were taught by the curate in the chancel and had damaged a monument 'with writing their copies upon it'. At Stourton (Notts) in 1638, the archdeacon was told that 'The North Ile of the westerne (part) of the church is separated and divided from the church by a wall of bordes and converted to a scholehouse where one Marshall teacheth schole'. The churchwardens of Minchinhampton (Glos), paid 6s 3d in 1651 'for stones and making a Chimnie in the Chansell for the schoole'. At Long Melford (Suffolk) in 1670, the Lady Chapel was being used as a 'Publick Schoole for Melford' and a multiplication table used by the children survives on the east wall; similarly at North Cadbury (Som), two alphabets can still be seen on a wall of the church, a reminder of its former use as a schoolroom.[24]

For many short-lived schools, documentary evidence is not very easy to find, though occasionally it occurs incidentally in unexpected places. The manorial records of Little Gransden (Cambs) for 1649 include the depositions of elderly witnesses in a dispute over land, and one stated that sixty years earlier he had attended a school in the chancel of Little Gransden church; there is no other documentary reference to the existence of this school.[25] At Winford near Bristol in 1625, during a case before the diocesan court over seating arrangements in the church, elderly inhabitants testified that within their memory there had been no seats in one aisle of the church, but that seats had been installed in order that a school might be kept in the church:

> The youth of the parish did usuallie stand theare to heare divine prayers and the old men of the parishe did theare use to walke upp and downe and talke together before and after prayers...theare was a schoolmaster who kepte schoole in the churche of Winford, and because the schollers should have fitt places to sitt in to learne theire lessons the formes and seates were erected and builte upp as well for theire use on the working daies as also for a convenient place for the schollers and other youth of the parish to sitt on on the sabbath and holie days to heare divine service, who before that stoode, some in one place and some in another in divers places of the church.[26]

The Wiltshire antiquarian, John Aubrey, recalled that he had attended a school in the parish church near Malmesbury, and that he had covered his books with parchment which came from the library of the former Benedictine abbey:

> Anno 1633, I entered into my grammar at the latin schoole at Yatton-Keynel, in the church, where the curate, Mr Hart, taught the eldest boyes Virgil, Ovid, Cicero etc. The fashion then was to save the forules of their bookes with a false cover of parchment, sc. old manuscripts, which I was too young

to understand; but I was pleased with the elegancy of the writing and the coloured initiall letters?[27]

During the early seventeenth century the traditional sports, games, plays and money-raising activities, such as church ales, continued to be held in churchyards and to be closely linked with the parish churches, as did the seasonal festivities connected with Christmas, Shrove Tuesday, Rogation-tide, Whitsun, Midsummer and similiar time-honoured holidays. Churchwardens' accounts which record the income for the church from such festivities, and the records of the Church courts concerning those who had gone beyond the traditional licence granted to such merry-making, together provide evidence of these activities and of their important part in parochial life. John Aubrey, writing in c. 1670, recalled a somewhat idealised picture of church ales in the early seventeenth century:

> There were no rates for the poor in my grandfather's days; but for Kington St Michael (no small parish) the church-ale of Whitsuntide did the business. In every parish is (or was) a church-house to which belonged spits, crocks, etc., utensils for dressing provisions. Here the housekeepers met, and were merry, and gave their charity. The young people were there too, and had dancing, bowling, shooting at butts, etc., the ancients sitting gravely by, and looking on. All things were civil, and without scandal?[28]

Notwithstanding the numerous objections to them on both religious and moral grounds, church ales were an efficient way of raising money for parish churches. Bishop Pierce of Bath and Wells wrote in their defence to Archbisop Laud in 1633:

> I finde that by Church-ales heretofore many poor Parishes have cast their Bells, repaired their Towers, beautified their Churches, and raised stocks for the Poor?[29]

At Mere (Wilts) for example, where it was the annual custom to choose a Cuckoo King and Queen to preside over the festivities at the Whitsun ales, and where there was a regular expenditure on gunpowder for fireworks to enliven the proceedings, almost all the income for the church came from this source.[30] The suppression of church ales and reliance upon compulsory church rates to produce the necessary parochial funds meant that money became much more difficult to collect and community life became much less colourful.

Such occasions certainly provided money for the churches, as can be seen from the churchwardens' accounts, but not all were 'civil, and without scandal.' At Blackthorne (Oxon) in 1584 the churchwardens were accused of disrupting the services by merry-making in the churchyard, and 'on Tewsdaye in Whitsun week at service tyme there came a stranger into the churche with a painted cloth on his back.' At Northallerton (Yorks) in 1612 Francis Milnes 'with divers others unknown did, on Easter day last, in the time of afternoon service, play in the churchyard there, at a game called Trippett, and did molest and disturbe the Minister theare reading Divine Service.'[31] Complaints about the election of Cuckoo Kings and Queens,

Lords of Misrule, Robin Hood and Little John, or about unruly conduct at May games, Whitsun ales, Midsummer feasts and other merry-making, are common from all parts of the country. Robert Herrick's well-known lines in praise of the annual round of feasts and revels reminds us of the continuing link between church festivals and secular holidays. Herrick was vicar of the Devonshire parish of Dean Prior on the borders of Dartmoor from 1629 to 1647 and again from 1661 until his death at the age of 83 in 1674. His picture of wakes, ales, dances and revels must have been typical of countless remote country parishes throughout England during the seventeenth century:

> For sports, for Pagentrie, and Playes,
> Thou hast thy Eves, and Holydayes…
> Thy Wakes, thy Quintels, here thou hast,
> Thy May-poles too with Garlands grac't:
> Thy Morris-dance; thy Whitsun-ale;
> Thy Sheering-feast; which never faile,
> Thy Harvest home; thy Wassaile bowle,
> That's tost up after Fox i'th' Hole;
> Thy Mummeries; thy Twelfe-tide Kings
> And Queens; thy Christmas revellings.

In Oxfordshire during the early seventeenth century there were accusations of 'interludes and playes in the church and brawlinge in the church about the same' at Duns Tew; of 'evell rule done in the church by the lorde and ladie on Midsomer Day' at Wootton; and of unruly dancing and bowling in the churchyards of Bourton, South Stoke and Goring. Churchyard games occasionally damaged the walls and windows of churches, as at Fordington (Dorset), on 1631 where the windows were broken by eight people who 'played at catt and Stoole ball in the churchyard Sundaies and holidays usually'. At Martock (Som) the hand-holds which enabled fives players to climb on to the church roof to retrieve the ball can still be seen cut into the north-west corner of the north aisle.[32]

A remarkable list of the activities which took place in a churchyard is provided by an elderly witness in a case before the church courts over land at Dundry near Bristol in 1636. He recalled that during all the time of his remembrance the churchyard

> was used for sportes and plays of severall sortes, as setting up of Maypoles
> and Summer Luggs (ie tug-of-war) in the same, daunceing, sporting,
> kissinge, bulbayting, coyting, bowling, shootinge att Butts, cudgleplaying,
> tennis playing, and divers other sportes and plays.

He also stated that a fair was held in the churchyard each year on the feast of St Giles (1 September). Clearly the church and churchyard were still very much the focus of community life at Dundry.[33]

By the late-sixteenth century there were many among both clergy and laity who deplored what they regarded as the desecration of the Sabbath and the excesses of church ales, Rogationtide processions, maypoles, Whitsun games and other traditional merry-making. Such men strongly supported the Puritan campaign against church ales, and greatly resented the way in which both James I and Charles I encouraged Sunday sports and games.

While we may regret the passing of these colourful activities, there was some force in the Puritan objections to them. It is a mistake to equate the rural pastimes of the seventeenth century with the decorous recreation of a twentieth-century church garden fête. A good deal of licence and drunken revelry undoubtedly accompanied festivities such as May Day revels, midsummer frolics and feast day wakes, and there are many references to disorders accompanying church ales, to bastards conceived after the festivities and to what the Devon magistrates in 1600 coyly referred to as 'many inconveniences which with modesty cannot be expressed'. At the same time it is not necessary to go as far as the Puritan William Prynne, who wrote that the main purpose of church ales was to enable the common people 'to dance, play, revel, drink and profane God's Sabbaths'. Both James I and Charles I supported the traditional view that sports and pastimes should be allowed and even encouraged on Sunday afternoons. After the Lancashire magistrates in 1617 had attempted to suppress Sunday sports, James I ordered that every minister throughout the country should read a declaration from the pulpit in favour of certain lawful sports to be used on Sundays after divine service. This declaration, sometimes known as the *Book of Sports*, was reissued by Charles I in 1633 after a renewed Puritan attempt, this time in Somerset, to prohibit Sunday games. The reading of this declaration gave great cause for disquiet to any Puritan clergy, for example to the curate of Beaminster, Dorset, who according to the churchwardens read the declaration in 1633 very unwillingly:

> Mr Spratt our curate was enjoyned to reade the King's Majesty's book touching the lawful recreations of the people upon Sundays after evening prayer, which book hee read accordingly; but having read it, spake of it in the manner; Neighbours (said hee) there is noe one commanded to use these recreations as in this booke is here specifyed, but these lawes are left to everyone's descretion whether you will use them or not use them, therefore I doe advise you rather to obey god's lawes rather than the lawes of the King, or words to that purpose.[34]

The Civil War and the Interregnum

On the question of church ales and Sunday sports the monarchy and the Anglican establishment won a temporary victory over the Puritan faction during the 1630s, and especially while the Church was ruled by Archbishop Laud. But the turn of the Puritans was to come, for with the success of the Parliamentary cause in the Civil War their religious and political ideas triumphed. During the course of the Civil War, as troops moved all over the country, there was a great deal of destruction and damage to Church property. Many of the Parliamentarians saw the Church and the Monarchy as joint enemies, and were eager to purge the parish churches of what they considered the surviving relics of popery, so that works of art and things of great beauty which had escaped destruction during the sixteenth century fell victim to Puritan zeal during the 1640s. Stained glass was smashed, statues were defaced or destroyed, vestments cut up or torn to bits and organs, service-books and carved woodwork burnt. Much of the desecration of churches which is conventionally ascribed to Oliver Cromwell in popular tradition was in fact caused by troops, generally parliamentarian but occasionally also royalist, out of the control of their officers.

Evidence for renewed upheavals, religious strife, the controversies of the Commonwealth period, the growth of nonconformity, doctrinal disputes and changes in church furnishing, clerical vestments and in the services can be found in churchwardens' accounts, vestry minutes, parish registers and other parochial sources. It illustrates the truth of the statement by Thomas Hobbes, that:

> Every man, nay every boy and wench that could read English, thought they spoke with God Almighty, and understood what he said, when by a certain number of chapters each day they had read the scriptures once or twice over..[35]

Most of the Anglican clergy had supported or at least sympathised with the royalist party and after the defeat of the King in 1646 many of the clergy, perhaps a third of the whole number, were ejected from their benefices as 'delinquents' or 'malignants' and replaced by Puritan ministers. The sufferings endured by some of the clergy were extremely harsh. The royalist incumbent at Pontefract was hanged by the parliamentary army, the aged vicar of Tarrington was shot through the head when he told a troop of parliamentarians that he supported 'God and the King'; many others suffered ill-treatment and pillage of their possessions as well as loss of their benefices, like Humphrey Betty of Little Petherick (Cornwall), who was driven out of his parish 'all naked'. (For information on the many clergymen who were ejected or persecuted during this period an essential starting point is A.G. Matthews, *Walker Revised,* 1848.) The use of the Book of Common Prayer was strictly forbidden, and in its place a *Directory* for public worship was issued, which left considerable latitude for individual ministers in the conduct of the services. The impact of the changes in the services in parish churches therefore varied from place to place. But as well as new services most congregations also witnessed other changes, for the triumph of the Puritans unleashed another holocaust of destruction. Screens, stalls, crosses, statues, organs, stained glass, paintings and vestments, which had escaped earlier attacks, were now broken or defaced. The royal arms were removed, and communion tables—which under Archbishop Laud's regime during the 1630s had been carefully enclosed with rails, 'altarwise', at the east end of the chancel—were brought out into the body of the church, where the congregation could gather around them; often seats were provided around the table to make the Holy Communion as much a commemorative service and as little like the sacrament of the Mass as possible. The pulpit and the sermon became the central focus of the church; and fonts were frequently torn out or defaced since they were associated with popish rites or were decorated with carvings of the saints. The parish register of Keeston, Kent, contains the entry for 23 April 1643, 'Our church was defaced, our font thrown downe and new formes of prayer appointed'. Likewise Ralph Josselin, the Puritan vicar of Earls Colne, Essex, recorded with satifaction in his diary for Michaelmas 1641 that he had been able to strip his church of the surviving medieval statues, stained glass and wall-paintings: 'upon an order of House of Commons to that purpose wee tooke downe all (images) and pictures and such like glasses'. Men like Josselin of course welcomed the changes, and rejoiced greatly when Parliament removed 'the heavy burthen of the booke of Common prayer'[36]

The most notorious iconoclast of this period was William Dowsing, who during 1643 and 1644 visited several score of churches in Cambridgeshire and Suffolk, breaking and destroying everything that could be held to be superstitious or papist—images, glass, pictures, crosses, and even carvings and brasses on tombs. Dowsing is however only the most infamous of a large number of similar fanatics who ranged through the country inflicting untold damage upon parish churches.

In the contemporary atmosphere of destruction and iconoclasm few parish churches escaped and there were few additions either to furnishings or buildings. An exception was the church at Staunton Harold in Leicestershire which was built by the royalist Shirley family during the Commonwealth government. The tower bears following inscription:

In the yeare 1653
When all things sacred were throughout ye nation
Either demollisht or profaned
Sir Robert Shirley, Barronet
Founded this church
Whose singular praise it is
to have done the best things in ye worst times
And
hoped them in the most callimitous
the righteous shall be had in everlasting remembrance.

In Falmouth (Cornwall), the parish church was built in 1662-4 largely at the expense of the Cornish royalist, Sir Peter Killigrew, and at Tunbridge Wells (Kent), royalist patrons of the spa waters contributed to the building of a new church; both were dedicated to King Charles the Martyr.

With the return of the king in 1660 came the re-establishment of the Anglican Church. The 'intruded' ministers were removed and in many parishes those they had replaced resumed their offices and their rights to tithes and other dues. Details of Puritan clergy who were ejected or resigned at the Restoration can be found in A.G. Matthews, *Calamy Revised*, 1934, while much other information may be found in the documentation produced by Parliamentary committees during the Commonwealth period. The use of the Book of Common Prayer was revived, and it was reissued with a few minor changes in 1662. The interior arrangement of parish churches was restored, with the altar at the east end of the chancel, decently railed. The essential link between the monarchy and the Church was emphasised by the erection of the royal coat of arms in parish churches throughout the country, and appropriate texts also appeared on the walls, drawing attention to the Christian duty of obedience to established authority, and the wickedness of rebellion; these included 'The powers that be are ordained of God' and 'My son, fear God and the King, and meddle not with them that are given to change'. A few of these survive and can still be found in parish churches. But the upheavals and changes of the previous 20 years had been too profound to admit of total restoration. Nonconformity had now to be recognised in almost every parish as an established fact of religious life, and no longer could the Anglican Church claim to include all Christians within each parish. It is from the Restoration of 1660 that the real beginning of the deep and significant division of English social life between 'church' and 'chapel' can be dated. The gulf thus created was to remain until the twentieth century, a division that touched all aspects of life and affected attitudes to society, to politics, to education and to economic life, and which had an immeasurable impact upon the development of the nation.

The role of the parish church and its officials in village life during the seventeenth and eighteenth centuries can be reconstructed in detail from the evidence of the many hundreds of surviving churchwardens' accounts. The churchwardens played a part in the parish in many ways more important than that of the parson. From the sixteenth century onwards they had heaped upon them a mass of secular duties relating to matters as diverse as the care of the poor, the maintenance of the highways and the control of vermin, all of them having little relevance to their main and original function of maintaining the church and providing the things necessary for the conduct of the services.[37] An indication of the variety of their concerns is seen in the churchwardens' accounts for Cerne Abbas (Dorset) in 1686. They paid for repairs and maintenance of the church, for a new Book of Common Prayer, for bread and wine for the sacrament and for the washing of the surplice and altar cloth; in addition they paid the ringers for ringing the bells on the King's birthday, on 5 November and on 29 May—the latter being the day on which the King's restoration was celebrated. They contributed money to repatriate various English sailors who had been captured by Turkish pirates in the Mediterranean; for the relief of 'Mary Francis and Benjamin Cimber and their children begging who had lost all their goods by fire'; they relieved 14 men who claimed to have been shipwrecked on the Dorset coast; they sent money to help the French Protestants who were being persecuted for their religion; they paid for the repair of the church clock and for repairs to the local roads. And throughout the year they rewarded those who brought birds and animals regarded as vermin; the total of vermin for the year was:

85 dozen sparrow heads (the term 'sparrow' presumably covered all small birds)

37 hedgehogs

9 polecats

9 stoats

4 foxes[38]

Some parish vestry meetings had an agreed scale of payments for birds and animals. At Thorncombe on the borders of Dorset and Devon during the late seventeenth century it was as follows:

Mischevious Farments and Other Birds

To be paid for as follows:

First to pay for the heads of Foxes	one shilling each
Martins	ditto
Pole Cats	4d per head
Stoats	2d per head
Kites and Hawks	4d per head
Jays and Whoops	4d per head
Crows and Magepyes	1d per head
Sparrows	2d per dozen

and to be Delivered at Every Parish Meeting or not paid for.[39]

Frequent reference has already been made to the records of the Church courts. They can be an excellent source of detailed information, since the concerns of the courts were wide, ranging from slander, through matrimonial and testamentary disputes, to doctrinal controversy. The most frequent punishments imposed were fines, public penance in the parish church or market place, and excommunication. Much of the evidence was taken from witnesses, recorded in great detail and often almost *verbatim*. The court records are therefore well worth looking for among the diocesan records, but the difficulty of using the material must also be stressed. The ecclesiastical court records are often enormous in extent, frequently difficult to read, the proceedings were recorded in Latin although the depositions are in English, and they are unindexed so that there is no easy method of finding material about a particular parish, nor of following the progress of a case through the complex procedure of the courts.[40]

Glebe 'terriers', which describe the parsonage house, the glebe land, the rights of the incumbent and sometimes also the church and its contents, often in some detail, are also a useful source and should not be neglected. Tithe disputes and tithe books kept by the parson or his agent can also give information about farming, crops, livestock, local customs and markets. They also show a different aspect of parish life, for tithes were a constant source of friction between the parson and his parishioners, and were often paid unwillingly. The agricultural writer Walter Blyth wrote in 1652:

The minister might go barefoot and his family a-begging, for what the common people would contribute to his subsistence.[41]

In many parishes during the seventeenth century the parson was involved in agricultural affairs because he was obliged by manorial custom to provide a bull and a boar for the parishioners' cows and pigs. For example, the custom of Poyntington (Dorset) was for the parson:

> to provide a bull for the tenants' cows, and for everie sowe which anie of the Inhabitants shall keepe to breed pigges, the parson is to keepe a sufficient bore to increase the same at his own Chardge.

In some places this duty fell upon the churchwardens or on one of the other parish officials.[42]

Finally, the church building itself, together with its surroundings, can often reveal many aspects of parish life during the seventeenth century. Extensions or alterations to the structure, changes in its decoration, especially painted scriptural texts or plasterwork, furnishings such as screens, altar rails or a pulpit frequently date from the seventeenth century. In spite of the Elizabethan injunction that all parish churches should possess 'a comely and honest pulpit', few Elizabethan pulpits survive. An exception is at Odstock (Wilts), dated 1580, which bears the ambiguous inscription:

> God bless and save our royal queen,
> The lyke on earth was never seen.

Far more churches have Jacobean or Laudian pulpits, often ornate structures in heavily-carved oak with sounding boards and an hour glass, and the prominent position accorded to the pulpit and reading desk shows clearly the priorities of the time. The lofty sounding board to the pulpit at Lyme Regis (Dorset) leaves no doubt concerning both the donor and his sentiments:

> To God's Glory Richard Harvey of London
> Mercer and Marchant Adventurer 1613
> Faith Is By Hearing

The sumptuously carved pulpit at Croscombe (Somerset) dated 1616, bears the words:

> Blessed are They that hear the Word of the Lord and Do it.

Contemporary attitudes are also demonstrated by the royal arms and by expressions of loyalty dating from the Restoration; the arms are often the work of a local sign writer and are notable for their vigorous execution and the aggressively masculine lion and unicorn. The early attempts to deal with the growing problem of poverty by voluntary collections are recalled by the poor boxes, some bearing the words which the parish clerk cried out to the congregation as they left the church, 'Remember the Poor'. Seventeenth-century 'dole' or charity cupboards, where bread for the poor was placed, survive in numerous churches, such as those at Milton Ernest (Beds) and Axbridge (Somerset), as do the bequest boards recording local charities and benefactors.[43]

The ornate tombs of the gentry and clergy inside the church and the monuments to farmers and other substantial parishioners in the churchyard are a reminder of the way in which churches were increasingly used for the ostentatious display of wealth, family pride and grief. The provision of west galleries for musicians recalls the increasing emphasis upon music and communal singing of psalms in the services; while galleries for the poor reveal the growing competition for seats within the church.

From all these sources, documentary and architectural, the local historian may uncover for most parishes at least something of the large part which the Church played in community life, the sort of services which were conducted by the clergy, the response of the parishioners, and the social activities of the parish. It may also be possible to chart the influence of Puritan ideas, the upheavals of the Civil War and Commonwealth, the growth of nonconformity in the parish, the increasingly secular concerns of the parish officers, notably the churchwardens, and the growing secularisation of the parish as the primary unit of local government.

Chapter Seven

THE EIGHTEENTH-CENTURY CHURCH & THE LOCAL COMMUNITY

The impact of the Established Church and its clergy upon each of the approximately 9,500 parishes of eighteenth-century England varied greatly, depending on the size and population of the parish, the personality and energy of the incumbent or curate, his residence or non-residence within the parish, the strength of dissent, the attitude and influence of a resident landowner, and other local factors. The Church generally played a much greater part in community life in rural areas than in large towns, and it was notably weak in the rapidly-growing industrial areas; its influence was frequently stronger in the south and east of England than it was in the large parishes of the north, and it was commonly more successful in agricultural districts than in populous industrial centres.

Historians have been united in condemning the inefficient organisation of the Hanoverian Church, its failure to adapt to the massive economic, social and demographic changes of the time, its subservience to the civil government, the fact that the bishops were political appointments and were expected to spend a large part of their time in the House of Lords, that most of the clergy were appointed by lay patrons and that many were non-resident or pluralists, and that there was such a great disparity of income between the wealthy, beneficed clergy and the miserable stipends paid to curates. Above all, the Church has been generally condemned for its calm acceptance of the *status quo* and its distrust of anything which smacked of fervour or 'enthusiasm' on the one hand, or of 'popery' on the other. The pious churchman, Dr Samuel Johnson, in his *Dictionary* of 1755 defined 'enthusiasm' as 'a vain belief of private revelation; a vain confidence of divine favour or communication'. In its flight from fervour the Church adopted a somnolent round of services, sermons and moral teaching, which emphasised the importance of social harmony and the maintenance of the established order, but which was unlikely to inspire deep commitment among the majority of people. Parish records such as the vestry books, the accounts of churchwardens and expenditure by overseers of the poor, as well as the numerous eighteenth-century visitation returns, clerical diaries, published sermons and the records of the church courts, all show the Church in each parish as less concerned with spiritual welfare and the salvation of souls than with the preservation of order and the maintenance of the social fabric. The Church as an institution was valued for its role in establishing morals and reforming manners in an age of rapid change and of increasing anxiety about public order. This was later emphasised by William Lyall, Archdeacon of Colchester, in a visitation address of 1833:

The belief in God is, in the moral world, what the principle of gravitation is in the physical — that which binds all the discordant elements into one harmonious system.

Likewise, the soldily-built lock-up at Swanage in Dorset bears the inscription:

Erected for the Prevention of Vice and Immorality by the Friends of Religion and Good Order AD 1803

The conservative social influence which many of the clergy perceived as a prime function of the Church was summed up by another prominent churchman, Joseph Addison, in 1711:

...if keeping the seventh day holy were only a human institution, it would be the best method that could have been thought of for the polishing and civilising of mankind. It is certain the country people would soon degenerate into a kind of savages and barbarians, were there not such frequent returns of a stated time in which the whole village meet together with their best faces and in their cleanliest habits, to converse with one another upon different subjects, hear their duties explained to them, and join together in adoration of the Supreme Being![1]

It was against this background that nonconformity flourished, and that the Methodists rebelled and eventually separated from the Church; and it was in order to change such attitudes that the Evangelical and Tractarian reforms of the nineteenth century were pressed upon the Church.

In view of the usual condemnation of the eighteenth-century Church, the first concern of a local historian should be to establish whether the accusations of uncaring inefficiency, bland acceptance of the social order, clerical neglect and subservience to the local gentry were true for his parish or district, to enquire whether the influence of the Church and the size of its congregation declined during the century, how much of its teaching and influence were reflected in the beliefs and attitudes of the laity, the part which it played in community life, and how far it was prepared to meet the challenge posed by all the revolutionary changes of the time. For such an enquiry many more sources are available than for previous centuries; far more sources and diocesan records survive, and much more personal material is available such as diaries, both clerical and lay, correspondence, account books, sermons, charity records and other evidence of contemporary concerns and attitudes. It is also possible to find more material on nonconformists and recusants, and on the religious beliefs and moral standards of the parishioners. An excellent starting point is John Ecton's *Liber Valorem et Decimarum* 1711, which is a directory of ecclesiastical benefices, arranged under dioceses and deaneries. Ecton's collection arose out of the work of Queen Anne's Bounty which was set up in 1704 to improve the income of the worst-paid livings, and further editions appeared during the eighteenth century, including an edition by Browne Willis in 1742 entitled *Thesaurus Rerum Ecclesiasticarum*, and an edition by John Bacon in 1786 under the title *Liber Regis*. These list patrons, incumbents, dedications, appropriations and income. Bishops' registers and lists of the institutions will supply the names of incumbents and details of the licensing of curates; also useful are Subscription Books for each diocese in which the beneficed clergy, curates and licensed preachers, as well as schoolmasters, physicians, surgeons and midwives, recorded their acceptance of the Thirty-Nine Articles and their loyalty to the monarch as required under the Act of Uniformity of 1662. Evidence for the residence or non-residence of the clergy, the appointment and payment of curates, the state of the church's buildings and their furnishings, the frequency of services and many other aspects of parish life, as well as details of papists and dissenters in each parish, can be found in the visitation records of bishops and archdeacons; numerous examples of these informative records have been printed by local societies, while many others survive among the episcopal and diocesan archives?

The extent of non-residence, and the effect which this had on the number and frequency of services, can be seen from the records of a visitation of the diocese of York in 1743; out of 836 parishes in the diocese, 393 had non-resident incumbents, while only 383 parish churches had two services each Sunday. A visitation of the diocese of Exeter in 1779 showed that of the 390 parishes in Devon, 159 incumbents were non-resident; and a visitation of Salisbury diocese in 1783 revealed that 124 out of the 262 parishes in Wiltshire had non-resident incumbents. Many parishes were served by curates, but often they had charge of more than one parish, and conducted at most one service at each church on Sundays. From all parts of the country the evidence shows that Holy Communion was celebrated no more than three or four times each year. Hannah More, who did so much to relieve poverty and lack of education among the farmers, colliers and glass-makers of north Somerset, described in 1796 a situation which was far from uncommon elsewhere:

> We have in this neighbourhood thirteen adjoining parishes without so much as a curate

and she commented on the children of the district that:

> hardly any had ever seen the inside of a church since they were christened?

An episcopal visitation of the diocese of Bristol in 1735 revealed some of the reasons for this non-residence, and also illustrates the details about the clergy and their attitudes which may be obtained from these records. The diocese included the county of Dorset, and the bishop found that the rector of Chilfrome 'has not resided since his institution and lives at Westbourn in Sussex. Mr Osborn, vicar of Bradpole, is his curate.' The rector of Langton Herring was also a fellow of Kings College, Cambridge, but resided at Eton where he was tutor to Lord Milton's sons. The incumbent of Wyke Regis also lived at Eton 'on account of his wife's ill-health, and for the education of his boys.' At Weston Buckhorn the bishop noted wryly that the rector 'does not reside and complains much of ill-health, tho' he looks the picture of health itself.' At Iwerne Minster the bishop noted that the vicar 'lives at

Offenham near Evesham; Mr Rumsey of Blandford Forum takes care of the church for half a guinea each Sunday.' Samuel Marsh, the incumbent of Worth Matravers, was described as 'wicked, mad, now on board a man of war. His wife and 4 children receive the income. Mr Pope of Corfe Castle serves the parish for 5s 0d a week to their satisfaction.' At several places the bishop noted that the curate also served two or three other parishes, and services were conducted only once a fortnight in consequence. In most parishes the Holy Communion was celebrated only three times a year, and the number of communicants recorded was pitifully small. In Dorset, as elsewhere, the episcopal visitation carefully recorded the number of dissenters—Baptists, Congregationalists, Quakers, Independents—as well as a few Catholic congregations, especially in parishes with a nearby Catholic gentry family.[4] The visitation records also contain much about the state of the church buildings, their furnishing and decoration, about education and charities, and about the spiritual life of the parish and the morals of the parishioners. They are thus an invaluable source for any local study.

For the well-paid, beneficed clergy the Church offered an attractive career, with comfortable living and a minimal number of duties, and it became a popular choice for the younger sons or close relatives of gentry families, especially if the family controlled the patronage of one or more benefices. Rising land values, increased agricultural production and higher prices for farm produce all helped to raise the value of tithes during the eighteenth century, and the value of many benefices more than doubled during the century. The opulent life-style of the clergy in numerous parishes is still evident from the fine Georgian rectories and vicarages which survive in so many places, and from the large ornate monuments with which they burdened the chancels of so many parish churches. At the other end of the clerical scale, the inadequacy of the stipends paid to many of the lower clergy was recognised as early as 1704, when Queen Anne's Bounty was established to supplement the incomes of the very poorest of the clergy[5]

An indispensable source of information on clerical incomes in each parish, the size and arrangement of the glebe lands, tithes, dues and offerings, the size of the parsonage house and other local matters, is to be found in the glebe terriers. These surveys of the endowments, profits and possessions of each benefice were first ordered to be made in 1571, and further terriers were compiled from time to time in each diocese. They were made by the clergy, churchwardens and substantial inhabitants and sent to the archdeacon and can now generally be found among the diocesan records, although copies were often kept among the parish papers. Where a series of terriers survive they give a valuable insight into the changing value of the glebe, the differences in landholding and farming methods, the changes in tithe, and the development of the parsonage house. The detailed descriptions of the parsonage house, its construction, roofing material, lay-out and outbuildings, and the successive improvements, enlargements or rebuilding which can be traced in a series of glebe terriers, are a dramatic index of the increasing prosperity of the clergy from the late seventeenth century[6]

Many of the clergy derived a major part of their income from their own glebe lands, and often were actively involved in farming. They would have immediately recognised the description of Parson Trulliber in Fielding's novel *Joseph Andrews:*

> stript into his waistcoat, with an apron on, and a pail in his hand, just come from serving his hogs; for Mr Tulliber was a parson on Sundays, but all the other six might properly be called a farmer.

A few of the eighteenth-century clergy were active in promoting agricultural improvements, new methods and crops, such as turnips and potatoes, or urging enclosures, model cottages, or methods of housing livestock. Others served as justices of the peace, or were engaged in their own studies, for the Hanoverian church produced an impressive array of scholars, ranging from Bishops Berkeley and Butler in philosophy, to Gilbert White the naturalist, William Stukeley the archaeologist, Jethro Tull the agriculturalist, and numerous historians. Samuel Carter, the vicar of St Martin's, Leicester, made a famous collection of material on the history of his neighbourhood; John Collinson in Somerset and John Hutchins in Dorset were both parish clergymen who wrote monumental histories of their counties, and there were numerous other clerics similarly involved in the study of local history, antiquities, archaeology and natural history. It was of such men that it was somewhat unkindly said:

> The country clergy are constant readers of the *Gentleman's Magazine,* deep in the antiquities of inn signs, speculations as to what becomes of swallows in the winter, and whether hedgehogs or other urchins are most justly accused of sucking milch cows dry at night?

Information about the clergy, their occupations, attitudes and the way in which they discharged the duties of their office, can be found in the numerous clerical diaries of the eighteenth century, several of which have been published. One of the best known is that of James Woodforde, *The Diary of a Country Parson.* Woodeforde's diary illustrates how the better-off clergy could live in a style little different from that of the country squire; they were received as equals by the gentry, to many of whom they were related; and they could devote their days to country sports, the management of their glebe lands, the collection of their tithes and to taking a leading part in local affairs, confining their religious duties to the Sunday services and occasional offices:

> His talk was now of tithes and dues;
> He smoked his pipe and read the news;
> Knew how to preach old sermons next
> Vamp'd in the preface and the text.
> At Christ'nings well could act his part,
> And had the service all by heart .. [8]

The tithes on which the majority of parochial clergy depended for their income were not entirely an ecclesiastical property, nor did all the income from them pass to the Church, for many of the extensive tithe rights which had been owned by the monasteries passed at the Dissolution into the hands of laymen, who were known as *lay impropriators*. The tithes of such parishes thus became private property which could be freely bought, sold or leased, and which were totally divorced from the local parish church and its incumbent. The collection of tithes in kind continued to be the practice in many parishes during the eighteenth century; the process occupied much time and proved to be a fruitful source of dispute between parsons and parishioners. The method of assessment in each parish depended essentially upon long usage or 'custom', and the complex customs were recorded in detail in glebe terriers. The bewildering and intricate processes which were evolved to ensure that the parson was not given the poorest livestock, or to provide for situations in which the farmer had less than ten titheable animals, serve only to emphasise the opportunities for controversy. For example, the glebe terrier of Pottingham (Staffs) made in 1698 explains how each tithing lamb was to be chosen:

> The custom of tithing lambs is this, the owners first chuse two & then the Vicar takes his tithe & then the owner takes out seven more to make them ten & so on till all are tithed. If there be seven od ones … the Vicar has one ordinarily allowing 3d a lamb for those which make up ten. But if there be six od ones or a lesser number, the Vicar takes either 3d a lamb or reserves them for the increase of the Insuing year.

A tithe notebook kept by the vicar of Minety (Wilts) during the late seventeenth and early eighteenth centuries (now in the Wiltshire Record Office) shows the watchful eye he kept on his parishioners' livestock, records the sales and purchases they made, whether the cows calved in the parish or the sheep were shorn there, and the attempts which the parishioners made to hoodwink him by moving livestock into neighbouring parishes, overwintering stock and selling them in the spring, or by attempting to conceal the true number of lambs, calves or pigs which they had bred[9]

Not until 1836 was the old system of tithe collection entirely changed to a money payment, and in view of the constant difficulties many of the clergy would have echoed the heartfelt complaint of William Jones, vicar of Broxbourne and Hoddesdon, in 1803:

> I am confident that I am defrauded by many of my parishioners of various vicarial dues and rights to which the laws of Heaven and earth entitle me … for the very word 'tithe' has ever been as unpleasing and odious to farmers especially as cuckoo to the married ear. Those who pay them, pay them very partially and I may say, grudgingly and of necessity![10]

Because of the difficulties and disputes over tithe collection, it was often the practice to agree upon a money payment or *modus,* though this did not always end the reluctance of farmers to pay. In many parishes, especially those which had large areas of common grazing, manorial custom continued to impose upon the parson the obligation of providing a bull and a boar for his parishioners. The practice of the manor of Affpuddle (Dorset) was similar to that of others throughout the country: 'By our custome we are to have a Bull and a Bore of one Parson continually to serve our turns'. Such customs also brought the clergy into close contact with the agricultural concerns of their parishioners.[11]

In spite of all the Victorian restorations, many eighteenth-century church interiors survive almost unchanged, and it is therefore possible readily to appreciate the context, setting and atmosphere of worship during the Hanoverian period. The enlargements and additions to the buildings, as well as the numerous complete rebuildings, and the frequent construction of galleries, show the attempts which were made to accommodate additional worshippers and to provide room for the increasingly elaborate private pews and large monuments of gentry families. Often the squire's pew, in a prominent position or even in the chancel itself, was handsomely furnished, had its own entrance, and unlike the rest of the church, was heated by its own fireplace. The family sat on comfortable chairs as though in an elegant drawing room, divorced from their tenants, and surrounded by the monuments of their ancestors. At Tong, near Bradford (Yorks), the Tempest family, who lived in the nearby hall, rebuilt the church in 1727 on the foundations of its Anglo-Saxon predecessor, and furnished it with box pews, galleries, three-decker pulpit and a squire's pew complete with its own fireplace. This excellent example of an eighteenth-century interior survived largely unchanged.[13] Many other good examples can still be seen, including Breedon-on-the-Hill (Leics), Chaddleworth (Berks), Whalley (Lancs), Hinton St George (Somerset) and Tibenham (Norfolk). Similarly, the naves were filled with the square box-pews of the wealthier members of the congregation; a practical advantage of these high-sided pews was that they protected the occupants from draughts, although the crowded pews and galleries gave an irregular untidy appearance to the church interior as can still be seen, for example, at Whitby (N. Yorks) or Minstead (Hants).[13] Gilbert White, the antiquarian and naturalist, who was curate of Selborne (Hants) from 1751 to 1793, wrote of the private pews in his church:

> nothing can be more irregular than the pews of this church which are of all dimensions and heights, being patched up according to the fancy of the owners.[14]

At Burton Bradstock (Dorset), where the pews were allocated to particular tenements, the parish vestry ordered in 1808 that

> the present Pews and Seats be all numbered and entered on the Church Book, expressing to whom they belong, and in what Right, at the expence of the Parish, and that all persons desirous of Painting their seats shall be at liberty to do so, provided they agree to follow a uniform and regular plan to be laid down by the Minister and Church Wardens.[15]

Pews and benches which are still inscribed with the names of the farms to which they belong can be seen at West Grinstead (Sussex) or Sutton Mallett (Somerset), while a good example of socially 'graded' seating survives at Icklingham (Suffolk), where the best quality pews are at the front, and the less elegant and more uncomfortable pews are further back, while at the rear of the church are plain benches without backs or any other refinement.

Those who could not afford the pew rents were accommodated on forms in the aisles, at the back of the church or in the galleries. Even more than in the seventeenth century, the order of seating in churches emphasised the rigid social structure; mirroring the rank and social status of the occupants, it was regarded as a matter of the greatest importance. The relative freedom from such snobbery of the early Methodists was one of their greatest attractions for the poor, although pew rents and concern for social status soon afflicted chapel as well as church. In 1743, however, the Duchess of Buckingham could write to Selina, Countess of Huntingdon:

> I thank your ladyship for the information concerning the Methodist preachers. Their doctrines are most repulsive, and strongly tinctured with impertinence and disrespect towards their superiors. It is monstrous to be told that you have a heart as sinful as the common wretches that crawl the earth. I cannot but wonder that your ladyship should relish any sentiments so much at variance with high rank and good peerage![16]

The right to private pews could have odd consequences. It meant that churchwardens were ever anxious to provide more seats which would produce income, but reluctant to provide space for the poor, for scholars or for singers and musicians. It also meant that in many populous places it was impossible to rent a seat in the church, especially since families insisted on places in the church commensurate with their dignity. When Lord Ashburnham settled at Ampthill (Beds), during the late-seventeenth century he complained to the bishop 'I cannot carry my family to church as I ought to do, for I have not due and proper accommodation'. Eventually a gallery was erected for him, designed by Sir Christopher Wren, with easy chairs, velvet cushions and silk hangings. In 1806 the editor of *The Royal Cornwall Gazette* wrote to the vicar of St Mary's, Truro, to complain that he could not obtain seats for himelf and his family in the church:

> I have been nearly three years resident in this town, and hope to finish my days here, I have a pretty numerous family, eight children (with a probability of more) besides apprentices. It is my wish to bring up this numerous family members of our Church Establishment, and, with this in view I have to find me room in the church. I am now again called upon for payment of the Church Rate, without yet being able to get my family accommodated within its walls …

The writer went on to threaten that his family would join the Dissenters, whose 'doors are ever open to seceeders, and who are always ready to extend their houses in proportion to the number of their guests.' If the editor of the influential local paper could not find room in the church, we can imagine the problems of less important members of the community.

The churchwardens' accounts and presentments, vestry minutes, terriers and faculty petitions and the registers of faculties granted by the bishop will all provide evidence for the state of the church building and for any major alterations to it. A faculty or licence granted by the bishop was necessary to authorise alterations or additions to the structure or extensions to churchyards. Eighteenth-century faculties often refer to the erection of pews, and of galleries to provide more accommodation, or to the building of burial vaults for local gentry families. It is clear from all sources that the church and churchyard were now rarely used for anything other than services or for the burial of the dead. The churchwardens depended upon rates and pew rents for the bulk of their income, and church ales or similar fund-raising activities had largely ceased; almost everywhere church houses were disused or had become dwellings, inns, schools or poor-houses, while in the churchyards the number of headstones and elaborate tombs was such that there was no longer an open space for public recreation.

Churchwardens' accounts generally give proof of the regularity of maintenance work on church buildings, and, although there are exceptions, it is not in general true to say that the sweeping Victorian restorations were made necessary by eighteenth-century neglect of the buildings; the restorations were carried out because of changed religious ideas and fashions, and because of the difficulties of bringing medieval buildings up to the standards of professional Victorian architects. From the evidence of churchwardens' accounts, inventories of church goods, vestry minutes, seating plans, terriers, lists of pew rents, correspondence and other local records, as well as from the evidence of the building itself, it is possible to reconstruct the earlier appearance of a church interior. For interior decoration eighteenth-century churchwardens favoured whitewash, which was cheap and easy to apply and symbolically brought light even to the darkest corners of the church; it also provided a base for suitable texts and sentences of scripture. At the east end of the church, around the altar, the Commandments, the Lord's Prayer and the Creed were generally displayed. The royal arms were also regularly exhibited in the church, and symbolised the essential link between Church and State.

Sermons were a more regular feature of the services than was the Holy Communion. The pulpit was frequently the most imposing feature of the interior. It was often a 'three-decker' complete with sounding board and three sections, each on a different level—from the top one the parson preached, from the middle he read the service, and in the lowest compartment the parish clerk was accommodated. Churchwardens regularly spent large sums on the decoration of the pulpit and on the pulpit cushion. Samuel Johnson observed that most people found it easier to listen to a sermon than to concentrate on prayer, and contemporary diaries illustrate the attention which was bestowed on good preachers. Not all the clergy were such, of course, but nonetheless long sermons were the custom and eighteenth-century hourglasses survive by many pulpits![17]

Churchwardens' accounts also record the practice, which grew rapidly during the eighteenth century, of having singers and musicians to accompany the services. A remarkable change occurred then in the music in English parish churches, and although the evidence is not easy to find, local historians should look carefully for references to singers, musical instruments, music and musicians, and for any indication of the way in which services were conducted and accompanied by music. From the mid-seventeenth century the practice of 'lining out' had become common for singing the metrical psalms, in the version by Thomas Sternhold and John Hopkins of 1562, whereby the parish clerk read out each line before it was sung by the congregation. The Directory of Public Worship, which replaced the Book of Common Prayer in 1645 and remained in use until the Restoration in 1660, had ordered:

> ... where many in the congregation cannot read, it is convenient that the minister, or some fit person appointed by him and the other ruling officers, do read the psalm, line by line, before the singing thereof.

This practice continued after the Restoration, and set an extremely slow tempo, especially since parish clerks who led the singing without the help of instruments developed a slow, drawn-out style, so that each psalm took an excessively long time. This curious and mannered way of singing was transformed during the eighteenth century. Organs had been common in larger, richer churches during the later Middle Ages, but from the reign of Elizabeth their use had declined rapidly. In a few places a lively musical tradition survived from the sixteenth century, and the Wiltshire antiquarian John Aubrey described the excellent musical accompaniment to the services at Bishops Cannings during the seventeenth century, where the vicar encouraged music, had obtained an organ, and

> made severall of his parishioners good musicians, both for vocall and instrumental musick; they sung the Psalms in consort to the organ.

Aubrey added that 'This parish in those days would have challenged all England for musique, foot-ball and ringing'.[18]

But most parishes witnessed a great decline in the musical accompaniment of services, and in singing either by choirs or by the whole congregation. Puritan clergy had frowned upon music as upon other rituals. During the late seventeenth century, however, more and more town churches acquired organs, often through the gifts of pious citizens, and using choirs of young men or of charity-school children, began to emulate the musical accompaniment to services which had always been a feature of cathedral worship. In country parishes religious societies of young men were founded and began to introduce a new style of singing. The movement was strengthened in 1698 by the foundation of the Society for Promoting Christian Knowledge which, among other aims, worked to improve music and singing in churches. Hymns were not common until the nineteenth century, and *Hymns Ancient and Modern* was not published until 1861, but in 1696 *A New Version of the Psalms of David* was published by Nahum Tate and Nicholas Brady, and soon became popular. Most country churches could not afford organs, but choirs began to be introduced from the early eighteenth century to lead the congregational singing, often using a pitchpipe to find and maintain the right pitch, and the old practice of 'lining out' began to be abandoned.[19]

References to choirs, to itinerant singing masters and visiting singers, can be found in many churchwardens' accounts from c.1700 onwards. For example, at Hope (Derbys) in 1707 the churchwardens' accounts record:

3s 0d paid for two books and £3 18s 2d on a singing master.

And at Lymington (Hants) in 1723:

> £1 1s 6d for Fordingbridge singers and £1 0s 0d to the singing master for learning poor boys.

In 1724 the choir from Dunstable (Beds) was paid a guinea for giving a demonstration of singing at Ampthill, and thereafter the churchwardens paid for boys to be taught to sing. Addison's fictitious but eminently believable squire, Sir Roger de Coverley, was said in 1711 to have improved his parishioners' singing in church, and to have

> employed an itinerant singing-master, who goes about the country for that purpose, to instruct them rightly in the tunes of the psalms; upon which they now very much value themselves, and indeed outdo most of the country churches that I have ever heard.

From the 1740s references begin to appear in churchwardens' accounts for country parishes to musical instruments being used to accompany the singing. The accounts of Youlgreave (Derbys), include the following:

1742 For hiring [hairing] the bow of the viole   8d
1751 Gave Ben Jones to buy Reeds for the Basoon 3s 0d

At Beaulieu (Hants), in 1750 the churchwardens were authorised by the vestry meeting 'to buy an Instrument called a Bassoon at our charge for the use of the singers of the parish of Bewley aforesaid'. Many other churchwardens' accounts from the mid-eighteenth century record the purchase of bassoons, viols, flutes, clarinets, cellos, oboes, serpents and fiddles and other instruments. Later in the century, barrel organs became popular, although the repertoire of most was limited to a few tunes. Their popularity can be judged from the number which survive, especially in East Anglia and the West Country[20]

By the early nineteenth century there were many country churches where the services were accompanied by small bands and the singing was led by an enthusiastic choir, both being accommodated in a gallery at the west end of the church, so that the congregation turned to 'face the music' during the singing of psalms and the newly-introduced hymns. The erection of galleries for singers and musicians became common during the eighteenth century, and although many were dismantled during nineteenth-century restorations or in order to accommodate an organ, evidence of their former existence can often still be seen in the form of corbels or supports, stairways, blocked doors and windows. Faculties might be obtained from the bishop of the diocese in order to erect a gallery, and the diocesan records will often supply evidence both of the date and the purpose for which galleries were built. For example, in Chichester diocese faculties for seventeen galleries were issued between 1700 and 1750, and at Mayfield church (East Sussex) beside the former palace of the Archbishop of Canterbury, a faculty was granted in 1731 to the churchwardens, who were said to be desirous to promote the singing of Psalms in the said church to the honour of Almighty God in the most decent orderly manner, and do judge that a gallery, to be built in the west end of the parish church, will be convenient to answer to that end?[21]

The impetus for much of this remarkable development of music in parish churches during the eighteenth century came from members of the congregation themselves, and often received little encouragement from the clergy who, like the Mayfield churchwardens, were mainly concerned with conducting the services in a 'decent orderly manner'. Thomas Hardy, whose family had included several church musicians, knew a great deal about traditional church music; although he later regretted that he had caricatured such musicians in his fictional account of the Mellstock choir in *Under the Greenwood Tree* (first published 1872), much of his picture is based on first-hand knowledge of the Dorset choirs and musicians at Puddletown and Stinsford. Hardy's fictional Mellstock choir and musicians counted it a great virtue in the parson that he was totally uninterested in their activities, and never interfered with the music or singing which accompanied the church services:

> 'And 'a was a very jinerous gentleman about choosing the psalms and hymns o' Sundays. "Confound ye", says he, "blare and scape what ye will, but don't bother me!"'[22]

Hardy drew many of his ideas from the stories told by his mother, who as a girl had lived in the Blackmore Vale at Melbury Osmund (Dorset). It is therefore interesting to find that in an episcopal visitation of *c.*1750 the bishop noted that at Melbury Osmund there was a dispute between the rector and the village musicians over the 'singing of psalms with various instruments'; the quarrel was settled by the bishop who forbade the use of musical instruments in the church, 'and both parties promised to live in concord for the future'[23]

In Somerset the melancholy and unpopular vicar of Camerton, John Skinner, was constantly at loggerheads with his choir and musicians, as his Journal shows:

> Sunday 14 July 1822
> During the evening service the Church was crowded; and the singers who have been in a state of constant intoxication since yesterday, being offended because I would not suffer them to chaunt the service after the First Lesson, put on their hats and left the Church.

Some joined the Methodists, but others later returned to the Church

> Sunday 14 February 1830
> The service in the evening was numerously attended, the congregation attracted by the Singers, who now muster a large band of various instruments. I do not like their mode of performing this part of the service near so well as that of the schoolgirls; but if it induces the people to come to Church, I will bear with them patiently?[24]

Notwithstanding the rapid growth of Dissent in many parishes during the eighteenth century and the eventual secession of the Methodists from the congregation of the parish churches, few people escaped completely from some involvement with the Established Church. Baptism was widely regarded as essential for the child's spiritual and physical well-being, even by those parents who seldom attended church themselves. Church schools and charities affected many; most parishioners were married in the parish church and few could avoid burial in the churchyard. Weddings and funerals, especially those of wealthier members of the community, were frequently accompanied by great solemnity and feasting. Huge memorials to the deceased were erected, often overwhelming the small churches in which they were placed, but telling us much about the wealth and attitudes of the families who paid for them. There are many examples of parish church interiors which are dominated by the monuments to local gentry families. The entire chancel at Warkton (Northants) is devoted to four large monuments to the Montague family which are far more prominent than the altar; at Sherborne (Glos) the church of this small Cotswold village is actually attached to the mansion of the Dutton family, and the altar is flanked by two large family tombs, on one of which a buxom, scantily-clad angel towers over a woebegone skeleton. Edenham church in Lincolnshire is filled with the tombs and memorials of the Bertie family; there are more family monuments in the churchyard, and others are to be found in the neighbouring church of Swinstead. The walls of Bath Abbey are covered in memorial tablets recording in elegant prose and verse the remarkable virtues of those who had failed to benefit from the waters of the spa and who are buried there. As one observer irreverently commented:

> These walls, adorned with monument and bust,
> Show how Bath waters serve to lay the dust[25]

Churchwardens' accounts also underline the importance of bell-ringing in the life of local communities. As in previous centuries, the upkeep of the bells demanded constant expenditure, and the large sums which were spent on ropes, frames, recastings, and on new bells, show its continuing popularity. The bells summoned the congregation to church and proclaimed the services when clocks were scarce and inaccurate; they tolled the curfew, they were rung for weddings and tolled for funerals, and celebrated national festivals, royal birthdays and British victories.

Even in the most remote parishes, the payments to ringers chronicle the excitements of the time, the victories, anniversaries and important national events, illustrating how quickly news of battles, peace treaties, political upheavals and royal fortunes spread, and the patriotic joy with which good news was received. The bells were also rung to greet prominent visitors such as royalty or the bishop, and they served as an alarm for fire or floods. Change-ringing developed greatly as an art during the eighteenth century and several national societies were founded to promote ringing; ringing contests between different parochial teams were a popular pastime, and the bell-ringers were an important section of church congregations with their own membership, rules and funds?[26]

In many parishes the Church continued to touch the lives of parishioners in other ways. Traditions included Easter or Christmas feasts, charity distribution or parochial revels. For example, at Kidlington (Oxon), a medieval bequest intended for the benefit of those who attended Midnight Mass on Christmas Eve continued to lay on a breakfast consisting of large quantities of beef, bread and beer at 3.00 am on Christmas morning even though celebration of Midnight Mass had ceased at the Reformation. The result of this oddly-timed feast was to make many of the participants too drunk to attend any Christmas Day service. At Marnhull, Dorset, it was the ancient custom for the parson to distribute bread, cheese and beer for consumption in the church on Easter Sunday after Evening Prayer; and at Souldrop (Beds) the rector contributed a stone of new cheese, together with bread and beer, for a Christmas feast[27]

Many charities continued to provide money, food, clothing and coals for the poor and were distributed by the parson, churchwardens or overseers, especially to those who regularly attended church or to the 'second poor', that is those who were not regularly in receipt of poor relief. The bequest boards which survive in many churches give evidence of these charities, as do the 'dole cupboards' or receptacles for food, bread and clothing which are still to be found in others. Whatever criticisms may be levelled at the eighteenth-century church, no one can doubt its concern for charity and the central role it played in the establishment of schools, hospitals, almshouses and foundations of all sorts; such local charities, bequests and benevolence will repay detailed investigation at local level. Hospital foundations such as those of Radcliffe in Oxford, Addenbrooke in Cambridge, or the following remarkable list of London hospitals, witness to the concern of the age for social welfare:

Westminster Hospital	1719	Lock	1746
Guy's	1723	Lying-in hospital	1749
St George's	1734	Queen Charlotte's	1752
London hospital	1740	Royal Maternity	1757
Foundling	1742	Westminster Lying-	
Middlesex	1745	in hospital	1765

As well as churchwardens' and overseers' accounts, and vestry minutes, some parishes also kept separate charity books recording the management of parochial benefactions and the payments made from them. In addition, sources which should on no account be neglected are the reports of the Charity Commissioners 1819-40, published as Parliamentary Papers and giving detailed and extremely useful information about the charities of each parish. An index and digest of these Reports was published as a Parliamentary Paper in 1843 (*Analytical Digest*, 1843, XVIII).

Parish registers of churchwardens' account books for the seventeenth and eighteenth centuries often include interesting lists of 'briefs' or authorisations to collect money for some deserving cause, together with a note of the amount collected. Briefs were issued by the Privy Council and became very common during the eighteenth century, and some parishes kept 'brief books' in which were listed the various calamities, good causes or pious purposes for which the collections were made; the system continued until the early nineteenth century, in spite of criticisms and scandals associated with professional 'undertakers' who collected the money from parishes. Sums were commonly collected for the redemption of captives, especially of seamen who had been captured by 'the Turks' that is by Barbary pirates in the Mediterranean; also for the relief of distressed Protestants in Europe, or for sufferers from fire, flood or other calamity in England, and for building, rebuilding or restoring churches. The briefs, giving details of the purpose for which money was required, were read out by the minister during the church service, and the collection was made by the parish clerk as the congregation left the church.[28] Many of the places and causes for which help was sought must have seemed very remote from those who were being asked to contribute. For example, in the remote Dorset parish of Symondsbury, during a few months of 1711 the following collections were made:

June	Collected towards the relief of the inhabetance of Haughley in Suffolk	1s-0d
July	Collected towards repairing Cockermouth church in the county of Cumberland	5½d
July	Collected towards rebuilding the Church of St Mary's at Colchester in Essex	9½d
August	For Wishaw church in Warwickshire	5d
September	For reliefe of the poor sufferers in Edinburgh	11½d
September	For sufferers at Market Rayson in the county of York	6½d
October	Towards rebuilding Long Melford church in Suffolk	3½d
November	Collected for rebuilding the church at Woolwich in the county of Kent	2s-2d

The parish and parish church were also closely involved with the farming community through the churchwardens' continuing responsibility for the control of vermin and obligation to pay a bounty on the heads of all destructive birds and animals brought to them. Meetings and ceremonies of all sorts continued to be held in parish churches throughout the eighteenth century. Vestry meetings commonly took place in churches, and the principal officers of the parish—the churchwardens, the overseers of the poor, and the supervisors of the highways—were elected at the Easter vestry in the parish church. Parish vestries also considered topics as various as the care of the poor, the apprenticing of pauper children, the conduct of the parish poor-house, the upkeep of the highways, the church clock, the repair and decoration of the church, the care of the churchyard wall, the maintenance of the bells, the administration of parish lands and charities and a host of other matters. Parish fire-fighting equipment, including the pump or 'engine', was regularly kept in the church, as was the parish bier, and churches were also used as the repositories for the parochial armour and weapons.[29] At Burton Bradstock, Dorset, the vestry minutes for 1813 record an agreement that:

the Fire buckets belonging to the Parish and furnished by the Sun Fire Office be placed in the Church, and that they be painted and lettered at the expense of the Parish.

At Crewkerne (Som), the fire engine was kept in the church and the churchwardens regularly paid men to 'play the engine' on feast days and national holidays, that is, to squirt water from the engine around the market square, thus neatly combining a holiday spectacle with practice for the firemen. At Crewkerne, as at many other places, the cost of maintaining the fire engine and keeping the leather pipes greased also fell upon the churchwardens. Since the church services were the only occasions when a major part of the parishioners regularly met together, they were used for giving out notices of all sorts, and the church door continued to be the recognised place for the display of important information. During the eighteenth century the Church courts continued to exercise jurisdiction over wills and testamentary matters, libel, slander, adultery, and disputes over tithes, church rates and church seating arrangements; while services in parish churches continued to be occasionally enlivened by the performance of public penance by some unfortunate parishioner who had fallen foul of the ecclesiastical authorities.

Schools continued to be held in churches; for example, in Cheshire at least six schools were kept in parish churches, and in many other places parish or charity schoolrooms were built in the churchyards. As in the seventeenth century, many schools were short-lived, depending upon the availability or enthusiasm of a curate or of suitably qualified laymen, and it is not always easy to find details of such establishments. Bishops' and archdeacons' visitation returns, churchwardens' presentments, or references in wills will provide evidence, as will the records of the SPCK and the licences granted to schoolmasters by diocesan bishops[30]

Topics for investigation

The study of the eighteenth-century church and its place in the life of each local community presents an opportunity and a challenge to the local historian. Ample and easily accessible evidence is likely to be available, both architectural and documentary, and will probably throw light on many aspects of local history and on the life of all classes of society. Among the topics worth pursuing are the following:

1 *The clergy:* their education, residence or non-residence, their curates, income, life-styles, attitudes, interests and concept of their responsibilities in the parish.

2 *The services:* their frequency and duration, attendance at them, sermons, communicants, special services, observation of State prayers, fasts, and intercessions.

3 *Music:* singers, instruments, accommodation within the church, their place in parish life and in the services, the parish clerk.

4 *The church fabric:* interior arrangement of the church, its furnishings and decoration, the care of the fabric, seating arrangements and galleries.

5 *Church life:* education, charities, marriage and burial customs, Rogationtide and other processions, beating the bounds, bell-ringing, church rates, pew rents, tithes and finances.

6 *The Church's influence:* on social life, morals, poor relief, education, recreation; the role of landowners, gentry families and of church officials, especially the churchwardens; and the extent to which this influence was superseded during the century by the growth of nonconformity, the rise of the Methodists, or by sheer indifference.

In exploring these subjects and considering the Church's place in the community, it is important to remember that the Church—its hierarchy, clergy, organisation, services and attitudes—did no more than mirror prevailing opinions in the upper classes of society to which it was so closely tied; these naturally attached great significance to birth, breeding, connections, wealth and the possession of land. It would be unjust as well as unhistorical to judge the standards of the Georgian age from the viewpoint of the twentieth century.

Chapter Eight

PARISH LIFE IN THE CHURCH REVIVAL OF THE NINETEENTH CENTURY

The nineteenth century saw many developments in the work and concerns of all the various denominations, as the churches tried, often unsuccessfully, to keep pace with the massive growth in population, especially in the towns, and struggled to cope with all the social and economic changes which the century witnessed. The nonconformist churches underwent a great expansion during the early decades of the century, and the Church of England was transformed by the Evangelical revival and by the Oxford or Tractarian Movement; everywhere the evidence of resurgence in Church life and activity and of the new sense of responsibility and professionalism among the clergy can be seen in the number of new or restored churches and chapels, in new parishes, mission churches, church schools, social clubs, reading rooms and parish halls. Brighter, more lively services were introduced, often accompanied, though not without much bitter controversy, by a more elaborate ritual, surpliced choirs, lights, statues, organs and far greater congregational participation, especially through hymn-singing. Parochial activities ranged from Sunday and Day schools, adult classes and youth groups, to missions, social work, church building, restoration, parish magazines, orphanages, clubs, friendly societies, soup kitchens and a much more socially-conscious policy towards the whole community. Religious controversy and theological argument became a popular pursuit, filling the correspondence columns of newspapers with heated discussion of Free Will, Original Sin, Predestination, Redemption, Grace, Ritual, Vestments and a host of similar topics, or later, with discussion of science and religion, evolution and the literal truth of the Old Testament.

Faced with this revival and expansion of church life, the number of questions which a local historian should ask is greatly increased, as is the number of available sources which can be consulted to provide answers. For any parish or district, urban or rural, the following are some of the major questions concerning the changes in church life during the nineteenth century:

1 How did the churches of all denominations cope with expanding population, new communities and changes in the old settlement pattern?

2 What evidence is there for increased activity, new attitudes, changes in the frequency and character of services, the introduction of hymn-singing, surpliced choirs, an organ, and for the involvement of the church with schools, charities, work among the poor, missions, societies and clubs?

3 To what extent were new parishes founded, new churches built or existing churches restored, mission churches established, pew rents abolished, and a new spirit and energy observable in the life of the church? How were the funds raised for these and other projects? How many people regularly attended or received the Holy Communion, and what support was there for causes such as foreign missions, the temperance movement, social work, education, coal and clothing clubs or other charities?

4 What was the effect of the rapid growth of Methodism and other forms of dissent upon the parish or locality, and is there any evidence that the Evangelical revival, both within and outside the Established church, turned men's minds away from violent action against political and social injustices and economic hardship during the early decades of the nineteenth century?

5 What were the relations between the Church of England and members of the various nonconformist churches, especially with the Methodists, for many dissenters continued to be married and buried by the Anglican rites, and many Methodists for long continued to attend the church services as well as those of the chapel? Was any pressure exerted by landowners or clergy to hinder the spread of dissent or the building of nonconformist chapels? What were the social differences between the membership of the various denominations?

6 What evidence is there for changes in the structure and furnishings of the church, or for the introduction of a cross and candlesticks on the altar, vestments, a surpliced choir, new stained glass windows, new bells, an organ, or more elaborate services, ritual and processions? What was the reaction among the parishioners to these changes?

7 Is there any evidence of active pressure by the clergy to suppress the long-established games, festivities and pastimes that had traditionally been associated with the parish churches?

8 How far did religion act as a social bond within the community; were all sections affected by the work of the churches; and how far was there an overall decline in religious adherence? For in spite of the strenuous activity of all the churches, there emerged for the first time in many communities a sizeable number of people who confessed allegiance to no particular creed or who attended no church, and who rejected Christian belief and remained untouched by all the missionary zeal of the nineteenth century.

Only local historians with a detailed knowledge of the social structure and relationships within their communities have the information to attempt the answers to many of these questions, and only by their enquiries can knowledge of these important matters be extended and refined. The following section describes some of the major sources which should be consulted to answer these and similar questions. Detailed information concerning the growth or decline of population, the proliferation of new settlements, the changes in the population of older centres and the rapid growth of new industrial and manufacturing communities, can from 1801 be gathered from the decennial Census returns. So too can the way in which the Church attempted to adapt its ancient system of parishes to meet the rapidly-growing needs of the nineteenth century, and valiantly attempted to accommodate more people by enlarging existing churches or building new ones.

The ancient but essentially static system of parishes, each with its own church and clergy, income and property-rights, and the long-established network of deaneries, archdeaconries and dioceses, was best suited to a rural society where change was slow; it was ill-fitted to cope with the rapid developments of the nineteenth century. The rights of patrons, the lucrative practice of charging rent for pews, the fears of tithe and rate payers, and private interests of all kinds, militated strongly against action by the Church to divide parishes or to supply the need of increased accommodation. Political considerations stood in the way of any division of dioceses which would have brought more effective episcopal control. Yet the problem was immense. The diocese of Lincoln stretched from the Humber to the Thames, the diocese of Exeter included the whole of Devon and Cornwall and was 140 miles in length with nearly 700 parishes. Early in the nineteenth century, the population of Leeds had grown to 64,000 while the Anglican churches could accommodate only 3,400; the parish of Manchester was one of the largest in the country including Manchester and Salford and 28 other townships, and by 1831 there were some 10,000 persons to each church. In Plymouth, the expansion of the naval and military base had greatly increased the population, so that by 1831 there were 61,000 people, with church accommodation for 3,500. The population of Frome (Somerset) in 1801 was 8,747 and by 1821 had grown to 12,411, but there was only one parish church, with seats for 800 people. In Southampton the population of St Mary's parish rose from 4,708 in 1821 to 14,885 by 1841, yet the church could accommodate only 650 people, and the parish was not divided until 1848. To make matters worse, the incumbent of St Mary's from 1797 until 1850 was the Reverend, the Earl of Guilford, a notorious pluralist and absentee, who seldom appeared in Southampton and left the care of the parish to a curate! The same situation was to be found in many rapidly-expanding towns. Even as late as 1858 there were only 1,400 church places in Bradford for a population of 78,000, and only 200 of the seats were free, the rest having been let to private individuals. The Church of England's response to this situation was an impressive campaign of church building. The process was given a great impetus by a government grant of one million pounds for this purpose in 1818. Ostensibly it was a thank-offering for victory at Waterloo, and resulted in the so-called 'Waterloo' churches; more realistically it was an attempt to provide some civilizing influence in the barren wastes of the new industrial towns, suburbs and villages. For whatever the motivation of the more zealous of the clergy, the government was largely impelled by the hope that the new churches might serve to check the violence and lawlessness among the lower classes in the crowded slums, and reduce the danger of civil disorder and rebellion. As Charles Blomfield, the reforming Bishop of London, put it in 1836, church building was 'a work of prudence no less than charity'. The following statistics tell their own story of increasing zeal and endeavour within the Church.

Anglican Church Building 1801-1870

	New churches	Churches rebuilt	Total churches consecrated
1801-10	28	15	43
1811-20	70	26	96
1821-30	235	73	308
1831-40	514	86	600
1841-50	759	170	929
1851-60	654	166	820
1861-70	791	319	1,110[2]

In all parts of the country the number of new churches built was remarkable. There were 106 new churches built in the diocese of Oxford during the episcopate of Bishop Samuel Wilberforce, 1845-69; in the new diocese of Manchester, Bishop Lee consecrated 110 new churches during the period 1848-69. Even in the predominantly rural diocese of Gloucester, 54 new churches were consecrated between 1832 and 1864; in Hampshire during the same period, there were 82 new churches, and in Surrey 87. In Wiltshire during the first fifty years of Queen Victoria's reign, 32 churches were enlarged, 98 were extensively restored, 51 were completely rebuilt and 45 entirely new churches were erected. One example of the many individuals who contributed so generously to church building and restoration was Mary Caroline, Marchioness of Ailesbury, who lived at Tottenham House in Savernake Forest from 1837 to 1879, and during that time was responsible for the rebuilding or complete restoration of nearly all the parish churches in that part of Wiltshire, as well as for the erection of four new churches, including the large and ornate St Katherine's church, built for the Savernake estate workers in 1861 to a design by T. H. Wyatt. In many places, architecture and furnishings not in accord with the restorers' conception of 'correctness' were ruthlessly removed, screens, box-pews, and other old furnishings were often swept away, and the interior appearance and atmosphere of the churches completely altered. While we may regret many of these changes and the over-drastic restorations, we cannot but admire the energy and enthusiasm of those who directed the work, or the generosity of those who paid for it.[3] Some individuals made a profound impact on parishes or districts by their charitable, educational and Evangelical work. For example, over a large area of north Somerset, the two remarkable sisters, Hannah and Martha More, devoted themselves to spreading Christianity and education among the lead miners of Mendip, the glass-workers and coal miners of Nailsea, the farmers and quarrymen of Cheddar, the calamine workers of Shipham, and other groups of impoverished, isolated workers who were almost totally neglected by the Church of England.[4]

Another measure of the revival in the Church of England is provided by the names and foundation dates of some of the societies founded to raise money and carry forward the church's revitalised missionary enthusiasm. The 'National Society for the Education of the Poor in the Principles of the Church of England' was founded to carry out the educational and religious ideas of Dr Andrew Bell in 1811, and within two years of its creation was educating 40,000 children; by 1831 nearly 400,000 children were in Anglican day-schools (the name 'National School' is still to be seen on many school buildings). The Church Building Society was founded in 1818; the Church Pastoral Aid Society in 1836; the Additional Curates Society in 1837. The founding of the following theological colleges for the training of the clergy also played an important part in fostering a new attitude of professionalism among the clergy.

Chichester   1839
Wells   1840
Birkenhead 1846
Cuddesdon 1854
Salisbury   1860

There are numerous records through which the changes of the nineteenth century may be followed at a local level, and these may be divided into diocesan, national and parochial sources. The following pages will consider the most important of these sources and those which are most useful to the local historian.

Diocesan records

Bishops' registers and the visitation returns of bishops and archdeacons remain a major source throughout the century, giving details of the number of services, the frequency of Holy Communion, the number of Dissenters and Catholics, and providing evidence for the establishment of Sunday schools, the provision of music, alterations to the church and its furnishings and other signs of a more active church life. The diocesan records may supply lists of confirmation candidates, the licences for curates together with details of their careers, responsibilities and stipend, and inventories of church furnishings, plate and other possessions. The bishops' records may also contain certificates of meeting houses, records of ordinations and institutions as well as the correspondence of bishops, archdeacons and rural deans, providing much information about church life in individual parishes, details of the clergy and their activities and otherwise unobtainable evidence for the rôle of the church in each parish. Particularly useful for tracing the architectural history of the parish church and the parsonage house are the diocesan records relating to faculties and mortgages. Faculties or licences granted by the bishop were, and still are, required for alterations and additions to the fabric of churches or churchyards. Earlier faculties generally relate to relatively minor works such as the erection of private pews, galleries, monuments or burial vaults, but nineteenth-century faculties often reveal the installation of organs, new pews or improved accommodation as well as details of major building work, extensions to churches and churchyards, alterations, restorations or even complete rebuilding; they often also include a petition giving the reasons why the work was required as well as useful plans and sketches of the new building. The diocesan records will often contain much detailed correspondence about new building work on parish churches; bills, estimates and plans may survive; while contemporary local newspapers give long accounts of the restoration and consecration of church buildings, and provide details of the work done and the ways in which money was raised. Journals such as *The Builder* (from 1834) and the *Ecclesiologist* (1841-68) published long and detailed accounts of new churches and church restorations[5]

Mortgage deeds are another informative but often neglected diocesan source. In 1776 an Act of Parliament, known as the Clergy Residences Repair Act, enabled the clergy to raise money for the repair or rebuilding of their parsonage houses by mortgaging the income from their benefices, glebe, tithes and other emoluments, usually through Queen Anne's Bounty. It was this facility which enabled so many parsonage houses to be rebuilt in a substantial and elegant style during the late eighteenth and early nineteenth centuries, and the diocesan records will often contain the mortgage deed as well as surveys of the old parsonage house, architects' reports, correspondence, plans and designs, together with details of the work done and its cost.

Diocesan records relating to the licensing and consecration of new places of worship can also be of great interest, revealing otherwise unknown details, especially of temporary places of worship which preceded permanent churches in outlying parts of populous parishes. For example, in the diocese of Bristol, several temporary galvanised iron buildings were used for worship in various parts of the rapidly-expanding city before the money could be raised for permanent church buildings. The iron churches were made by Acramans, a local firm of ironfounders, who later specialised in the supply of complete galvanised iron churches to many colonial settlements, especially in Australia. The petitions to the bishop and the licences granted for such temporary churches, or for new permanent buildings, reveal much about the spiritual needs of populous districts and the Church's attempts to minister to such places. At New Holland (Lincs) where the coming of the railway led to a rapid growth in population, licence was granted in 1848 for the first-class waiting room of the station to be used for public worship, and later the National schoolroom was licensed for the same purpose. There are likely to be several other diocesan records which add to the picture of church life in a particular parish, among them churchwardens' presentments—although these are generally much less informative for the nineteenth century—the visitation reports of archdeacons, rural deans and diocesan architects, ecclesiastical court proceedings, terriers, lists of church furnishings and records of confirmations, as well as letters and papers relating to individual benefices or clergy.[6]

For those parishes which were 'peculiars' of a Dean and Chapter or of a particular cathedral prebend, similarly useful records may be found among the cathedral archives.

Also useful are early directories and the diocesan calendars or handbooks which, for most dioceses, were printed from the 1850s and give much detail about churches, schools, congregations and the clergy. From 1855 the clergy can be also traced through the pages of Crockford's *Clerical Directory* which provides potted biographies of all the clergy and details of all benefices.

National records

A major source for church history during the nineteenth century, and one which is too frequently ignored by local historians, is the great series of papers and reports or 'Blue Books' on contemporary affairs of all sorts produced for Parliament. Evidence collected by Parliamentary commissioners, Royal Commission reports and Parliamentary accounts and papers provide invaluable and detailed local evidence, as does the material on local churches and church attendance collected at the same time as the population census of 1851. Most of this material can only be found in large reference libraries, although microfiche copies are making the evidence increasingly available, and because of the amount of material, the manner in which the accounts and papers are arranged and cited, and the lack of detailed indexes to local evidence, they are not easy to use without some practice. But for most local historians the 'Blue Books' will amply repay the time spent on them; they will be found to contain useful material about even the smallest and most remote places and will give details of local life, society, economic affairs, population, religion and church life. There are several guides and lists to help the researcher, including P. and G. Ford, *a Guide to Parliamentary Papers,* 1859 edition; M. F. Bond, *The Records of Parliament: A Guide for Genealogists and Local Historians,* 1964; M. F. Bond, *Guide to the Records of Parliament,* 1971. The most useful starting-point for local historians is the Historical Association pamphlet by W. R. Powell, *Local History from Blue Books: A Select List of the Sessional Papers of the House of Commons,* 1962, which as well as explaining the arrangement and listing of the Parliamentary Papers also gives a list of libraries having complete holdings, although other libraries have since acquired microfiche copies. For the historian of churches and Church life the Parliamentary papers contain copious information about church buildings, nonconformist chapels, schools, almshouses, charities, the clergy, the treatment of the poor and many other subjects. Some papers were printed by command of the Crown, in which case they were given a 'Command Number' which is normally shown in square brackets, or they were printed by order of Parliament and were given a sessional number. Thus they are normally cited by

1 Title
2 Command number or Sessional number
3 Year of Session in round brackets
4 Volume number in the official bound set for that session.

Among the most valuable is the *Report of the Royal Commission on Ecclesiastical Revenue* [67] H.C. 1835 xxii which includes lists of churches and church accommodation, incumbents, curates, patrons, income, parsonage houses, etc. for each parish, and *Reports of the Royal Commission on the Church* H.C. 54 (1835) xxii; H.C. 86, 280, 387 (1836) xxxvi. Information on new or restored churches can be obtained from *Churches and Chapels consecrated within the last 10 years* H.C. 620 (1840) xxxix; and *Returns of Churches Built or Restored at a cost of over £500 since 1840* H.C. 125 (1876) lviii. Valuable statistics and comments on the provision of education in each parish can be obtained from the significantly-named *Reports of the Select Committee on the Education of the Lower Orders* H.C. 136, 356, 426, 427, 428 (1818) iv; and from *Report of the Select Committee on Education* H.C. 572 (1834) ix.

The usefulness of the information on schools is exemplified by the returns for 1818 and 1834 from the two Dorset parishes of Halstock and Ryme Intrinseca.

1818

Ryme Intrinseca
Population 135

'1 Sunday school for 24 children. The poor are without sufficient means of education.'

Halstock
Population 433

'A Sunday school established on Dr Bell's system composed of about 60 children, supported by subscription. The master's salary is £5 per annum. The poorer classes are provided with the means of education by the Sunday School and shew a disposition to avail themselves of it.'

1834

Ryme Intrinseca
Population 171

'One Daily school commenced 1828. 8 males and 4 females are educated at their parents expense.
One Sunday school supported by the Rector with private assistance, 8 males and 19 females.'

Halstock
Population 554

'One Day and Boarding School commenced 1833 — 18 males and 9 females are educated at their parents expense.
One Sunday school commenced 1820 — 60 children of both sexes, the master is paid from parochial rates.'

Other Parliamentary papers give details about school buildings, grants, endowments, the further development of educational provision and many other educational subjects. Equally informative are the Parliamentary papers on poor relief, charities, friendly societies, housing, industries, agriculture, the employment of women and children, and social and economic conditions generally.[7]

The Census of Religious Worship 1851

An indispensable source, which should on no account be overlooked, is the Census of Places of Religious Worship compiled in 1851 at the same time as the population census. Returns were sent in from almost all places of worship and all denominations, and the originals are at the Public Record Office (Class H.O. 129). The census provides details of the churches and chapels, endowments, accommodation, pew-renting, average attendances for the previous twelve months, and the number present at services on 30 March 1851; many also contain informative remarks by the minister responsible for making the return. There has been controversy at the time and since about the reliability of the returns and especially of the attendance figures, and debate about the national implications of the figures; a few of the clergy refused to make returns of attendance, and a number of others returned suspiciously round figures, while in many churches and especially in nonconformist chapels the number of people said to have attended either exactly coincided with or else exceeded the accommodation available. At Gayton le Wold, (Lincs), for example, the incredible number of 80 persons was said to have been present at a Wesleyan Methodist meeting held in 'the kitchen of a dwelling house, used for domestic purposes and licensed for a place of religious worship on the Sabbath'. At Somerton, Somerset, the Congregational minister excused himself from making any returns because his eyesight was so bad that he could not see beyond the first few seats. But whatever their shortcomings, for local historians the returns provide a unique glimpse of the religious observance of each community mid-way through the nineteenth century. The possibilities as well as the difficulties of using the material from this Census have been explored by R. A. Ambler, 'The 1851 Census of Religious Worship', *Local Historian* xi, 1975; and by R. A. Ambler, ed., 'Lincolnshire Returns of the Census of Religious Worship 1851', *Lincoln Record Society,* 72, 1979. It is well worth the trouble and expense of consulting these returns in the Public Record Office (Class H.O. 129), and some local libraries now have photocopies of their localities. A digest of the information collected by the census was published as a Parliamentary paper, *Census of 1851: Religious Worship, England and Wales, Report and Tables,* (1852-3) xxxix.

For the local historian the returns for each parish give a list of the churches of all denominations, their size and the accommodation they provided—both rented and free seats as well as standing room—and the attendances both of adults and of scholars from the Sunday school. In conjunction with the population figures for 1851 they show the number within each community actually attending a place of worship, and the proportion of the whole which could have been accommodated. They supply evidence of the strength of the various nonconformist churches and of Catholism, the divisions which led to secessions and the growth of separate nonconformist congregations, and the appearance of new groups such as the Mormons. The date of the erection of nonconformist churches is also given if it was after 1800, and we are told whether the building was used exclusively for public worship. The returns to the religious census also make it possible to see the contrast between 'closed' villages where most of the land was owned by one, two or, at most, three landowners who imposed their ideas of social orderliness and church attendance upon their tenants, and 'open' villages where there were many small proprietors and landless labourers with much less concern for church-going and where there likely to be far more nonconformist chapels.[8]

The comments made by incumbents and nonconformist ministers on the census forms are often illuminating. For example, in Lincolnshire several of the clergy observed that many people continud to attend both Anglican and Methodist services; others referred to the problems of very large parishes, inadequate churches, growing population in some centres, and other difficulties which they faced in carrying out their duties. The little church in the remote Dorset village of Alton Pancras was packed with 153 worshippers at morning service, 190 in the afternoon and 124 at an evening lecture, and the vicar commented, 'Well attended; many come from other places where Puseyism scatters the congregation'.

Above all the returns illustrate just how many places of worship of different denominations existed by 1851, even in quite small villages; they also reveal that, although attendances were often large, there was still a large proportion of people who did not attend any place of worship and remained untouched by any of the churches. For example, the large north Somerset parish of Chew Magna had a population of 2,124 in 1851, and those who wished to attend religious worship had a choice of seven different establishments—two Anglican churches, a Wesleyan Methodist chapel, a Wesleyan Reform chapel, a meeting house of the Society of Friends, a Baptist chapel and a 'preaching room' of the Brethren. All except the last had Sunday schools, and most were also active in charitable and benevolent works. It is not possible to tell from the figures given in the census how many people attended more than one service during the day, nor of course how many had been encouraged by the ministers to attend just because a census was to be taken, but the proportion of the inhabitants of Chew Magna who attended any place of worship on that day was certainly less than 40 per cent, and was probably a good deal less. Likewise, in the market town of Crewkerne in south Somerset, the population of 4,500 people had a choice of attending the large parish church or one of the four nonconformist chapels—Methodist, Unitarian, Bible Christian, or the recently-established Mormons. On the census Sunday some 1,300 people attended one or other of these places of worship, representing less than 30 per cent of the total inhabitants. In contrast, at Nettlecombe in the Brendon Hills of west Somerset, where the whole parish was dominated by the Trevelyan family, there were no nonconformist chapels and more than 60 per cent of the inhabitants attended the parish church on 30 March 1851, notwithstanding the fact that it was situated beside the manor house, inside the park, and was more than a mile even from the nearest houses of the parishoners. Another typical 'squire's village' was Belton near Grantham (Lincs) where almost all the land belonged to the lord of the manor, Earl Brownlow, whose large mansion and extensive park dominated the parish. The Earl was patron of the living, a relative was the rector, and there was no nonconformist chapel in the parish; most of the population of 182 were tenants or workers on the estate. On Sunday 30 March 1851, 135 of the parishioners, 74 per cent, attended the parish church.

Such places were the exception, and in general the results of the census came as a sad shock to many churchmen, for they revealed in cold statistics the extent to which the Church of England had lost the loyalty of working people, and how few attended any form of religious worship. The census showed that only about 21 per cent of the population attended an Anglican church, and that the proportion in many of the larger towns was pitifully small. Already the church was faced with the situation which Flora Thompson was later, during the 1880s, to describe in *Lark Rise to Candleford*:

> If Lark Rise people had been asked their religion, the answer of nine out of ten would have been 'Church of England', for practically all of them were christened, married and buried as such, although in adult life few went to church between the baptisms of their offspring?

Further shocks were in store for churchmen as attendances declined even more sharply during the second half of the century, especially in the big towns. Already in 1830 Lyall's *Principles of Geology* had cast doubt on the biblical account of the Creation, and Charles Darwin's *Origin of Species* in 1859, followed by *The Descent of Man* in 1871, led many to question the whole foundation of their beliefs. By *c*.1900 Charles Booth's survey of London showed that fewer than 20 per cent of the population attended any place of worship.

In conjunction with earlier diocesan visitation returns, the 1851 Census can be used to show the growth in nonconformity, and the gradual withdrawal of the Methodists from the Church of England. John Wesley himself had urged his followers to remain within the Church of England; in an episcopal visitation of the diocese of Exeter in 1779, for example, the clergy were uncertain as to whether Methodists should be described as dissenters or not, and many echoed the reply of the vicar of Treneglos: 'Dissenters none, unless they may be called dissenters who go by the name of Methodists'. Forty years later, an episcopal visitation of 1821 revealed the same uncertainty, as for example:

St Keyne: No dissenters, some Methodists.
Blisland: No dissenters, few Methodists who have a meeting house, but who generally come to church.
Manaccan: No dissenters or Methodists, except a few of the Wesleyan persuasion who regularly attend church and never absent themselves from the Holy Sacrament.

By 1851 the separation between the churches was still not complete in some places. At Elsham (Lincs) in 1851 the vicar commented that there were many dissenters 'who at times come to church'; and the record of Swaby noted that people attended both the parish church and the Wesleyan chapel. As late as 1881 the vicar of Stonesby (Leics) could write that 'In country villages they go to church and chapel also'.[10]

Parochial sources

For the nineteenth century a whole new range of documentary sources generated by parish churches, parochial clergy and church officers becomes available, giving the local historian a great deal of information about the part played by the Church in all aspects of parish life. In addition to the continuing series of churchwardens' accounts and vestry minutes which still include much basic data, registers of services survive for some parishes showing the increasing frequency of services, the more elaborate ritual, musical accompaniment, special services and preachers, and the much more regular celebration of Holy Communion. Parish magazines, almanacs or calendars were often started by energetic incumbents towards the end of the century, and can be extremely informative about local events of all kinds, secular as well as religious, although the survival of such ephemeral material is very much a matter of chance.[11] At Bowerchalke on the Wiltshire chalklands south-west of Salisbury, the incumbent from 1878 until his death in 1924 was Edward Collett, an energetic high churchman who revolutionised the religious life in his small parish of some 460 people. Every week from 1881 until a few weeks before his death he produced his own magazine, entitled the *Bowerchalke Parish Paper*, which he printed himself on his own hand press and sold for ¼d per copy. The whole life of the village is reflected in these pages: church services, festivals, local events, births and deaths, national occurences and local news.[12] Many other similar magazines were produced in parishes all over the country, and although copies have not always survived, where they have they are an incomparable source of local history.[13]

Records relating to Sunday schools, confirmation classes, youth activities, clubs and societies and church restoration, inventories of church furnishings and gifts of such things as crosses, candlesticks, candelabra, surplices, vestments, hangings for the altar or of stained glass windows, can also be found, although the survival of such material has also been very haphazard and much was destroyed during the various salvage campaigns of the Second World War. Occasionally diaries, journals, correspondence, reminiscences or notes made by incumbents and others have also survived to fill in details of the religious life of the parish and of the activities and attitudes of the church and clergy. For example, the Rev. R. S. Hawker, who became vicar of Morwenstow on the north Cornish coast in 1834, later (in 1865) recalled his early days in the parish, revealing much about the state of the Church and about his own attitudes:

> I found myself the first resident vicar [of Morwenstow] for more than a century....My people were a mixed multitude of smugglers, wreckers and dissenters of various hues. A few simple-hearted farmers had clung to the grey old sanctuary of the church and the tower that looked along the sea, but

the bulk of the people in the absence of a resident vicar had become the followers of the great preacher of the last century [John Wesley] who came down into Cornwall and persuaded the people to alter their sins.

Hawker's attitude to the Methodists was echoed by many of the Cornish clergy, at a time when Methodism was spreading rapidly, especially among the mining population, and when chapels with names such as Bethel, Zion, Salem, Ebenezer, Providence, Emanuel or Bethesda were being built in almost every hamlet, 'crowding our land with tabernacles of Christian assembly and our tongue with the idioms of Zion'.[14] Already by 1833 Henry Phillpotts, the newly-appointed Bishop of Exeter, could say in his Primary Visitation Charge to the Cornish clergy, 'In a few words— *We have lost the people*. The religion of the mass has become Wesleyan Methodism'. Not all clergy were hostile however; some had welcomed John Wesley and allowed him to preach from their pulpits, and, as was shown earlier in this chapter, many of the Methodists, especially in rural areas, for long continued to attend services at their parish churches.[15]

The Rev. George Rundle Prynne, who was to achieve fame as an energetic and highly-successful vicar of St Peter's, Plymouth, and who attracted much publicity for his introduction of ritual, vestments, statues and other innovations, including the founding of an order of Anglican nuns in his parish, recorded his boyhood visits to the church services at Fowey in Cornwall during the 1830s:

> I can remember the grand old church to which I was taken every Sunday, and the great square pew in which I was boxed up, and the seats all round from which the family circle looked at each other, or when they knelt, turned their backs on each other. The whole church was fitted with pews of a similar character. I remember the parson's desk, and the clerk's desk, and their alternate reading of the verses and the psalms in which very few of the congregation ever joined, for the clerk's responses, though in a monotone, were not musical or easy to join in. The altar was blocked out of sight altogether by the high square pews, but the Holy Communion was celebrated there once a month, I was told. There was a high gallery at the west end of the nave which was reached by a by a steep flight of stairs, and to this gallery, which had the Royal Arms in front of it, the clerk went to give out some verses of one of the metrical psalms composed by Messrs. Tate and Brady. Hymns of any kind were not considered orthodox or correct in those days. The aged vicar then went to the pulpit in a black gown and read a sermon, and so the service ended. it was certainly not a lively function..[16]

The dullness and predictability of the Established Church services, the long theological sermons and the inelasticity of the Church's organisation, all contributed to the rapid success of the nonconformist churches. The staid Prayer Book services, often hurried through by a curate, with the help of a self-important parish clerk, offered little to miners, fishermen, farm labourers, railway navvies or dockers when set against the fellowship, liveliness, hymn-singing and warmth of the chapel, where they could find an outlet for the emotions, food for the imagination and an opportunity to take part in the services and in the running of the chapel. The atmosphere of somnolence and tedious sermons also impressed the novelist and poet Thomas Hardy, who as a child attended the services at Stinsford church in Dorset:

> On afternoons of drowsy calm,
> We stood in the panelled pew,
> Singing one-voiced a Tate and Brady psalm,
> To the tune of Cambridge New.

An amosphere of a rather different sort was noted by the son of the curate of Writhlington (Somerset), who recalled that when he was a child in c.1860 their family pew was situated directly above the burial vault of the Goldfinch family, who were lords of the manor:

> ...in the vaults below were their coffins mouldering to decay. On the walls was an ominous green slime. The floor of our old pew had several holes, and a frowsy smell ascended to my sisters' and my noses, as we nearer the floor than our elders. If the day chanced to be very fine, a ray of light struck from the window through the said holes to the bulging coffins, and showed us their nauseous state...I place to the account of those dead Goldfinches a bad typhus fever from which we children suffered.

He also recalled the continuing trust in numerous supersitions and charms, even in his own family, and the fact that a rash which afflicted him and his sisters was dressed with oil from the church bells in the belief that this had healing properties![17]

Some clerical reminiscences reveal all too clearly the difficulties which the clergy faced in the growing strength of Dissent, the indifference of many of their parishioners, the problems of making any improvements in the wretched economic and social conditions to be found in many towns and villages, and the isolation of their calling, especially in remote rural parishes. Edward White Benson, who became the first Bishop of the newly-created diocese of Truro in 1877 and was later to become Archbishop of Canterbury, encountered many isolated, lonely and frustrated clergy in the large and remote parishes of his Cornish diocese. The Bishop's son, A.C. Benson, accompanied his father on tours of the diocese, and recalled one parish where:

> the vicar told us a pitiable tale of isolations and privations...his congregation had dwindled...and his loneliness was such that he rented a pew on Sunday evenings in the Wesleyan chapel...as very few people in the parish would speak to him.
> At another parish the vicar...took us into his poor home; on the walls of his study were medical diplomas gained by himself; he had been, he told us, a practising physician but, fired by a missionary enthusiasm, had taken Orders and offered himself to Bishop Phillpotts who had sent him to his present living nearly thirty years before 'to fight with beasts' as he sternly said. His congregation had steadily dwindled ever since; he was old and broken, ill of a mortal disease. In the study stood a huge heap of unbound books, his only literary labour, the Second Book of Kings (I think) versified into rhyming heroic couplets. He had paid for the printing but as no copies had been sold, and he had not the heart to have it destroyed, he had caused it to be returned

to him, and it had been there ever since; he presented my Father and myself
with as clean a copy as he could find![18]

Several clerical diaries of the nineteenth century have appeared in print,
such as those of Francis Kilvert, John Skinner, William Jones, James
Woodforde and others. Such diaries, together with the many other
unpublished reminiscences and recollections of this sort, are an invaluable
source of local history, and bring alive the background, circumstances and
atmosphere of church life, the services, the clergy and the role of the church
in the community in a way few earlier sources can match.

A good account of the central part played by the Church in a small rural
community during the nineteenth century is contained in O. Chadwick,
Victorian Miniature.[19] Using unpublished diaries and letters, this traces the
often acrimonious relationship between the parson and the squire in the
Norfolk village of Ketteringham near Norwich. It gives a fascinating
insight into the workings of the social order in an English village, and is a
model of the way in which good local history can illuminate important
aspects of social and ecclesiastical history.

A very different, but equally instructive, example of the way in which
information from numerous sources can be combined to tell the story of a
parish during the ninteenth century is to be found in M. Spurrell, 'Stow
Church Restored 1846-1866', *Lincoln Record Society*, 75, 1984. This is a
collection of documents including churchwardens' accounts, vestry
minutes, local newspaper reports and the correspondence of the incumbent,
the bishop, archdeacon, local gentry and the Ecclesiastical Commissioners,
which tells the story of the restoration of the important Saxon church of St
Mary at Stow in Lincolnshire. It vividly illustrates the effect upon the parish
of the arrival of a young, energetic clergyman, George Atkinson; he was
the first resident incumbent for more than sixty years, and when he came to
Stow in 1836 found that Church life was at a low ebb, the church building
was falling into ruin and that 'dissent and indifference to religion
extensively prevailed'. His efforts to remedy this situation, while extremely
successful, were not always popular, and in particular, the wealthy farmers
of the parish went to great lengths to frustrate his plans for an extensive and
costly restoration of the Saxon parish church. This collection is another
model for local historians of the way in which the surviving documentary
sources can be used, to bring alive the problems faced by the Church of
England and by an enthusiastic incumbent in a country parish during the
nineteenth century.

Occasionally, contemporary descriptions of church services may also be
found. Newspapers devoted much space to Church affairs, and Joseph
Leech, the editor of a Bristol newspaper, published a long series of articles
during the 1840s on church services in the district under the pseudonym
'Church-Goer'. He described the liturgy, the music, the musical
instruments, singing and sermons in great detail and often very critically. As
a stranger in each parish, he often found it difficult to get a seat because so
many pews were rented:

...every pew is like a preserve; you must not put your hand on the first door you meet.

At Yatton, he was obliged to sit with the poor on a bench at the back; it was so unusual to see a well-dressed man occupying such a position that

> even the school children who, headed by the master carrying a music book in his hand, entered in a long file...and came pat, pat, clatter, clatter in their wooden shoes up the aisles,...looked over their snub noses at me as if I had two heads?[20]

Another aspect of the new attitude to their calling among the clergy, which can be discerned through the parochial sources in many parishes, is the part they played in protesting against abuses in employment, housing or social conditions, and in promoting schemes of emigration, and the example they set as reformers and champions of the poor in their parishes. This new attitude marks a great change from that of most eighteenth-century clergy, who thought it one of their principal duties to instil into the laity that calm acceptance of the established social order which is imposed by the Catechism:

> To order myself lowly and reverently to all my betters...to do my duty in that state of life, unto which it shall please God to call me.

David Davies, who was rector of Barkham (Berks) from 1782 until his death in 1819, worked assiduously to improve the wretched conditions of the farm labourers in his parish, and his book *The Case of Labourers in Husbandry*, published in 1795, is a sympathetic plea for better wages and conditions during a time of desparate need and soaring corn prices. Davies stressed the disastrous social consequences of enclosures and of the 'improved' farming methods, and described from first-hand experience the plight of the great number of landless labourers:

> ...an amazing number of people have been reduced from a comfortable state of partial independence to the precarious condition of mere hirelings, who when out of work immediately come on the parish?[21]

The social concerns of the clergy are also exemplified by notable clerical reformers such as Charles Kingsley, by prominent lay churchmen like Lord Shaftesbury, or by F.D. Maurice and the Christian Socialists. At a humbler level many parish clergy were active in promoting the physical well-being of their parishioners. For example, in the West Country Canon Girdlestone, rector of Halberton, (Devon) fought strongly for higher wages for the farm labourers of his parish, arranged better-paid jobs in other counties for many of them and encouraged several hundred labourers from North Devon to emigrate. William Barnes, the Dorset poet, did much to provide education for the poor and lectured tirelessly over a wide area, using the new railways; he also campaigned for temperance and better housing, higher wages and the encouragement of greater self-respect amongst the labourers and their families. Lord Sidney Godolphin Osborne, rector of Durweston near Blandford Forum 1841-75, became famous for his letters to the *Times* signed S.G.O., in which he pleaded for better conditions for the poor. At Langley Burrell (Wilts), Francis Kilvert was curate from 1872 to 1876; he conducted two services with a sermon each Sunday, ran a Sunday school, had services on weekdays and festivals, visited the sick, taught in the village school every day, gave evening lectures every week, and was completely involved in the life of his small parish. Kilvert's busy routine and total involvement in community life could have been matched by hundreds of fellow clergymen, but would have amazed his eighteenth-century predecessors. All over the country there were countless other concerned and caring clergymen actively trying to promote the social and economic welfare of their parishioners as well as caring for their spiritual needs. Such men are in sharp contrast with the notoriously harsh clerical magistrates of the previous century.[22]

The Victorian restoration of English parish churches has become notorious for its well-intentioned but over-zealous concern to sweep away what were regarded as the inappropriate accretions of past centuries and to make the churches worthy of the new standards of worship and pastoral care. In their enthusiasm and piety Victorian restorers saw in the form and design of medieval churches a symbolism which would have astonished the medieval masons who were concerned only to meet the practical needs of contemporary clergy and congregations. The unfortunate result was the wholesale destruction of ancient pews, screens and galleries, the ruthless scraping of stonework, and the insertion of new and highly-coloured glass and tiles, with new pine furniture from approved ecclesiastical suppliers.

Nineteenth-century churchwardens' accounts and other parochial papers frequently go into great detail about the extent of work done on the churches and about the active church life, fund-raising and social concerns which lay behind all the building work. For example, the parish records of St John's, Devizes (Wilts) from 1830 include an account of the installation of gas lighting 'in the most durable and scientific manner', the purchase of elaborate heating apparatus which must have made church attendance a much more comfortable experience during the winter, and details of the thorough church restoration, of architects' reports and the raising of a loan on the security of Devizes Corporation. The chancel was restored in 1844, and in 1862-3 the nave, which had been leaning dangerously, was rebuilt and extended by one bay on the advice of Sir Gilbert Scott. In addition the Devizes parish records contain faculties for alterations to both church and churchyard and the construction of a vestry, details of the local controversy over church rates and the objections of the dissenters, seating plans, expenses for the organ and the organist's salary, contributions to the fund for additional curates, and an account of the weekly offertory collections. There are also details of charities, church day- and Sunday-schools, active social work in the parish, and special collections for a host of causes, among them the victims of the Irish famine during 1845-7 and of fires in Quebec and Newfoundland, and the hanging of the church with black on the death of Prince Albert in 1861.[23]

Great attention was also paid to improving the appearance of churchyards and removing unseemly buildings. At St James's, Trowbridge (Wilts), where £7,000 was spent on the restoration of the church, a sexton's house, fire-engine house and Free School were all removed from the churchyard, and a row of cottages which adjoined it was demolished. Increases in population and the fact that the same plots were no longer constantly re-used for burials, led to the necessity in many parishes of enlarging the churchyards or of creating new cemeteries at some distance from the church?[24]

We may regret the over-thorough Victorian restorations or the complete rebuilding of so many medieval churches, but we cannot doubt the energy and zeal which carried them through or the generosity with which money was given to such projects; as well as the episcopal records of faculties and consecrations, the files of local newspapers often yield abundant evidence of the restoration and rebuilding of churches, and of money-raising activities, the names of benefactors and architects, and details of the consecration of the new or restored building. Drawings, paintings and early photographs can also provide much information about earlier or pre-restoration churches and churchyards. Alongside the drastic alterations in the appearance of English churches came great changes in the conduct of public worship, as ritual, vestments and other accessories which had not been seen since the Reformation were brought back into use. Again, parochial sources may give information about the purchase or gifts of chasubles, albs or copes, and the introduction of a surpliced choir, crosses, candlesticks, lecterns, altar frontals, or even of incense and the Reserved Sacrament.

A century later, it is very difficult to comprehend the depth of feeling engendered by the introduction of services, ritual, vestments, lighted candles, crosses, ornaments and ceremonial, which were thought by many to be papist and which many feared would lead to a reconciliation with the Catholic Church. Although such embellishments have since become common, fervent feelings of anti-popery, nourished over three centuries, did not die easily, and preaching in a surplice, or having a cross and candles on an altar, were enough to start riots in various parts of the country during the 1840s and 1850s, as well as numerous suits in the ecclesiastical courts against what were regarded as illegal ornaments, liturgy, or ritualism?[25] To take just one example, Brighton (Sussex) became a leading centre of High Church or 'Anglo-Catholic' activity; church life was revitalised, mission churches built, an active programme of social concern was instituted, and the churches became a crucial factor in local community life. But these impressive developments were accompanied by many innovations in worship, ritual, vestments, music, sung services, ornaments and ceremonies which attempted to restore the sumptuous trappings of the pre-Reformation liturgy. The result at Brighton, as in many other places, was ferocious riots, protests and protracted legal action, which divided the clergy and laity alike and gravely weakened the impact of the Church. The Brighton controversy and riots were at their height during the decade 1865-75, but as late as 1900 a leading protester felt strongly enough to stand for Parliament as a Protestant and anti-ritualist candidate, and to continue court action against various church ornaments and furnishings?[26]

What the local historian should attempt is to gauge the feeling and reaction in the parish to such changes. Strong feelings there undoubtedly were, but only an intimate knowledge of the local sources will reveal the reactions of ordinary conservative parishioners to the changes in services, decoration and furnishing in their churches. The introduction of a surpliced choir and the replacement of the village musicians and their violins, viols, serpents, bassoons and flutes by a barrel-organ, harmonium or organ must have caused much argument in rural parishes and is well worth exploration. Likewise, the replacement of the Tate and Brady metrical psalms announced by the parish clerk with communal singing from *Hymns Ancient and Modern*, which was first published in 1861, must have aroused much comment and reaction amongst the parishioners. At Langley Burrell (Wilts), where Francis Kilvert dismissed the village musicians and installed an harmonium, he recorded in his diary:

> 29 October 1874
> This morning was an epoch in the history of Langley Church, and the first sound of an instrument within the old walls, an event and sensation not soon to be forgotten?[27]

At Purton (Wiltshire) an organ was acquired in 1851 and the west gallery musicians with their flutes and viols immediately left the church; this sort of replacement of the village band and choir in the gallery by an organ and a surpliced choir situated in the chancel occurred all over the country. Like so many other changes, it must have had a profound impact on those involved, but only local historians with an intimate knowledge of parochial sources can reveal the full details. The services of the Church of England may have gained something in decorum and perhaps also in musical quality, but they lost immeasurably in colour and liveliness as well as in popular appeal when the vitality of the village band was replaced by the dull uniformity of organ music?[28]

The Victorian sense of propriety also tended to discourage many traditional events which had always been associated with parish churches. These included wakes and feasts on patronal festivals, club walks and friendly society processions, revels, rushbearing, bell-ringing contests, and ancient customs associated with Boxing Day, Plough Monday, May Day and Whitsun, as well as ceremonies with their roots in a long-forgotten, pre-Christian past such as 'clipping the church' or dancing around it on Shrove Tuesday. Such events had often been an excuse for excessive drinking and unseemly behaviour and many of the clergy attempted to substitute organised games or the sedate pleasures of garden fêtes and tea parties. Sadly, the result in many parishes was finally to sever the ancient link between the parish church and the secular activities, recreations and traditional observances of the parish community.

It is not the intention of this book to pursue the story of the Church's role in society into the twentieth century, or to chart the continuing decline in church attendances. Nor is this the place to discuss the immensely important question that now confronts both Church and society: how to care for the large number of church buildings which are no longer required for worship or where the congregations are inadequate to maintain the fabric. But in spite of the manifold contemporary problems of the Church, there are heartening signs that in many places, parish churches are beginning once more to play a significant role in the social, as well as in the religious, life of the communities which they serve. During the nineteenth century and for long afterwards, secular use of parish churches was unusual and it was seldom considered proper to use the buildings for anything other than religious worship. The contemporary efforts to find new and additional functions for parish churches as social and recreational centres, and to use them for parish meetings, concerts, plays and assemblies of all sorts, as well as for services, are hopeful signs that a continuing and worthwhile secular as well as religious function can once again be found for English parish churches.

Those who raised the money and organised the building of the great heritage of English medieval parish churches would have seen little incongruity in using them as venues for concerts, plays, conferences and exhibitions as well as in their essential rôle as places of worship. But above all, they would have emphasised that the buildings must be used to the greater glory of God, and must serve as visible, daily reminders of Man's relationship to the Almighty. The constant, recurring ideal of church builders throughout the centuries is admirably summed up in the words of those who planned and built, on a lavish scale, the extravagant and expensive Gothic chapel for Lancing College in 1854:

> It will lead men to ask what can have been the inducements which have called forth so large a sacrifice of money and of labour, for which there can be no adequate worldly return, and in that inquiry find the true solution.

APPENDIX

Some Examples of Documentary Sources

1. *Extract from the contract for the building of a tower at Arlingham church (Glos), 1372*

[Note that the money had been raised by the parishioners who also agree to provide all the materials, that the whole project was organised and supervised by the churchwardens, and that considerable discretion was left to the mason to build 'in a good and workmanlike manner'. The original is in Latin.]

Contract made between John de Yate, Sir Roger the vicar, William de Erlyngham, Robert de Middleton...and all the parishioners of Arlingham, on the one part, and Nicholas Wyshonger, mason of Gloucester, on the other part.

The said Nicholas Wyshonger agrees to build, construct and finish the bell tower of the church of Arlingham in the same manner as it has been started within three years, with 4 buttresses competently built, as they have been started.

He is to construct and make corbels inside the walls to carry the floors of the said tower; and set a door on the east side of the tower so that a man can get on to the roof of the church. He is to build a handsome window (*una fenestra artificialer constructa*) on the west side of the tower between the first and second stage; and four small windows, one at each side of the top stage.

At the top of the tower there shall be battlements well and handsomely built, with gutters all around the top of the said tower. He shall also make a spiral stairway reaching to the top stage whereby a man may easily ascend and descend, with doors at the top and bottom, and windows and all other things necessary. And the said Nicholas shall build and perfect the same in a good and workmanlike manner. And for each foot of height so built the parish shall pay him at the rate of 17 shillings and a bushell of wheat, to be paid in four instalments in each of the three years.

The parishioners shall provide all materials, stone, sand, lime, and other materials necessary to the said work, except tools, and shall bring them to a suitable place within 40 feet of the said tower.

The said Nicholas shall bear the cost of the workmen's wages, but the parishioners shall provide board and lodging for him and his men.

(L.P. Salzman, *Building in England*, 1952; 2nd edn.1967, OUP)

2. Extracts from the Register of Robert Hallum, bishop of Salisbury 1407-17

11 July 1409   Licence to William Fynamor and Agnes his wife to have divine service celebrated in the oratory of their house at Whetham in the parish of Calne. They are to attend the parish church at the great festivals.

1 April 1410   Commission to the sub-dean of Salisbury cathedral to order the proper observance of Sundays and feast days. People are engaging in business, shops are open for trade, the tavern is frequented rather than the church, feasts and drunkeness abound rather than tears and prayers.

8 May 1410   Commission to the Dean of Salisbury to denounce as excommunicate Richard Wade of Heytesbury for having falsely accused John Dunning, rector or Chittern of adultery with Joan Wade wife of the said Richard Wade.

30 Oct. 1411   Commission to the archdeacon of Wiltshire to denounce as excommunicate the persons who broke into the church of Grittleton and killed a certain Robert who had fled there for sanctuary. Penance later imposed on the persons responsible—to come to the west door of Salisbury cathedral wearing only linen shirts and to enter the cathedral, each bearing a candle, and in the presence of the Dean and congregation, to prostrate themselves before the altar.

2 May 1412   Proceedings against Thomas Punche of Reading on charges of Lollardy.

9 Aug. 1412   Suspension of prebendal church of Charminster for not ringing their bells when the bishop came to their church to confirm children.

16 June 1415   Licence to the inhabitants of Corsley to have a churchyard consecrated and to bury their dead at Corsley, because of the distance to Warminster and the difficulty of carrying bodies there, especially in the winter.

undated   Complaint from John Rygges, rector of Holy Trinity, Dorchester, that no chaplain is willing to serve in the dependent church of St Peter, preferring instead to celebrate anniversary masses.

28 June 1410   Enquiry into the dilapidations which Richard Betty B.C.L. alleges were left in the chancel of the church at Stallbridge by his predecessor, Benet Nycol, in repairs, books, ornaments and buildings of both church and rectory. Repairs will cost £58 14s 4d.

3. *Inventory of the goods and ornaments of the parish church of St Mary at Bridgwater 1447*

[Compiled by the Vicar, William atte Well, and the churchwardens John Martyn and William Snothe. Note the large number of valuable objects and the contrast this presents with the few belongings of post-Reformation parish churches, as shown for example at North Nibley in 1639, see 5 below.]

In primis, 1 Crosse with ii images of Mary & John, of sylvere and gylte.

1	Fote and staffe to the same crosse of coper and gylte.
ii	sensurys of sylver and gylte
	crewetes of sylvere
ii	Candelstyckes of sylver
i	ship of sylver
ii	crosses of laton & gylte
iv	corporas
i	Relique of St Stephey closid in sylvere
ii	Coupis of sylvere for the sacrament
ii	candelstycks of laton
i	holywaterbokett with i spryngell of laton
iii	massebokys
ii	grayles
ii	processionaries
i	colitare
i	mortylage (i.e. list of benefactors)
i	Antiphoner
i	portuas
i	antiphoner for the deacon
i	manuell
i	ordinall
	Suits of blue, green, white and gilt vestments
i	olde pall of sylke
i	veyl for lent
	Alle the apparell for the hye altar with lipardes of golde
ii	cloths to hang before the hye altar with the xii apostles
v	altar frontals
i	selpulchre cover
xvi	pillows of sylke
x	altar cloths
xviii	towelles

iii   altar cloths dysteyned of the Assumptcion of oure Lady
i   steyned cloth to hang afore the rode lofte.

(Somerset Record Society, 48, 1933)

4. *Extracts from the Churchwardens' Accounts of St Ewen's, Bristol 1548*

[Note how these payments during the first year of Edward VI's reign show the ancient ceremonies continuing while at the same time the altars screens and images are being destroyed and the wall-paintings obliterated with whitewash.]

For reading the Passion	id
For watching the Sepulchre (i.e. the Easter Sepulchre)	viiid
For frankinsence	iiid
For mending the holly-water spryngell and new herynge (hairing) the other	iid
(Payments for the refreshment of those who took part in the procession on Corpus Christi day)	
Paid the workmen for takeing downe the tabernacles with the Images	xd
Paid to a mason for dressinge upp the walls by the hye Altar	is vid
For Whit-lyminge the Chancell	is viiid
For the Injunctions and homylies	is viiid
Paid to the Somner at the King's visitation	iiiid
Paid for a byble	xiiiis iiiid
Paid for bearing the banners in Rogation weeke	iiiid
Paid for takeinge downe the Roode and the reste of the Images	is iiiid
Paid the Somner for bringing the holy oil	iiiid
Paid for taking downe the Easter sepulchre	iiiid
(Paid for ale, cheese, butter, bread and cakes for a parish feast in the Church House	14s 2d)

(J.H. Bettey, *Bristol Parish Churches during the Reformation, Bristol Historical Association*, 1979).

5. *Examples of Churchwardens' Expenses from North Nibley, Glos, 1639*

[Note the increasing number of secular payments. The churchwardens' income came from a rate on householders, Easter offerings and from rent for the Church House which was no longer used for church ales.]

For maimed soldiers	£1 1s 0d
For goal money	6s 0d
Expenses at the Visitation	£1 2s 0d
Bread and Wine for Easter, Whitsun, Michaelmas and Christmas	£1 4s 5d
Paid for bell ropes	5s 4d

Given to two poor men	4d
Given to a poor man that cam out of Irland	2d
Paid for work on the church and churchyard	14s 6d
Paid for mending the clapper of the bell	4d
Given to five poor people that cam with a passe	6d
Paid to Robert Cooper for keeping of the Clock and ringing the bell evenings and mornings	13s 4d

6. *Inventory of Church Goods from North Nibley, 1639*

The greate bible of the new translation
The book of common prayer
The book of homilies
A parchment register book
A silver communion cup and cover
A great Pewter flaggon
Erasmus paraphrases
The workes of Bishop Jewell
A parchment roll for the church rate
A parchment roll for the payment of the poore
A surplesse
The book of cannons
A carputt for the communion table
A table of consanguinitie
Fourteen bonds to save the parish harmless from Incommers
Twentie seaven indentures for apprentices
A green cushion for the pulpett
A greene pulpitt cloth

(Gloucestershire Record Office P230/CW2/1)

7. *Notes on parishes in his diocese made in 1735 by Thomas Secker, bishop of Bristol*

Wyke Regis

200 Presbyterians, 8 Quakers, 4 Anabaptists. Church in very bad repair, dangerous going to it, timber both in tower and church rotten. They are now mending the South aisle, but being chiefly Dissenters do the work unwillingly... seats infested and rotted with droppings...

Hampreston

Large parish, 12 or 14 families papists, most of them poor, no gentlemen amongst them. Rector, William Forster, hath been a bad man, resides in the town (Poole), parsonage house burnt down 30 years ago. Collections made to enable him to rebuild it and wood given him, some of which he sold.

Milborne St Andrew	Vicar John Sanger, drank too much formerly, is now mad.
Wareham	200 or 300 Presbyterians with a licensed meeting house. The former Rector was a Lunatick and this occasioned the increase in Presbyterians.
Burstock	Incumbent Thomas Pope, good, sensible, Tory. Resident in this small parish. Divine service every Sunday, children catechised ever afternoon service. Sacrament four times a year.
Worth Matravers	Incumbent, Samuel Marsh, wicked, mad, now on board a man of war. His wife and 4 children receive the income. Mr Pope of Corfe Castle serves the parish for 5s 0d a week to their satisfaction.
Wimborne	Incumbent, Thomas Hooper, very good, much esteemed, whig, resident. Good house and fine gardens.
Fontmell Magna	Incumbent Dr Thomas Dibben disordered in his head, resident. No curate. Mr Dibben also rector of Fifehead Neville.
Lyme Regis	Incumbent Mr Syms, good. His predecessor Mr Hallet had been minister there for 60 years, seldom used the surplice or conformed in any respect strictly to the rules of the Church. This did not lessen the number of Dissenters, and now ten out of 16 and the generality of the Town are such.
Fifhead Magdalen	Vicar Narcissus Whitaker, tory, good, resident. Also vicar of Bradford Abbas.
Moor Critchell	Incumbent James Webb, good, never declares himself in party matters.
Tarrant Gunville	Incumbent Daniel King, good, rich, votes with the Whigs, resident.
Blandford Forum	Incumbent Thomas Riley, weak, Tory, resident, old. The church burnt with the town in 1731.
Chettle	Incumbent Charles Dobson, resident, very drunken and wicked, hath been in jayl.

(Bristol Record Office EP/A/2/2)

REFERENCES

Chapter 1   pages 11—24

1 Charles Thomas, *Christianity in Roman Britain to AD 500*, Batsford, 1981; M.W. Barley and R.P.C. Hanson, *Christianity in Britain 300-700*, Leicester, 1968

2 J. Godfrey, *The Church in Anglo-Saxon England*, Cambridge, 1962, 34-67.

3 C. Thomas, op.cit., 240-274; R. Morris, *The Church in British Archaeology*, Council for British Archaeology Research Report, 47, 1983; W. Rodwell, *The Archaeology of the English Church*, Batsford, 1981.

4 T. Taylor, *The Life of St Samson of Dol*, 1925.

5 M.D. Anderson, *History and Imagery in British Churches*, J. Murray, 1971.

6 P. Hunter Blair, *Anglo-Saxon England*, Cambridge, 1977, 123; D. Whitelock, *English Historical Documents 500-1042*, Eyre Methuen, 1955, 75, 363, 722.

7 D. Whitelock, op.cit., 155, 643.

8 ibid., 654-5.

9 G.W.O. Addleshaw, *The Beginnings of the Parochial System*, St Anthony's Hall Publications, 1954.

10 C.A. Ralegh Radford, 'Pre-Conquest Minster Churches', *Archaeological Journal*, 130, 1973, 120-40.

11 J. Godfrey, op.cit., 315.

12 D. Whitelock, op.cit., 395, 412; F. Barlow, *The English Church*, Longman, 1963, 183-5.

13 W. Rodwell, op.cit.; P.V. Addyman and R.K. Morris, eds., *The Archaeological Study of Churches*, Council for British Archaeology, 1976.

14 B.R. Kemp, 'The Mother Church of Thatcham', *Berkshire Archaeological Journal*, 63, 1976-8, 15-22.

15 *Victoria County History*, Somerset, IV, 1978, 28-9; R.W. Dunning, 'The Minster at Crewkerne', *Somerset Archaeological Society Proceedings*, 120, 1976, 63-8.

16 M. Aston, *Interpreting the Landscape*, Batsford, 1985, 49.

17 R. Morris, *The Church in British Archaeology*, 1983, 75; B.R. Kemp, 'The Monastic Dean of Leominster', *English Historical Review*, 83, 1968, 510; B.R. Kemp, 'The Churches of Berkeley Hernesse', *Transactions of Bristol and Gloucestershire Archaeological Society*, 87, 1968, 96-110; P.H. Sawyer, ed., *Medieval Settlement*, Edward Arnold, 1979.

18 Dorothy Owen, 'Chapelries and rural settlement', in P.H. Sawyer, ed., *Medieval Settlement*, 1979, 67.

19 D.J. Bonney, 'Early boundaries and estates in Southern England', in P.H. Sawyer, ed., *Medieval Settlement*, 1976, 72-82.

20 M. Deansley, 'Early English and Gallic Minsters', *Transactions of the Royal Historical Society*, Ser. 4, 3, 1941, 25-69; C. Platt, *The Parish Churches of Medieval England*, Secker and Warburg, 1981, 1-5.

21 C. Ralegh Radford, 'Pre-Conquest Minster Churches', *Archaeological Journal*, 130, 1973, 120-40.

22 D. Whitelock, op.cit., 695.

23 H.M. & J. Taylor *Anglo-Saxon Architecture,* C.U.P., vols 1 and 2, 1965; H.M. Taylor, *Anglo-Saxon Architecture,* C.U.P., 3, 1978.

24 W. Rodwell, *The Archaeology of the English Church,* Batsford, 1981; P.V. Addyman and R.K. Morris, eds., *The Archaeological Study of Churches,* Council for British Archaeology, 1976.

25 C.H. Talbot, *The Anglo-Saxon Missionaries in Germany,* Sheed & Ward, 1954, 153-77.

26 Adrian Oswald, *The Church of St Bertelin at Stafford,* City of Birmingham Museum, 1966.

27 C. Platt, op.cit., 17-20.

28 J. Campbell, 'The Church in Anglo-Saxon Towns', in D. Baker, ed., *The Church in Town and Countryside, Studies in Church History,* 16, 1979, 119-35.

29 D. Whitelock, op.cit., 601-2.

30 R. Morris, *The Church in British Archaeology,* 1983; M. Gelling, *Signposts to the Past,* Dent, 1978.

31 A. Ross, *Pagan Celtic Britain,* Routledge and Kegan Paul, 1971.

32 M. Deansley, *The Pre-Conquest Church in England,* 1962, 276-327; D. Parsons, ed., *Tenth-Century Studies,* Phillimore, 1975.

33 H.M. Taylor, op.cit., 3, 766-72; W. Rodwell, op.cit.,

34 F. Arnold-Forster, *Studies in Church Dedications,* 3 vols., 1899; F. Bond, *Dedications and Patron Saints of the English Churches,* O.U.P., 1914.

35 H. Benson, 'Church Orientations and Patronal Festivals', Antiquaries *Journal,* 36, 1956, 205-13.

36 H.C. Darby, *Domesday England,* CUP, 1977.

37 *Victoria County History,* Wiltshire, II, 1955, 23-34.

38 R. Lennard, *Rural England 1086-1135,* OUP, 1959, 292-4.

Chapter 2   pages 25—41

1 E. Mason, 'The Rôle of the English Parishioner 1100-1500', *Journal of Ecclesiastical History,* 27, 1976, 17-18.

2 W.E. Lunt, ed., *The Valuation of Norwich,* 1926; S. Ayscough and J. Caley, eds., *Taxatio Ecclesiastica Angliae et Walliae auctoritate Papae Nicholia 1V, 1291,* Record Commission, 1802,; G. Vanderzee, ed., *Nonarum Inquisitiones in Curia Scaccarii,* Record Commission, 1807.

3 P.J. Drury and W.J. Rodwell, 'Investigations at Asheldham, Essex', *Antiquaries Journal,* 58, 1978, 133-51; A. Hamilton Thompson, *The Ground Plan of the English Parish Church,* 1911; W. Rodwell, *The Archaeology of the English Church,* Batsford, 1981.

4 M. Brett, *The English Church under Henry I,* 1975, 138-40.

5 J. Godber, *The History of Bedfordshire 1066-1888,* Bedfordshire C.C., 1969, 6, 39.

6 B.R. Kemp, 'The Monastic Dean of Leominster', *English Historical Review,* 83, 1968, 510.

7 R. Lennard, *Rural England 1086-1135,* OUP, 1959, 396-404.

8 C.N.L. Brooke, 'The Missionary at Home: The Church in the Towns 1000-1250', in G.J. Cummings, ed., *Studies in Church History,* 6, 1970, 53-83.

9 D.M. Owen, *Church and Society in Medieval Lincolnshire,* 1971, 5.

10 T. Rowley, *The Shropshire Landscape,* Hodder & Stoughton, 1972, 49, 81.

11 C. Taylor, *Village and Farmstead,* George Philip, 1983, 114-5, 206.

12 P. Wade-Martins, 'The Origin of Rural Settlement in East Anglia', in P. Fowler, ed., *Recent Work in Rural Archaeology,* 1975, 128, 140-8.

13 M. Aston and J. Bond, *The Landscape of Towns,* 1976, 76.

14 R.A.R. Hartridge, *A History of Vicarages in the Middle Ages,* 1930; G.W.O. Addleshaw, *Rectors, Vicars and Patrons,* 1956.

15 A. Watkin, ed., The Great Chartulary of Glastonbury, *Somerset Record Society,* 59, 1947, 63, 1952, 64, 1956.

16 B. Schofield, ed., The Rolls and Register of Bishop Oliver Sutton 1280-99, *Lincoln Record Society,* 39, 1948, 54.

18 Calendar of the Manuscripts of the Dean and Chapter of Wells, *Historical Manuscripts Commission,* 1907, I, 355-8.

19 ibid.

20 M.D. Anderson, *History and Imagery in British Churches,* 1971; A. Caiger-Smith, *English Medieval Mural Paintings,* 1963.

21 C. Phythian-Adams, *Local History and Folklore,* Bedford Square Press, 1975; K. Basford, *The Green Man,* 1978; J. Andersen, *The Witch on the Wall,* 1977; J.H. Bettey and C.W.G. Taylor, *Sacred and Satiric: Medieval Stone-Carving in the West Country,* Redcliffe Press, 1982; A. Weir and J. Jerman, *Images of Lust: Sexual Carvings on Medieval Churches,* Batsford, 1986.

22 F. Arnold-Forster, *Studies in Church Dedications,* 3 vols., 1899; F. Bond, *Dedications and Patron Saints of English Churches,* 1914.

23 T. Rowley, *The Shropshire Landscape,* Hodder & Stoughton, 1972, 48, 77.

24 A. Hamilton Thompson, *The English Clergy and their Organisation in the Later Middle Ages,* 1947.

25 *Historical Manuscripts Commission Report,* 1907, 545-6.

26 W. Sparrow Simpson, Visitations of Churches belonging to St Paul's Cathedral, *Camden Society Miscellany,* 9, 1895, and *Camden Society,* N.S., 55, 1895.

27 W.H.R. Jones, Register of St Osmund, *Rolls Series,* 78,1883-4, I, 275-314.

28 M. Brett, *The English Church under Henry I,* 1975, 220-1.

29 D.M. Owen, *Church and Society in Medieval Lincolnshire,* 1971, 136-7.

30 *Victoria County History,* Wiltshire III, 1956, 23, citing the Register of Richard Metford, Bishop of Salisbury 1395-1407.

31 R.R. Darlington, ed., Vita Wulfstani, *Camden Society,* 40, 1928, 6, 47, 94.

32 M. Bell, ed., Wulfric of Haselbury, *Somerset Record Society,* 47, 1933.

33 ibid.

34 R. Lennard, *Rural England 1086-1135,* 1959, 336.

35 R. Graham, *St Gilbert of Sempringham and the Gilbertines,* 1901.

36 W.A. Pantin, *The English Church in the Fourteenth Century,* 1962, 195-202.

37 G.H. Cook, *The English Medieval Parish Church,* 1954, 94-5; A. Hamilton Thompson, *The Ground Plan of the English Parish Church,* 1911.

38 L.F. Salzman, *Building in England,* 1952, 437-8, where the church is confused with Sandon in Essex.

39 T.B. Dilks, ed., Bridgwater Borough Archives 1200-1377, *Somerset Record Society,* 48, 1933, 65-7.

40 C.D. Ross, ed., The Cartulary of Cirencester Abbey, 1964, I, xxxi-ii, II, 419, 425, 500, 560.

41 D.M. Owen, *Church and Society in Medieval Lincolnshire* 1971, 103.

42 J.G. Nichols, ed., *Topographer and Genealogist,* III, 1858, 251-2.

43 J.H. Bettey, *Wessex from 1000 AD,* Longmans, 1986, 86-7.

Chapter 3 pages 42—53

1 A. Hamilton Thompson, *The English Clergy and their Organisation in the Later Middle Ages,* OUP, 1947.
2 J.M. Horn, ed., The Register of Robert Hallum, Bishop of Salisbury 1407-17, *Canterbury and York Society,* 72, 1982, 3.
3 ibid.
4 ibid. 6.
5 H.C. Maxwell-Lyte and M.C.B. Davies, eds., The Register of Thomas Bekynton, Bishop of Bath and Wells 1443-65, *Somerset Record Society,* 49, 1934, 105.
6 *Victoria County History,* Somerset, 5, 1985, 62.
7 J.M. Horn, ed., op.cit, 139.
8 C. Gordon Browne, ed., The Register of Edmund Lacy, Bishop of Exeter 1420-55, *Devon and Cornwall Record Society,* 1915.
9 F.W. Weaver, ed., Cartulary of Buckland Priory, *Somerset Record Society,* 25, 1909, 95-6.
10 H.C. Maxwell-Lyte and M.C.B. Davies, eds., op.cit.
11 D.P. Wright, ed., The Register of Thomas Langton, Bishop of Salisbury 1485-93, *Canterbury and York Society,* 74, 1985, 63.
12 C.T. Flower and M.C.B. Dawes, eds., Register of Simon Ghent, *Canterbury and York Society,* 69, 1976, 213.
13 A. Watkins, ed., Archdeaconry of Norwich: Inventory of Church Goods, temp. Edward III, 2 vols., *Norfolk Record Society,* 1947-8.
14 W.G. Hoskins, *Local History in England,* Longmans, 1959, 60-70.
15 J. Raine, ed., The Fabric Rolls of York Minster, *Surtees Society,* 35, 1859.
16 T.C.B. Timmins, ed., The Register of John Chandler, Dean of Salisbury 1404-17, *Wiltshire Record Society,* 39, 1983.
17 D.P. Wright, ed., The Register of Thomas Langton, Bishop of Salisbury 1485-93, *Canterbury and York Society,* 74, 1985.
18 D.M. Owen, *Church and Society in Medieval Lincolnshire,* 1971, 122.
19 J.M. Horn, ed., op.cit. 221-3.
20 J.H. Bettey, *Bristol Parish Churches during the Reformation,* Bristol Historical Association, 1979, 4.
21 W.K. Clay, *A History of the Parish of Landbeach, Cambridge,* 1861.
22 A.J. Camp, *Wills and Their Whereabouts,* 1974; J.S.W. Gibson, *Wills and Where to Find Them,* 1974; E.L.C. Mullins, ed., *Texts and Calendars: An Analytical Guide to Serial Publications,* 1958.
23 D.M. Owen, op.cit. 105-6.
24 J. Chandler, *Endless Street, A History of Salisbury and Its People,* Hobnob Press, Salisbury, 1983, 197.
25 E. Peacock, ed., Instructions for Parish Priests by John Myrc, *Early English Text Society,* 31, 1868.
26 M. Hicks, 'Chantries, Obits and Almshouses: The Hungerford Foundations 1325-1478' in C.M. Barron and C. Harper-Bill, eds., *The Church in Pre-Reformation Society,* Boydell Press, 1985, 123-33.
27 J.H. Bettey, *Church and Community in Bristol during the Sixteenth Century,* Bristol Record Society, 1983, 5.
28 J. Chandler, op.cit., 197.

Chapter 4   pages 54—66

1 J.C. Cox, *Churchwardens' Accounts,* 1913, 15-43.
2 R.C. Dudding, ed., *The First Churchwardens' Book of Louth 1500-1524,* 1941.
3 J.J. Wilkinson, ed., Accounts for Building Bodmin Parish Church, *Camden Society Miscellany,* 7, 1875.
4 W.O. Ault, 'Manor Court and Parish Church in Fifteenth-Century England', *Speculum,* 42, 1967.
5 W.K. Clay, op.cit..
6 *Royal Commission on Historical Manuscripts,* 3rd Report, 1892, 2, 341-5.
7 L.F. Salzman, *Building in England,* 1952, 499, 547-8, 575.
8 ibid., 514-15.
9 J.H. Bettey, *Church and Community in Bristol during the Sixteenth Century,* Bristol Record Society, 1983, 7-8; C. Phythian-Adams, 'Ceremony and the Citizen: The Communal Year at Coventry 1450-1550', in P. Clark and P. Slack, eds., *Crisis and Order in English Towns,* 1972.
10 *Royal Commission on Historical Manuscripts,* 5th Report, 1876, 1, 488-533.
11 W. Rodwell, *The Archaeology of the English Church,* 1981; P.V. Addyman and R.K. Morris, eds., *The Archaeological Study of Churches,* Council for British Archaeology, 1976.
12 C. Woodforde, *English Stained and Painted Glass,* 1954; A. Caiger-Smith, *English Medieval Mural Paintings,* 1963.
13 E.E. Williams, *The Chantries of William Canynges in St Mary Redcliffe, Bristol,* Bristol, 1950.
14 J. Fowler, *Medieval Sherborne,* Dorchester, 1951.
15 G.R. Owst, *Preaching in Medieval England,* 1926; J.W. Blench, *Preaching in England 1450-1600,* Blackwell, 1964.
16 M. Aston, *Interpreting the Landscape,* Batsford, 1985, 78-81.
17 J.E. Jackson, Rowley *alias* Wittenham, *The Wiltshire Archaeological Magazine,* 13, 1872, 227-51; *Victoria County History,* Wiltshire, 7, 1953, 69-75.
18 R.W. Dunning, *Christianity in Somerset,* Bridgwater, 1976, 13.
19 J.H. Bettey, *Church and Community in Bristol during the Sixteenth Century,* Bristol Record Society, 1983, 8.
20 W.K. Clay, op.cit.
21 J.C. Cox, Churchwardens' Accounts, 1913.
22 ibid. 267-86; A. Hanham, ed., Churchwardens' Accounts of Ashburton 1479-1580, *Devon and Cornwall Record Society,* N.S. 15, 1970.
23 J. Godber, *History of Bedfordshire 1066-1888,* 1969, 105.
24 E. Hobhouse, ed., Pre-Reformation Churchwardens' Accounts. *Somerset Record Society,* 4, 1890.
25 D.M. Owen, op.cit..
26 W.O. Ault, op.cit..
27 M.D. Anderson, *History and Imagery in British Churches,* 1971.
28 Quoted by A. Caiger-Smith, *English Medieval Mural Paintings,* 1963, 46.
29 E. Carleton Williams, 'The Dance of Death in Painting and Sculpture in the Middle Ages', *Journal of the British Archaeological Association,* 3rd Series, 1, 1937, 230-8.
30 H.J.F. Swayne, ed., *Churchwardens' Accounts of St Edmund's, Salisbury, 1443-1702,* Salisbury, 1896, 38, 40;
   J.H. Bettey, *The English Parish Church and the Local Community,* Historical Association, 1985, 12,.
31 J. Chandler, op.cit. 195.

32 This description is reproduced in Sir William Parker's *History of Long Melford,* 1873.

Chapter 5   pages 67—89

1 E. Hobhouse, ed., Churchwardens' Accounts 1349-1560, *Somerset Record Society,* 4, 1890.
2 A.G. Dickens, *The English Reformation,* Batsford, 1964.
3 *Guide to the Contents of the Public Record Office,* HMSO, 3 vols., 1963-8.
4 G.H. Woodward, ed., Calendar of Somerset Chantry Grants 1548-1603, *Somerset Record Society,* 77, 1982;
D.M. Palliser, *Tudor York,* OUP, 1979, 239-41.
5 J.H. Bettey, *Church and Community in Bristol during the Sixteenth Century,* Bristol Record Society, 1983, 5.
6 Public Record Office, Exchequer K R Church Goods, *List and Index Society,* lxix, lxxvi, 1971-2.
7 C. Phythian-Adams, 'Ceremony and the Citizen: the Communal Year at Coventry 1450-1550', in P. Clark and P. Slack, eds., *Crisis and Order in English Towns 1500-1700,* 1972;
J.H. Bettey, *Church and Community in Bristol during the Sixteenth Century,* 1983, 7.
8 W.E. Tate, *The Parish Chest,* 1960, 35-42.
9 J. Godber, *History of Bedfordshire 1066-1888,* 1969, 184.
10 J.C. Cox, *Churchwardens' Accounts,* 1913.
11 F.H. Crossley, *English Church Monuments 1150-1550,* 1921.
12 E. Hobhouse, ed., *Somerset Record Society,* 4, 1890.
13 J.H. Bettey, *Church and Community,* Moonraker Press, 1979, 60-75.
14 P. Northeast, ed., Boxford Churchwardens' Accounts 1520-1561, *Suffolk Records Society,* 23, 1982.
15 J.H. Bettey, *Church and Community,* Moonraker Press, 1979, 68.
16 A, Hanham, ed., Churchwardens' Accounts of Ashburton 1479-1580, Devon and Cornwall Record Society, N.S., 15, 1970.
17 W.K. Clay, *A History of the Parish of Landbeach,* CUP, 1861.
18 W.G. Hoskins, *Devon,* Collins, 1954, 235; D.M Palliser, 'Popular Reactions to the Reformation', in F. Heal and R. O'Day, eds., *Church and Society in England from Henry VIII to James I,* 1977, 35-56; C. Cross, *Church and People 1450-1660,* 1976.
19 D. Hey, *Yorkshire AD 1000,* Longman, 1986, 129.
20 K.G. Powell, The Beginnings of Protestantism in Gloucestershire, *Bristol and Gloucestershire Archaeological Society Transactions,* 90, 1971, 141-57.
21 Gloucester City Library, *Hockaday Transcripts of Diocesan Records.*
22 G.H. Cook, *The English Medieval Parish Church,* 1954, 268.
23 Wiltshire Record Office, *Churchwardens' Presentments for the Dean's Peculiars.* For similar examples see J.S. Purvis, *Tudor Parish Documents of the Diocese of York,* 1948.
24 G.R. Elton, *Sources of History: England 1200-1640,* 1969, 104-5.
25 R. Houlbrooke, *Church Courts and the People during the English Reformation,* OUP, 1979; F.G. Emmison, *Elizabethan Life, Morals, and the Church Courts,* 1973.
26 J.H. Bettey, *Church and Community in Bristol during the Sixteenth Century,* Bristol Record Society, 1983, 18-19.

27 ibid., 17.

28 ibid., 17-19.

29 ibid., 11-12.

30 M. Spufford, *Contrasting Communities,* CUP, 1974, 320-44; P. Clark, *Towns and Townspeople 1500-1780,* Open University Press, 1977, 58, 76, 420; L. Munby, *Life and Death in Kings Langley 1498-1659,* Kings Langley W.E.A., 1981; A.G. Dickens, *Lollards and Protestants in the Diocese of York 1509-1558,* OUP, 1959, 171-2, 215-18; D.M. Palliser, *The Reformation in York 1534-1553,* St Anthony's Press, York, 1971 18-21, 28-9.

31 J. Vanes, ed., The Ledger Book of John Smythe 1538-50, *Bristol Record Society,* 28, 1975.

32 G.E. Fussell, ed., Robert Loder's Farm Accounts 1610-20, *Camden Society,* 3rd., 53, 1936.

33 Thomas Fuller, *The Worthies of England,* 1952 ed., 23.

34 D.M. Palliser, 'Popular Reactions to the Reformation', in F. Heal and R. O'Day, eds., *Church and Society in England from Henry VIII to James I,* 1977, 35-36.

35 J. Fowler, *Medieval Sherborne,* Dorchester, 1951.

36 Quoted by Sir William Parker, *History of Long Melford,* 1873.

37 J. Smyth, A description of the Hundred of Berkeley, 1885 edn. 35; J.S. Purvis, ed., *Tudor Parish Documents of the Diocese of York,* CUP, 1948, 173-9 197-201.

38 C. Cross, ed., The Letters of Sir Francis Hastings 1574-1609, *Somerset Record Society,* 69, 1969; C. Phythian-Adams, 'Ceremony and the Citizen: the Communal Year at Coventry 1450-1550', in P. Clark and P. Slack, eds., *Crisis and Order in English Towns 1500-1700,* 1972; P. Clark, *The English Alehouse: A Social History 1200-1830,* Longman, 1983.

39 M. Spufford, *Contrasting Communities,* CUP, 1974, 319.

40 J. Chandler, *Endless Street: A History of Salisbury,* Hobnob Press, Salisbury, 1983, 201-2..

41 C. Hill, *Society and Puritanism in Pre-Revolutionary England,* Secker and Warburg, 1964, 420-2; I. Luxton, 'The Reformation and Popular Culture', in F. Heal and R. O'Day, eds., *Church and Society in England: Henry VIII to James I,* Macmillan, 1977, 57-77.

Chapter 6   pages 90—108

1 Bristol Record Office, Churchwardens' Presentments 1675.

2 E.H. Bates Harbin, ed., Somerset Quarter Sessions Records 1625-39, *Somerset Record Society,* 24, 1908, 34.

3 R.F.B. Hodgkinson, ed., Act Books of the Archdeacons of Nottingham, *Transactions of the Thoroton Society,* 31, 1927, 108-53.

4 George Herbert, *The Country Parson; A Priest to the Temple,* 1652 and later editions, Chapter XXV.

5 D. Hey, ed., *English Rural Community,* Leicester UP, 1974.

6 M. Aston, 'Deserted farmsteads on Exmoor', *Somerset Archaeological Society Proceedings,* 127, 1983, 71-104; Joyce Popplewell, 'A Seating Plan for North Nibley Church in 1629', *Bristol and Gloucestershire Archaeological Society Transactions,* 103, 1985, 179-84.

7 R.B.F. Hodgkinson, ed., op. cit.; E.R.C. Brinkworth, 'The Laudian Church in Buckinghamshire', *University of Birmingham Historical Journal,* 5, 1955-6, 31-59; W.E. Tate, *The Parish Chest,* CUP, 1960, 89-92.

8 K.A. Esdaile, *English Church Monuments 1510-1840,* Batsford, 1946; B. Kemp, *English Church Monuments,* Batsford,

9 Wiltshire Record Office, Records of the Dean's Peculiars, (Charminster).

10 J.S. Purvis, *Tudor Parish Documents of the Diocese of York,* St Anthony's Press, 1948; R.F.B. Hodgkinson, op. cit.; E.R.C. Brinkworth, op. cit..

11 K. Wrightson, *English Society 1580-1680,* Hutchinson, 1982; A. Macfarlane, ed., *The Diary of Ralph Josselin 1618-1683,* OUP, 1976; J.M. Lloyd Thomas, ed., *The Autobiography of Richard Baxter,* Everyman edn., 1931, 3-6

12 W.B. Willcox, *Gloucestershire 1590-1640,* Yale UP, 1940; W.E. Tate, *The Parish Chest,* CUP, 1960; J.G. Davies, *The Secular Use of Church Buildings,* SCM Press, 1968.

13 H.B. Walters, *Church Bells of England,* OUP, 1912. The Proceedings of County Archaeological Societies often contain detailed descriptions of the bells of each parish, together with useful accounts of their inscriptions, donors and founders.

14 Somerset Record Office, Crewkerne Churchwardens' Accounts.

15 J.H. Bettey, *Wessex from AD 1000,* Longman, 1986, 186.

16 R.W. Dunning, *The Monmouth Rebellion,* Somerset County Library, 1985.

17 Dorset County Record Office, Churchwardens' Accounts of Wyke Regis.

18 Wiltshire Record Office, Churchwardens' Presentments for the Dean's Peculiars (Netherbury).

19 S.A. Peyton, Churchwardens' Presentments, *Oxfordshire Record Society,* 10, 1928, li.

20 J.C. Cox, *Churchwardens' Accounts,* Methuen, 1913; W.E. Tate, *The Parish Chest,* CUP, 1960, 34, 74.

21 J.H. Bettey, *Wessex from AD 1000,* Longman, 1986, 166.

22 W.B. Willcox, *Gloucestershire 1590-1640,* Yale UP, 1940, 234-5; E. Bradby, *History of Devizes,* Barracuda Books, 1985, 60.

23 E.H. Bates Harbin, ed., Somerset Quarter Sessions Records 1625-39, *Somerset Record Society,* 24, 1908; E. Trotter, *Seventeenth Century Life in the Country Parish,* 1919.

24 J.G. Davies, *The Secular Use of Church Buildings,* SCM Press, 1968; R.F.B. Hodgkinson, Act Books of the Archdeacons of Nottingham, *Thoroton Society Transactions,* 31, 1927; K. Wrightson, *English Society 1580-1680,* Hutchinson, 1982, 183-256.

25 M. Spufford, *Contrasting Communities,* CUP, 1974.

26 J.H. Bettey, *Church and Community in Bristol during the Sixteenth Century,* Bristol Record Society, 1983, 20.

27 J. Aubrey, *Natural History of Wiltshire,* ed. K. Ponting, David and Charles, 1969, 78.

28 J. Aubrey, *The Topographical Collection,* ed. J.E. Jackson, 1862, 272-74.

29 Margaret Stieg, *Laud's Laboratory, the Diocese of Bath and Wells in the Early Seventeenth Century,* Bucknell UP, 1982.

30 T.H. Baker, 'The Churchwardens' Accounts of Mere', *Wiltshire Archaeological Magazine,* 35, 1908, 23-92.

31 S.A. Peyton, Churchwardens' Presentments, *Oxfordshire Record Society,* 10, 1928; E. Trotter, *Seventeenth Century Life in a Country Parish,* 1919.

32 C. Hill, *Society and Puritanism in Pre-Revolutionary England,* Secker and Warburg, 1964; J.H. Bettey. *The English Parish Church and the Local Community,* Historical Association, 1985, 32.

33 J.H. Bettey, *Church and Community in Bristol during the Sixteenth Century,* Bristol Record Society, 1983, 22.

34 Wiltshire Record Office, Churchwardens' Presentments for the Dean's Peculiars (Beaminster).

35 C. Hill, *The Century of Revolution,* Nelson, 1961, 173.

36 A. Macfarlane, *The Diary of Ralph Josselin 1618-1683,* OUP, 1976.

37 J.C. Cox, *Churchwardens' Accounts,* Methuen 1913; W.E. Tate, *The Parish Chest,* CUP, 1960.

38 Dorset Record Office, Churchwardens' Accounts for Cerne Abbas.

39 Dorset Record Office, Thorncombe Parish Accounts.

40 J.S. Purvis, *An Introduction to Ecclesiastical Records,* St Anthony's Press, 1953.

41 E. J. Evans, *The Contentious Tithe,* Routledge and Kegan Paul, 1976.

42 W.E. Tate, *The Parish Chest,* CUP, 1960, 185, 245, 258.

43 G.W.O. Addleshaw and F. Etchells, *The Architectural Setting of Anglican Worship,* Faber, 1948.

Chapter 7　pages 109—125

1 Quoted by N. Sykes, *Church and State in England in the Eighteenth Century,* CUP, 1934, 231.

2 For example. H.A. Lloyd Jukes, ed., Primary Visitation of the Diocese of Oxford by Dr Thomas Secker, 1738 *Oxford Record Society,* 38, 1957; S.L. Ollard and P.C. Walker, eds., Archbishop Herring's Visitation Returns 1743, *Yorkshire Archaeological Society,* 71, 75, 77, 79, 1929-31; E. Ralph and J.H. Bettey, eds., Bishop Secker's Diocese Book, in P. McGrath, ed., Bristol Miscellany, *Bristol Record Society,* 37, 1985; M. Ransome, ed., Wiltshire Returns to the Bishop's Visitation Queries 1783, *Wiltshire Record Society,* 27, 1972.

3 M.G. Jones, *Hannah More,* CUP, 1952, 153-5.

4 E. Ralph and J.H. Bettey, eds., op. cit.; J.H. Bettey, Bishop Secker's Diocesan Survey, *Dorset Archaeological Society Proceedings,* 95, 1973-4, 74-5.

5 G.F.A. Best, *Temporal Pillars: Queen Anne's Bounty, the Ecclesiastical Commissioners and the Church of England,* CUP, 1964.

6 D.M. Barratt, ed., Ecclesiastical Terriers of Warwickshire Parishes, *Dugdale Society,* 22, 1955.

7 W. Addison, *The English Country Parson,* Dent, 1947.

8 N. Sykes, op. cit., 229; J. Woodforde, *The Diary of a Country Parson,* edited by J. Beresford, 5 vols., 1924-31; J. Skinner, *The Journal of a Somerset Rector,* edited by H. Coombs and H.N. Bax, OUP, 1930; T. Brockbank, Diary and Letter-Book 1671-1709, edited by R. Trappes-Lomax, *Chatham Society,* 1930; W. Cole, *The Bletchley Diary 1765-7,* edited by F.G. Stokes, 1931; W. Jones, *Diary 1777-1821,* edited by O.F. Christie, 1929; J. Ayres, ed., *Paupers and Pig Killers, The Diary of William Holland 1799-1818,* Alan Sutton, 1984.

9 Wiltshire Record Office 1190/17; see also E. Evans, *The Contentious Tithe,* Routledge and Kegan Paul, 1976; W.E. Tate, *The Parish Chest,* CUP, 1960.

10 O.F. Christie, ed., *The Diary of William Jones 1777-1821,* Brentano, 1929.

11 W.E. Tate, op.cit., 117, 185, 245, 258.

12 D. Hey, *Yorkshire from 1000 AD,* Longman, 1986, 205-6.

13 G.W. Addleshaw and F.E. Etchells, *The Architectural Setting of Anglican Worship,* Faber, 1948, 86-97.

14 G. White, *The Natural History and Antiquities of Selborne,* 1836 edn, 329.

15 Dorset Record Office, Burton Bradstock Churchwardens' Accounts, 1797-1832.

16 A.D. Gilbert, *Religion and Society in Industrial England,* Longman, 1976.

17 G.W. Addleshaw and F.E. Etchells, op. cit., 68-83; N. Sykes, op.cit., 231-83.

18 J. Aubrey, *Natural History of Wiltshire,* edited by K.G. Ponting, David and Charles, 1969, 109.

19 N. Temperley, *The Music of the English Parish Church,* 2 vols., CUP, 1979; V. Gammon, '"Babylonian Performances": The Rise and Suppression of Popular Church Music 1660-1870', in E. and S. Yeo, eds., *Popular Culture and Class Conflict 1590-1914,* Harvester Press, 1981, 62-88.

20 J.C. Cox, *Churchwardens' Accounts,* Methuen, 1913, 195-210; W. Addison, *The English Country Parson,* Dent, 1947; H.E.R. Widnell, *The Beaulieu Record,* Pioneer Publications, 1973, 117-119.

21 V. Gammon, op.cit., 70; G.W. Addleshaw and F.E. Etchells, op.cit., 98-100.

22 T. Hardy, *Under the Greenwood Tree,* Macmillan, 1974 edition, 75.

23 E. Ralph and J.H. Bettey, op.cit., 76.

24 H. Coombs and H.N. Bax, *Journal of a Somerset Rector,* OUP, 1930, 8, 235.

25 Quoted by N. Penny, *Church Monuments in Romantic England,* Yale UP, 1977, 40.

26 H.B. Walters, *Church Bells of England,* OUP, 1912.

27 J.G. Davies, *The Secular Use of Church Buildings,* SCM Press, 1968, 159-69.

28 For other examples see W.E. Tate, op.cit., 108-118, 187-239.

29 J.G. Davies, op.cit., 75, 186.

30 ibid.; M.G. Jones, *The Charity School Movement,* 1938; E. McClure and W.O.B. Allen, *Two Hundred Years: The History of the SPCK 1698-1898,* 1898; D. Robson, 'Education in Cheshire in the Eighteenth Century', *Chatham Society,* 3rd Ser., 13, 1966.

Chapter 8 pages 126—145

1 J.H. Bettey, *Wessex from AD 1000,* Longman, 1986, 277.

2 These figures are adapted from A.D. Gilbert, *Religion and Society in Industrial England,* Longman, 1986, 130.

3 B.F.L. Clarke, *Church Builders of the Nineteenth Century,* SPCK, 1938; G.W.O. Addleshaw and F. Etchells, *The Architectural Setting of Anglican Worship,* Faber & Faber, 1948, 203-18.

.4 M.G. Jones, *Hannah More, CUP, 1952, 151-71.*

5 G.W.O. Addleshaw and F. Etchells, op.cit., 203-8; A. Rogers, *Approaches to Local History,* Longman, 2nd. Ed., 1977 148-9.

6 D.M. Owen, *The Records of the Established Church in England,* British Record Association, 1970, 28-30.

7 W.R. Powell, *Local History from Blue Books: A Select List of the Sessional Papers of the House of Commons,* Historical Association, 1962; P. and G. Ford, *A Guide to Parliamentary Papers,* Blackwell, 1955.

8 B.I. Coleman, *The Church of England in the Mid-Nineteenth Century,* Historical Association, 1980; A. Rogers, op.cit., 135-39, 144-47; R.W. Ambler, 'The 1851 Census of Religious Worship', *The Local Historian* xi, 7, 1975, 375-81.

9 F. Thompson, *Lark Rise to Candleford,* OUP, 1946 ed., 189.

10 R.W. Ambler, ed., Lincolnshire Returns of the Census of Religious Worship 1851, *Lincoln Record Society,* 72, 1979, xxiv; B.I. Coleman, 'Southern England in the Religious Census of 1851', *Southern History,* 5, 1983, 154-88; D.M Thompson,'The Churches and Society in Nineteenth-

Century England,' in G.J. Cuming and D. Baker, eds., *Studies in Church History,* 8, Blackwell, 1972, 274-5; A.M. Everitt, *The Pattern of Rural Dissent: The Nineteenth Century,* Leicester UP, 1973.

11 R.W. Dunning,'Nineteenth Century Parochial Sources', in D. Baker, ed., *Studies in Church History,* 11, 1975, 301-8.

12 R.L. Sawyer, *The Bowerchalke Papers,* 1985, unpublished typescript, Wiltshire Library Service, Trowbridge.

13 R.W. Dunning, op.cit., 308; W.B. Stephens, op.cit., 265.

14 Truro Diocesan Conference Proceedings, 1877.

15 A.M. Everitt, *The Patterns of Rural Dissent,* Leicester UP, 1972.

16 A.C. Kelway, *George Rundle Prynne,* Longmans, Green & Co., 1905, 6-7.

17 Somerset Record Office, DD/HY Box 12.

18 A.C. Benson, *Edward White Benson,* 1902, 478-80.

19 O. Chadwick, *Victorian Miniature,* Hodder & Stoughton, 1960.

20 J. Leech, *The Church-Goer,* 4 vols., Bristol, 1845, 1850, 1851, 1888.

21 P. Horn, *David Davies: A Georgian Parson and His Village,* Beacon Publications, 1981, 80.

22 A.D. Gilbert, op.cit., 56; O. Chadwick, *The Victorian Church,* 2 vols., A. & C. Black, 1966, 1969; W.R. Ward, *Religion and Society in England,* 1972.

23 Wiltshire Record Office, Devizes Churchwardens' Accounts 1830-??; E. Bradley, *The Book of Devizes,* Barracuda Books, 1985, 114.

24 K. Rogers, *The Book of Trowbridge,* Barracuda Books, 1985, 117.

25 N. Yates, *The Oxford Movement and Anglican Ritualism,* Historical Association, 1983; G.W.O. Addleshaw and F. Etchells, op.cit., 203-222.

26 E.P. Hennock, 'The Anglo-Catholics and Church Extension in Victorian Brighton', in M.J. Kitch, ed., *Studies in Sussex Church History,* University of Sussex, 1981, 173-88; N. Yates, '"Bells and Smells": London, Brighton and South Coast Religion Reconsidered', *Southern History,* 5, 1983, 1??, 122-53.

27 F. Kilvert, *Diary 1870-79,* ed. W. Plomer, 3 vols., 1938-40.

28 V. Gammon, '"Babylonian Performances": the Rise and Suppression of Popular Church Music 1660-1870', in E. & S. Yeo, eds., *Popular Culture and Class Conflict 1590-1914,* Harvester Press, 1981, 62-88; N. Temperley, *The Music of the English Parish Church,* 2 vols., CUP, 1979.

GLOSSARY

Advowson   The right of appointing a priest to a parish or other ecclesiastical benefice. The person or institution holding the advowson is the 'patron', who presents the priest to the bishop for institution and induction.

Appropriation   The practice which was common in the Middle Ages whereby the tithes and other endowments of a parish church were annexed to a monastic house.

Apse   Semicircular or polygonal end of a chancel or a chapel.

Aumbry   A small recess or cupboard in the wall of a church in which sacred vessels and books were kept.

Baldric   A thick leather thong by which the clapper was attached to a bell.

Benefice   An ecclesiastical office, generally a rectory, vicarage or perpetual curacy.

Box Pews   Pew with high, wooden sides, common in parish churches during the seventeenth and eighteenth centuries.

Brief   A letter from the bishop or other ecclesiastical official authorising collections for charity or some good cause.

Canon Law   The ecclesiastical law or law of the Church.

Cartulary   Register of the deeds, charters, grants, property, estates and possessions of a monastic house or lay landowner.

Censer   Vessel used for the burning of incense during services.

Chantry   An endowment which maintained a priest to say or sing Mass for the soul of the founder and his family. Also applied to the chapel or altar at which such Masses were celebrated. These foundations were suppressed in 1547 and the endowments of some 2,374 chantries and guild chapels passed to the Crown.

Chapel of Ease   A chapel established by a lord of a manor or other benefactor, with the consent of the bishop, to serve a remote place which was too far from the parish church for people to walk there regularly for services.

Chaplain   An unbeneficed priest employed in a private household or institution.

Chrism   Holy oil used in some of the sacraments.

Church Ales   Parish gatherings and festivities which were often major fund-raising activities for parish churches and an important part of community life.

Church House   Buildings in which church ales and other parish functions were held.

Churchwardens   Principal lay officials of each parish church and legal guardians of all church property. From the sixteenth century, a heavy burden of secular duties was imposed upon them by Parliament.

Clerestory   The upper storey of the nave walls of a church, with windows giving additional light to the interior.

Consistory Court   The bishop's court for the administration of ecclesiastical law within his own diocese.

Corbels   Blocks of carved stone projecting from just below the roof eaves of a church, often seen in Norman buildings.

Curate Literally a priest with the cure of souls in a parish, but generally applied to an assistant or unbeneficed clergyman, nominated by the incumbent and licensed by the bishop.

Dispensation Licence granted by a bishop for non-observance of ecclesiastical regulations, for example, permission to eat flesh during Lent.

Easter Sepulchre Recess or structure, generally on the north side of the altar, which was used during the Middle Ages in the dramatic representation of the death, burial and resurrection of Christ during Good Friday, Holy Saturday and Easter Sunday.

Faculty A licence issued by the bishop permitting alterations or additions to churches or churchyards.

Glebe Land devoted to the maintenance of the incumbent of a parish. It could be cultivated by the incumbent himself or let to a tenant.

Hatchment Board or canvas with armorial bearings, often diamond-shaped. It was carried in the funeral procession of an armigerous parishioner and then hung up in the parish church.

Impropriate The term used to describe benefices of which the tithes were annexed by lay proprietors or institutions. Used of benefices which passed into the hands of lay rectors after the Reformation, as distinct from parishes which were 'appropriated' to monastic houses during the Middle Ages.

Incumbent The priest in charge of a parish, generally a rector, vicar or perpetual curate.

Induction The admission of a new incumbent into the revenues of his parish, thus giving him legal possession of the income, tithes, rights and endowments. It was performed by the archdeacon or other person authorised by the bishop.

Injunctions Orders issued to clergy and churchwardens by the Crown or by ecclesiastical authorities.

Institution The admission of a new incumbent into the spiritual functions in his parish. Performed by the bishop of the diocese.

Lay Rector A layman who received the appropriated tithes of a parish, often through having acquired former monastic property. A lay rector was responsible for the upkeep of the chancel of the parish church.

Minster Early church centres staffed by groups of Anglo-Saxon clergy living in a community and serving the surrounding area, before the establishment of the parochial system.

Missal A Mass book giving the words of the Mass for the different seasons and festivals throughout the year.

Modus A fixed payment or arrangement in lieu of tithes in kind.

Mortuary A customary levy due to the parish priest from the estate of each deceased parishioner.

Obit A memorial Mass, often celebrated annually on the anniversary of a person's death.

Oratory A chapel licensed for private devotion or family use.

Ordinal A service book giving the order of services throughout the year.

Ordinary An ecclesiastical superior, archdeacon, bishop or archbishop.

Parish Clerk A layman who assisted the parish priest with minor duties — making the responses, reading the epistle or gospel, leading the singing and helping in the running of the church.

Patron The possessor of the advowson or right to present a new incumbent to the bishop.

Pax or **Pax Brede** A small plate of wood, metal or ivory with a representation of the Crucifixion or some religious subject. It was used during Mass for the kiss of peace.

Peculiar   A place exempt from the jurisdiction of the bishop in whose diocese it is situated and subject to some other ecclesiastical superior.

Perambulation   The procession around the parish bounds, often at Rogationtide.

Perpetual Curate   The title given to a priest who was nominated by a lay rector to serve a parish where there was no regularly endowed vicarage. Unlike stipendiary curates or chaplains, perpetual curates were appointed in perpetuity and, once licensed by the bishop, could not be dismissed or removed by the patron.

Piscina   Small basin and drain generally set in the wall on the south side of an altar and used for washing the Communion or Mass vessels.

Pluralism   The holding of more than one benefice by the same incumbent. The accumulation of several benefices by individual clergymen, who used poorly-paid curates to conduct the parish duties, became a scandalous abuse during the eighteenth century.

Porticus   Side chapel, common in Anglo-Saxon minster churches.

Prebend   A cathedral benefice or estate from which the income was derived to support a prebendary or canon of the cathedral.

Presentation   The nomination of a clergyman to the bishop by a patron.

Presentments   Statements made on oath in an ecclesiastical court, or reports made by churchwardens in response to the visitation queries of a bishop or an archdeacon.

Pyx   A receptacle in which the Sacred Host was reserved.

Rector   The incumbent of a parish where the tithes had not been appropriated to a monastery, and who thus received the full income from the parishioners' tithes. The rector was responsible for the upkeep of the chancel of the parish church.

Recusant   One who refused to conform to the Established Church or attend its services. Generally used of Roman Catholics.

Rood   The cross or crucifix.

Rood Screen   The screen which divided the nave and the chancel in a medieval parish church; above it was a loft or gallery and above that the rood and often also the figures of Our Lady and St John.

Sedilia   Seats, usually three in number, set into the south wall of the chancel near the altar, and often elaborately carved and decorated. They were used by the priest and his attendants during sermons or the sung parts of the liturgy.

Sequestration   The legal process whereby the emoluments of a vacant benefice are safeguarded by the appointment of sequestrators who administer the income for the benefit of the next incumbent.

Sheila-na-Gig   A grotesque and blatantly sexual female figure to be found carved in stone on parish churches, especially in the Romanesque period. The purpose is uncertain, but the figure may be intended as a warning against sexual licence.

Terrier   Inventory of landed possessions and other property.

Three-decker Pulpit   Elaborate pulpit common during the eighteenth century which combined in one structure the pulpit, the clergyman's reading desk and a smaller desk for the parish clerk.

Tithe   The tenth part of the produce of the land of a parish allotted to the rector for his maintenance.

Transcripts Duplicate copies of the entries in parish registers furnished annually to the archdeacon or bishop by the churchwardens.

Trendal A hoop or circle suspended before the rood to hold candles.

Trental A series of Masses celebrated daily for thirty days after a person's death.

Tympanum The space between the lintel of a doorway and the arch above it, which was used, especially in Romanesque churches, for a display of carving or the depiction of some religious subject.

Vestry Meeting of ratepayers or of the governing body of a parish.

Vicar Literally *'vicarius'* or substitute. Originally the priest of a parish where the tithes were appropriated by a monastic house. The monastery thus became the rector of the parish and appointed a vicar to perform the parochial duties. The vicar generally received only a portion of the parochial tithes, but enjoyed the same spiritual status as a rector.

Visitation Periodic tour of inspection by a bishop or archdeacon during which enquiries were made into the affairs of each parish.

SELECT BIBLIOGRAPHY

G.W.O. ADDLESHAW and F. ETCHELLS, *The Architectural Setting of Anglican Worship,* Faber & Faber, 1948

M.D. ANDERSON, *Drama and Imagery in Medieval Churches,* J. Murray, 1963

M.D. ANDERSON, *History and Imagery in British Churches,* J. Murray, 1971

M. ASTON, *Interpreting the Landscape: Landscape Archaeology in Local Studies,* Batsford, 1985

J.H. BETTEY, *The English Parish Church and the Local Community,* Historical Association, 1985

J.H. BETTEY and C.W.G. TAYLOR, *Sacred and Satiric: Medieval Stone Carving in the West Country,* Redcliffe Press, 1982

R. and C. BROOKE, *Popular Religion in the Middle Ages,* Thames and Hudson, 1984

F. BURGESS, *English Churchyard Memorials,* Lutterworth Press, 1963

A. CLIFTON TAYLOR, *English Parish Churches as Works of Art,* Batsford, 1974

G.H. COOK, *The English Medieval Parish Church,* Phoenix House, 1955

J.C. COX, *Churchwardens' Accounts,* Methuen, 1913

F.L. CROSS and E.A. LIVINGSTONE, eds., *The Oxford Dictionary of the Christian Church,* OUP, 1974

J.G. DAVIES, *The Secular Use of Church Buildings,* SCM Press, 1968

D. P. DYMOND, *Writing a Church Guide,* Church Information Office, 1977

D. P. DYMOND, *Writing Local History,* Bedford Square Press, 1981

R. MORRIS, *The Church in British Archaeology,* C.B.A. Research Report 47, 1983

D.M. OWEN, *Church and Society in Medieval Lincolnshire,* Lincolnshire Local History Society, 1971

C. PLATT, *The Parish Churches of Medieval England,* Secker and Warburg, 1981

J.S. PURVIS, *An Introduction to Ecclesiastical Records,* St Anthony's Press, 1953

G. RANDALL, *Church Furnishing and Decoration in England and Wales,* Batsford, 1980

P. RIDEN, *Local History,* Batsford, 1983

W. RODWELL, *The Archaeology of the English Church,* Batsford, 1981

A. ROGERS, *Approaches to Local History,* Longman, 2nd edn., 1977

L.F. SALZMAN, *Building in England,* OUP, 1967

W.B. STEPHENS, *Sources for English Local History,* CUP, 1981

W.E. TATE, *The Parish Chest,* CUP, 1960

INDEX